VIA LATINA

AN

EASY LATIN READER

BY

WILLIAM C. COLLAR

HEAD-MASTER ROXBURY LATIN SCHOOL

WITH

VOCABULARY

BY

CLARENCE W. GLEASON

Master in Roxbury Latin School

BOSTON, U.S.A., AND LONDON
GINN & COMPANY, PUBLISHERS
𝕿𝖍𝖊 𝕬𝖙𝖍𝖊𝖓𝖆𝖚𝖒 𝕻𝖗𝖊𝖘𝖘
1897

PREFACE.

THE Latin problem, so far as it relates to secondary schools, remains but partially solved. The beggarly results of much study of Latin in preparation for college are not denied, and cannot be, for they are patent. In 1896 nearly a third of the applicants for admission to Harvard failed on the final examination in Latin, and in 1895 a little more than one-third. But it is very well known that the pass mark on the entrance examination is very low. It is said to be no more than forty per cent, and there are indications that it is sometimes lower. If one-third fail to obtain the lowest admissible mark, probably it would be safe to assume that another third do not get higher than from forty to sixty per cent, leaving only a third of the entire number who are able to pass the Harvard test in a creditable, or even satisfactory, manner.

One might appeal to the experience of teachers. How many are there who do not find what seem reasonable expectations and hopes disappointed? How many who do not often contemplate with amazement and mortification the wretched fruit of honest study and sound instruction? It must be sorrowfully admitted that our boys and girls do not learn to speak Latin, or to understand it, or to write it, or even to read it.

What is the secret of this failure, disappointment, and discontent? I believe the answer is to be found in the prevailing underestimate of the difficulty of learning Latin. Latin was never an easy language, but it was certainly easier for the generations that did not question its educational value, than for this, that questions and doubts everything. Not recognizing its inherent difficulty, we commit two capital mistakes. We do not allow sufficient time, and we do not provide for an easy and gradual progression.

Both these errors are glanced at in the report of the Latin Conference to the "Committee of Ten" in 1892. In recommending a lengthening of the Latin preparatory course, the Conference says : "The aggregate of one thousand or twelve hundred hours is much below the average in the schools of England, France, and Germany. The explanation of the undeniable fact that, in the countries just named, Latin has been more successfully employed than with us as an instrument for training the mind to habits of intellectual conscientiousness, patience, discrimination, and thoroughness, — in a word, to habits of clear and sound thinking, — doubtless lies partly in the more liberal allowance of time."

Touching the second error, the Conference deprecates the immediate transition from a first-year book of forms and simple constructions to the reading of a classic author in Latin, and especially the absurdity of a plunge at once into the *Gallic War*. It recommends the use of easy reading to prepare the learner, by an enlarged vocabulary and practice in translating Latin not beyond his powers, for the severer task that confronts him when he takes up Nepos, Caesar, or Ovid.

If these suggestions of the Conference were carefully carried out, the study of Latin with us would be revolu-

tionized. Why should it not be? What could with more
certainty predetermine failure in any subject than to give
to it no more than two-thirds, or even half, the time
needed for its mastery? How can we hope to do in four
or five years what foreign schools, taught by accomplished
scholars and trained teachers, need eight or nine years to
achieve? If it is worth while to study Latin at all it must
have a larger allotment of time. How is this possible
with our present crowded programmes? There is only
one way. Latin must be begun one, two, or even three
years earlier than is common in this country. Instead
of beginning at fourteen, the average age now, the study
should not be deferred beyond the eleventh or twelfth
year.

Here, I say, is our first capital error, but we aggravate
it by another, as has been already indicated. We do
not mount our Hill of Difficulty by a winding way and a
gentle incline. No, we strike a bee line for the top,
regardless of obstacles, over height and hollow,

> " Thorough bush, thorough brier,"

with the natural result of waste of time, weariness, dis-
gust, and defeat.

We rightly aim to teach our pupils to read, that is, to
understand, Latin, as well as to translate into pure English, because such are the means for acquiring power
through the best training. Training in reading is training in insight; and insight is to be gained by the learner's
application of his powers to texts that are not too easy,
of which there is little danger in Latin, nor too stubborn
and complicated. It is a question of grading difficulties,
of suiting the task you set the pupil to his capacity at

successive stages. Just here lies the *nodus* of the problem that must be worked out to a practical solution. If we succeed, there will be a two-fold gain, — a more rapid advance, and increased pleasure for the learner, not because less effort will be required of him, but because with the same effort he will be carried forward so much farther.

To find and prepare suitable reading to follow the first half year or year in a Latin course is not easy. A reading book for that stage should fulfill three conditions : it should not be too hard, it should be interesting, and it should lead by a gradual ascent to the level of one or another of the classic authors usually taken first. Furthermore, it should be designed and used for rapid reading, not for analysis and parsing. It should accordingly be annotated with a view to make the learner quick to observe and compare different meanings of the same word, and synonymous and contrasted words, to the end that the first and greatest difficulty, that of the Latin vocabulary, may be partially surmounted. Not that this should be the sole purpose, but it should be put first.

Many teachers have found that *The New Gradatim* fulfills all these conditions ; but for those who do not use that book, as well as for those who do, but who are of the opinion that additional *ad interim* reading is desirable, this Reader has been prepared.

WM. C. COLLAR.

ROXBURY LATIN SCHOOL,
    April 2, 1897.

VIA LATINA.

THE ARGONAUTS.

The celebrated voyage of the Argonauts was brought about as follows. Pelias had expelled his brother Æson from his kingdom in Thessaly, and had attempted to take the life of Jason, the son of Æson. Jason, however, escaped, and grew up to manhood in another country. At last he returned to Thessaly, and Pelias, fearing that he might attempt to recover the kingdom, sent him to fetch the Golden Fleece from Colchis, supposing this to be an impossible feat. Jason, with a band of heroes, started in the ship Argo (called after Argus, its builder), and after many adventures reached Colchis. Here Ætes, king of Colchis, who was unwilling to give up the Fleece, set Jason to perform what seemed an impossible task, namely, to plough a field with certain fire-breathing oxen, and then to sow it with dragon's teeth. Medea, the daughter of the king, however, assisted Jason by her skill in magic, first to perform the task appointed, and then to procure the Fleece. Medea then fled with Jason, and, in order to delay the pursuit of her father, sacrificed her brother Absyrtus. After reaching Thessaly, Medea caused the death of Pelias, and, with her husband, was expelled from Thessaly. They removed to Corinth, and here Medea, becoming jealous of Glauce, daughter of Creon, caused her death by means of a poisoned robe. After this, Medea was carried off in a chariot sent by the sun-god, and Jason was soon afterwards accidentally killed.

1. The Wicked Uncle.

Erant ōlim in Thessaliā duo frātrēs, quōrum alter Aesōn, alter Peliās appellātus est. Hōrum Aesōn prīmum rēgnum obtinuerat, at post paucōs annōs Peliās, rēgnī cupiditāte adductus, nōn modo frātrem suum expulit, sed 5 etiam in animō habēbat, Iāsonem, Aesonis fīlium, interficere. Quīdam tamen ex amīcīs Aesonis, ubi sententiam Peliae intellēxērunt, puerum ē tantō perīculō ēripere cōnstituērunt. Noctū igitur Iāsonem ex urbe abstulērunt et cum posterō diē ad rēgem rediissent eī renūntiāvērunt 10 puerum mortuum esse. Peliās, cum haec audīvisset, etsī rē vērā māgnum gaudium percipiēbat, speciem tamen dolōris praebuit et quae causa esset mortis quaesīvit. Illī tamen, cum bene intellegerent dolōrem ēius falsum esse, nēsciō quam fābulam dē morte puerī finxērunt.

2. A Careless Shoe-String.

15 Post breve tempus Peliās, veritus nē rēgnum suum tantā vī et fraude occupātum āmitteret, amīcum quendam Delphōs mīsit, quī ōrāculum cōnsuleret. Ille igitur quam celerrimē Delphōs sē contulit et quam ob causam vēnisset dēmōnstrāvit. Respondit ōrāculum nūllum esse in prae- 20 sentiā perīculum ; monuit tamen Peliam ut, sī quis venīret calceum ūnum gerēns, eum cavēret. Post paucōs annōs accidit ut Peliās māgnum sacrificium factūrus esset ; nūntiōs in omnīs partīs dīmīserat et certum diem conveniendī dīxerat. Diē cōnstitūtō māgnus numerus hominum 25 undique ex agrīs convēnit ; inter aliōs autem vēnit etiam

---

6 sententiam : *cōnsilium.*   14 nēsciō quam : *aliquam.*
11 percipiēbat : *sentiēbat.*   18 quam ob causam : *cūr.*
12 praebuit : *ostendit.*   19 in praesentiā : *nunc.*

Iāsōn, quī ā puerō apud Centaurum quendam vīxerat. Dum tamen iter facit, calceum alterum in trānseundō nesciō quō flūmine āmīsit.

3. The Golden Fleece.

Iāsōn igitur, cum calceum āmissum nūllō modō recipere posset, alterō pede nūdō in rēgiam pervēnit. Quem cum 5 vīdisset Peliās, subitō timōre adfectus est; intellēxit enim hunc esse hominem quem ōrāculum dēmōnstrāvisset. Hōc igitur iniit cōnsilium. Rēx erat quīdam nōmine Aeētēs, quī rēgnum Colchidis illō tempore obtinēbat. Huīc commissum erat vellus illud aureum quod Phrīxus 10 ōlim ibi relīquerat. Cōnstituit igitur Peliās Iāsonī negō- tium dare ut hōc vellere potīrētur ; cum enim rēs esset māgnī perīculī, spērābat eum in itinere peritūrum esse. Iāsonem igitur ad sē arcessīvit et quid fierī vellet dēmōn- strāvit. Iāsōn autem, etsī bene intellegēbat rem esse 15 difficillimam, negōtium libenter suscēpit.

4. The Building of the Good Ship Argo.

Cum tamen Colchis multōrum diērum iter ab eō locō abesset, nōluit Iāsōn sōlus proficīscī. Dīmīsit igitur nūn- tiōs in omnīs partīs, quī causam itineris docērent et diem certum conveniendī dīcerent. Intereā, postquam omnia 20 quae sunt ūsuī ad armandās nāvīs comportārī iussit, negōtium dedit Argō cuīdam, quī summam scientiam rērum nauticārum habēbat, ut nāvem aedificāret. In hīs rēbus circiter decem diēs cōnsūmptī sunt ; Argus enim

---

2 alterum: *ūnum.*   11 cōnstituit: p. 2, l. 7.
3 nesciō quō: p. 2, l. 14.   14 arcessīvit: *vocāvit.*
8 iniit: *fēcit.*   15 etsī: p. 2, l. 10.

qui operī praeerat tantam dīligentiam praebēbat, ut nē nocturnum quidem tempus ad labōrem intermitteret. Ad multitūdinem hominum trānsportandam nāvis paulō erat lātior quam quibus in nostrō marī ūtī cōnsuēvimus et ad 5 vim tempestātum perferendam tōta ē rōbore facta est.

5. The Anchor is Weighed.

Intereā is diēs appetēbat quem Iāsōn per nūntiōs ēdīxerat et ex omnibus regiōnibus Graeciae multī, quōs aut reī novitās aut spēs glōriae movēbat, undique conveniēbant. Trādunt autem in hōc numerō fuisse Herculem, 10 Orpheum, citharoedum praeclārissimum, Thēseum, Castōrem multōsque aliōs, quōrum nōmina nōtissima sunt. Ex hīs Iāsōn, quōs arbitrātus est ad omnia subeunda perīcula parātissimōs esse, eōs ad numerum quīnquāgintā dēlēgit et sociōs sibi adiūnxit. Tum paucōs diēs commo- 15 rātus, ut ad omnīs cāsūs subsidia comparāret, nāvem dēdūxit et tempestātem ad nāvigandum idōneam nactus māgnō cum plausū omnium solvit.

6. A Fatal Mistake.

Haud multum post Argonautae, ita enim appellātī sunt qui in istā nāvī vehēbantur, īnsulam quandam nōmine 20 Cȳzicum attigērunt et ē nāvī ēgressī ā rēge illīus regiōnis hospitiō exceptī sunt. Paucās hōrās ibi commorātī ad sōlis occāsum rūrsus solvērunt; at postquam pauca mīllia passuum prōgressī sunt tanta tempestās subitō coörta est ut cursum tenēre nōn possent et in eandem

---

1 **praebēbat**: p. 2, l. 12.   9 **trādunt**: *dīcunt.*
4 **cōnsuēvimus**: *solēmus.*   15 **subsidia**: *auxilium.*
6 **appetēbat**: *appropīnquābat.*   16 **tempestātem**: *tempus.*

partem insulae unde nūper profectī erant māgnō cum
perīculō dēicerentur. Incolae tamen, cum nox esset
obscūra, Argonautās nōn āgnōscēbant et nāvem inimīcam
vēnisse arbitrātī, arma rapuērunt et eōs ēgredī prohibē-
bant. Ācriter in lītore pūgnātum est et rēx ipse, quī cum 5
aliīs dēcucurrerat, ab Argonautīs occīsus est. Mox tamen,
cum iam dīlūcēsceret, sēnsērunt incolae sē errāre et arma
abiēcērunt; Argonautae autem, cum vidērent rēgem occīsum esse, māgnum dolōrem percēpērunt.

7. The Loss of Hylas.

Postrīdiē ēius diēī Iāsōn, tempestātem satis idōneam 10
esse arbitrātus, summa enim tranquillitās iam cōnsecūta
erat, ancorās sustulit et pauca mīllia passuum prōgressus,
ante noctem Mӯsiam attigit. Ibi paucās hōrās in ancorīs
exspectāvit; ā nautīs enim cōgnōverat aquae cōpiam
quam sēcum habērent iam dēficere, quam ob causam 15
quīdam ex Argonautīs in terram ēgressī aquam quaerēbant. Hōrum in numerō erat Hylas quīdam, puer fōrmā
praestantissimā, quī dum fontem quaerit ā comitibus
paulum sēcesserat. Nymphae autem, quae fontem colē-
bant, cum iuvenem vīdissent, eī persuādēre cōnātae sunt 20
ut sēcum manēret; et cum ille negāret sē hōc factūrum
esse puerum vī abstulērunt.

Comitēs ēius, postquam Hylam āmīssum esse sēnsērunt, māgnō dolōre adfectī, diū frūstrā quaerēbant; Herculēs autem et Polyphēmus, quī vestīgia puerī longius 25
secūtī erant, ubi tandem ad lītus rediērunt, Iāsonem sol-
visse cōgnōvērunt.

2 dēicerentur: *dēferrentur*.	19 colēbant: *incolēbant*.
9 percēpērunt: p. 2, l. 11.	22 abstulērunt: p. 2, l. 8.
15 dēficere: *deësse*.	26 solvisse: p. 4, l. 17.

8. Dining Made Difficult.

Post haec Argonautae ad Thrāciam cursum tenuērunt
et postquam ad oppidum Salmydessum nāvem appulerant
in terram ēgressī sunt. Ibi cum ab incolīs quaesīssent
quis rēgnum ēius regiōnis obtinēret, certiōrēs factī sunt
5 Phīneum quendam tum rēgem esse. Cōgnōvērunt etiam
hunc caecum esse et dīrō quōdam suppliciō adficī, quod
ōlim sē crūdēlissimum in fīliōs suōs praebuisset. Cūius
supplicī hōc erat genus. Mīssa erant ā Iove mōnstra
quaedam, speciē horribilī, quae capita virginum, corpora
10 volucrum habēbant. Hae volucrēs, quae Harpȳiae appel-
lābantur, Phīneō summam molestiam adferēbant; quotiēns enim ille accubuerat, veniēbant et cibum appositum
statim auferēbant. Quae cum ita essent, haud multum
āfuit quīn Phīneus fame morerētur.

9. The Harpies Beaten.

15 Rēs igitur in hōc locō erant, cum Argonautae nāvem
appulērunt. Phīneus autem, simul atque audīvit eōs in
suōs fīnīs ēgressōs esse, māgnō opere gāvīsus est. Sciēbat
enim quantam opīniōnem virtūtis Argonautae habērent
nec dubitābat quīn sibi auxilium ferrent. Nūntium igitur
20 ad nāvem mīsit, quī Iāsonem sociōsque ad rēgiam vocāret.
Eō cum vēnissent, Phīneus dēmōnstrāvit quantō in perīculō suae rēs essent et prōmīsit sē māgna praemia datūrum esse, sī illī remedium repperissent. Argonautae
negōtium libenter suscēpērunt et ubi hōra vēnit cum rēge
25 accubuērunt; at simul āc cēna apposita est, Harpȳiae

---

1 cursum tenuērunt: p. 4, l. 24.   18 opīniōnem: *fāmam.*
7 praebuisset: p. 2, l. 12.   24 hōra: *tempus.*
15 nāvem appulērunt: l. 2.   25 accubuērunt: l. 12.

cēnāculum intrāvērunt et cibum auferre cōnābantur.
Argonautae prīmum gladiīs volucrīs petiērunt ; cum
tamen vidērent hōc nihil prōdesse, Zētēs et Calais, quī
ālīs īnstrūctī sunt, in āera sē sublevāvērunt, ut dēsuper
impetum facerent. Quod cum sēnsissent Harpȳiae, reī 5
novitāte perterritae, statim aufūgērunt neque posteā umquam rediērunt.

10. The Symplegades.

Hōc factō, Phīneus, ut prō tantō beneficiō meritās
grātiās referret, Iāsonī dēmōnstrāvit quā ratiōne Symplēgadēs vītāre posset. Symplēgadēs autem duae erant 10
rūpēs ingentī māgnitūdine, quae ā Iove positae erant eō
cōnsiliō, nē quis ad Colchida pervenīret. Hae parvō
intervāllō in marī natābant et sī quid in medium spatium
vēnerat incrēdibilī celeritāte concurrēbant. Postquam
igitur ā Phīneō doctus est quid faciendum esset, Iāsōn 15
sublātīs ancorīs nāvem solvit et lēnī ventō prōvēctus mox
ad Symplēgadēs appropinquāvit ; tum in prōrā stāns
columbam quam in manū tenēbat ēmīsit. Illa rēctā viā
per medium spatium volāvit et priusquam rūpēs cōnflixē-
runt incolumis ēvāsit caudā tantum āmīssā. Tum rūpēs 20
utrimque discessērunt ; antequam tamen rūrsus concur-
rerent, Argonautae, bene intellegentēs omnem spem salūtis
in celeritāte positam esse, summā vī rēmīs contendērunt
et nāvem incolumem perdūxērunt. Hōc factō, dīs grātiās
libenter ēgērunt, quōrum auxiliō ē tantō perīculō ēreptī 25
essent ; bene enim sciēbant nōn sine auxiliō deōrum rem
ita fēlīciter ēvēnisse.

16 **sublātīs ancorīs**: p. 5, l. 12.
17 **appropinquāvit** : cf. p. 4, l. 6.
20 **incolumis** : *salva.*

23 **contendērunt** : *labōrāvē-*
runt.
24 **grātiās** . . . **ēgērunt** : l. 9.

11. A Heavy Task.

Brevī intermīssō spatiō, Argonautae ad flūmen Phāsim
vēnērunt, quod in fīnibus Colchōrum erat. Ibi cum nāvem
appulissent et in terram ēgressī essent, statim ad rēgem
Aeētem sē contulērunt et ab eō postulāvērunt ut vellus
5 aureum sibi trāderētur. Ille cum audīvisset quam ob
causam Argonautae vēnissent, īrā commōtus est et diū
negābat sē vellus trāditūrum esse. Tandem tamen, quod
sciēbat Iāsonem nōn sine auxiliō deōrum hōc negōtium
suscēpisse, mūtātā sententiā prōmīsit sē vellus trāditūrum,
10 sī Iāsōn labōrēs duōs difficillimōs prius perfēcisset; et
cum Iāsōn dīxisset sē ad omnia perīcula subeunda parātum esse, quid fierī vellet ostendit. Prīmum iungendī
erant duo taurī speciē horribilī, quī flammās ex ōre ēdē-
bant. Tum, hīs iūnctīs, ager quīdam arandus erat et
15 dentēs dracōnis serendī. Hīs audītīs Iāsōn, etsī rem esse
summī perīculī intellegēbat, tamen, nē hanc occāsiōnem
reī bene gerendae āmitteret, negōtium suscēpit.

12. The Magic Ointment.

At Mēdēa, rēgis fīlia, Iāsonem adamāvit et ubi audīvit
eum tantum perīculum subitūrum esse rem aegrē ferēbat.
20 Intellegēbat enim patrem suum hunc labōrem prōposuisse
eō ipsō cōnsiliō, ut Iāsōn morerētur. Quae cum ita
essent, Mēdēa, quae summam scientiam medicīnae habēbat, hōc cōnsilium iniit. Mediā nocte clam patre ex urbe
ēvāsit et postquam in montīs fīnitimōs vēnit herbās
25 quāsdam carpsit; tum sūcō expressō unguentum parāvit

---

2 **nāvem appulissent**: p. 6,   15 **etsī**: p. 2, l. 10.
l. 15.   23 **cōnsilium iniit**: p. 3, l. 8.
9 **sententiā**: *cōnsiliō.*   23 **clam patre**: *īnsciente patre.*

quod vī suā corpus aleret nervōsque cōnfirmāret. Hōc factō Iāsonī unguentum dedit, praecēpit autem ut eō diē quō istī labōrēs cōnficiendī essent corpus suum et arma māne oblineret. Iāsōn, etsī paene omnīs māgnitūdine et vīribus corporis antecellēbat, vīta enim omnis in vēnā- 5 tiōnibus atque in studiīs reī mīlitāris cōnstiterat, cēnsēbat tamen hōc cōnsilium nōn neglegendum esse.

13. Sowing the Dragon's Teeth.

Ubi is diēs vēnit quem rēx ad arandum agrum ēdīxerat, Iāsōn ortā lūce cum sociīs ad locum cōnstitūtum sē con- tulit. Ibi stabulum ingēns repperit in quō taurī inclūsī 10 erant ; tum portīs apertīs taurōs in lūcem trāxit et summā cum difficultāte iugum imposuit. At Aeētēs, cum vidēret taurōs nihil contrā Iāsonem valēre, māgnō opere mīrātus est ; nēsciēbat enim fīliam suam auxilium eī dedisse. Tum Iāsōn omnibus aspicientibus agrum arāre coepit, 15 quā in rē tantam dīligentiam praebuit, ut ante merīdiem tōtum opus cōnfēcerit. Hōc factō, ad locum ubi rēx sedēbat adiit et dentīs dracōnis postulāvit. Quōs ubi accēpit, in agrum quem arāverat māgnā cum dīligentiā sparsit. Hōrum autem dentium nātūra erat tālis ut in 20 eō locō ubi īnsitī essent virī armātī mīrō quōdam modō gīgnerentur.

14. A Strange Crop.

Nōndum tamen Iāsōn tōtum opus cōnfēcerat ; imperā- verat enim eī Aeētēs ut armātōs virōs, quī ē dentibus gīgnerentur, sōlus interficeret. Postquam igitur omnīs 25

9 **sē contulit**: p. 2, l. 18. **20 sparsit**: cf. *īnsitī*, l. 21.
16 **praebuit**: p. 4, l. 1. **21 īnsitī**: cf. *serendī*, p. 8, l. 15.

dentīs in agrum sparsit, Iāsōn lassitūdine exanimātus
quiētī sē trādidit, dum virī istī gīgnerentur. Paucās
hōrās dormiēbat; sub vesperum tamen ē somnō subitō
excitātus rem ita ēvēnisse ut praedictum erat cōgnōvit;
5 nam in omnibus agrī partibus virī ingentī māgnitūdine
corporis, gladiīs galeīsque armātī, mīrum in modum ē
terrā oriēbantur. Hōc cōgnitō Iāsōn cōnsilium quod
dederat Mēdēa nōn omittendum esse putābat. Saxum
igitur ingēns, ita enim praecēperat Mēdēa, in mediōs virōs
10 cōniēcit. Illī undique ad locum concurrērunt et cum
quisque sibi id saxum nēsciō cūr habēre vellet māgna
contrōversia orta est. Mox strictīs gladiīs inter sē pūgnāre coepērunt et cum hōc modō plūrimī occīsī essent
reliquī volneribus cōnfectī ā Iāsone nūllō negōtiō inter-
15 fectī sunt.

15. Flight of Medea.

At rēx Aeëtēs, ubi cōgnōvit Iāsonem labōrem prōposi-
tum cōnfēcisse, īrā graviter commōtus est, intellegēbat
enim id per dolum factum esse, nec dubitābat quīn Mēdēa
auxilium eī tulisset. Mēdēa autem, cum intellegeret sē
20 in māgnō fore perīculō, sī in rēgiā mānsisset, fugā salūtem
petere cōnstituit. Omnibus igitur ad fugam parātīs mediā
nocte īnsciente patre cum frātre Absyrtō ēvāsit et quam
celerrimē ad locum ubi Argō subducta erat sē contulit.
Eō cum vēnisset, ad pedēs Iāsonis sē prōiēcit et multīs
25 cum lacrimīs obsecrāvit eum, nē in tantō discrīmine mulierem dēsereret, quae eī tantum prōfuisset. Ille, quod

---

1 lassitūdine : *dēfatīgātiōne.*
4 ēvēnisse : p. 7, l. 27.
9 praecēperat : p. 9, l. 2.

22 īnsciente patre : p. 8, l. 23.
22 ēvāsit : p. 8, l. 24.
25 discrīmine : *perīculō.*

memoriā tenēbat sē per ēius auxilium ē māgnō perīculō
ēvāsisse, libenter eam excēpit et postquam causam veniendī audīvit hortātus est nē patris īram timēret. Prōmīsit autem sē quam prīmum eam in nāvī suā āvēctūrum.

16. The Seizure of the Fleece.

Postrīdiē ēius diēī Iāsōn cum sociīs suīs ortā lūce 5
nāvem dēdūxit et tempestātem idōneam nactī ad eum
locum rēmīs contendērunt, quō in locō Mēdēa vellus
cēlātum esse dēmōnstrāvit. Eō cum vēnissent Iāsōn in
terram ēgressus est et sociīs ad mare relictīs quī praesidiō
nāvī essent ipse cum Mēdēā in silvās viam cēpit. Pauca 10
mīllia passuum per silvam prōgressus vellus quod quaerē-
bat ex arbore suspēnsum vīdit. Id tamen auferre rēs
erat summae difficultātis; nōn modo enim locus ipse
ēgregiē et nātūrā et arte mūnītus erat, sed etiam dracō
quīdam speciē terribilī arborem custōdiēbat. At Mēdēa, 15
quae, ut suprā dēmōnstrāvimus, medicīnae summam scientiam habuit, rāmum quem ex arbore proximā dēripuerat
venēnō infēcit. Hōc factō ad locum appropinquāvit et
dracōnem, quī faucibus apertīs adventum exspectābat,
venēnō sparsit. Proinde, dum dracō somnō oppressus 20
dormit, Iāsōn vellus aureum ex arbore dēripuit et cum
Mēdēā quam celerrimē pedem rettulit.

17. Back to the Argo.

Dum tamen ea geruntur, Argonautae, quī ad mare
relictī erant, animō anxiō reditum Iāsonis exspectābant;

5 ortā lūce: p. 9, l. 9. 20 proinde: *igitur*, p. 2, l. 8.
7 rēmīs contend.: p. 7, l. 23. 22 pedem rettulit: *sē contulit*,
16 scientiam: p. 8, l. 22. p. 2, l. 18.

bene enim intellegēbant id negōtium summī esse perīculī.
Postquam igitur ad occāsum sōlis frūstrā exspectāverant,
dē ēius salūte dēspērāre coepērunt nec dubitābant quīn
aliquī cāsus accidisset. Quae cum ita essent, mātūran-
5 dum sibi cēnsuērunt, ut auxilium ducī ferrent, et dum
proficīscī parant lūmen quoddam subitō cōnspiciunt
mīrum in modum inter silvās refulgēns. Māgnō opere
mīrātī quae causa esset ēius reī ad locum concurrunt.
Quō cum vēnissent, Iāsonī et Mēdēae advenientibus
10 occurrērunt et vellus aureum lūminis ēius causam esse
cōgnōvērunt. Omnī timōre sublātō, māgnō cum gaudiō
ducem suum excēpērunt et dīs grātiās libenter rettulērunt
quod rēs ita fēlīciter ēvēnisset.

18. Pursued by the Angry Father.

Hīs rēbus gestīs, omnēs sine morā nāvem rūrsus cōn-
15 scendērunt et sublātīs ancorīs prīmā vigiliā solvērunt ;
neque enim satis tūtum esse arbitrātī sunt in eō locō
manēre. At rēx Aeētēs, quī iam ante inimīcō in eōs
fuerat animō, ubi cōgnōvit fīliam suam nōn modo ad
Argonautās sē recēpisse sed etiam ad vellus auferendum
20 auxilium tulisse, hōc dolōre gravius exārsit. Nāvem
longam quam celerrimē dēdūcī iussit et mīlitibus impo-
sitīs fugientīs īnsecūtus est. Argonautae, quī bene
sciēbant rem in discrīmine esse, summīs vīribus rēmīs
contendēbant. Cum tamen nāvis quā vehēbantur ingentī
25 esset māgnitūdine, nōn eādem celeritāte quā Colchī prō-

5 **cēnsuērunt** : *putāvērunt,*   12 **grātiās rettulērunt** : p. 7, l. 9.
p. 10, l. 8.   15 **sublātīs ancorīs** : p. 7, l. 16.
  7 **māgnō opere** : p. 6, l. 17.   19 **sē recēpisse** : *sē contulisse,* p.
12 **excēpērunt** : p. 11, l. 2.   2, l. 18.

gredī poterant. Quae cum ita essent, minimum āfuit quīn ā Colchīs sequentibus caperentur neque enim longius intererat quam quō tēlum adicī posset. At Mēdēa, cum vīdisset quō in locō rēs essent, paene omnī spē dēpositā, īnfandum hōc cōnsilium cēpit. 5

19. A Fearful Expedient.

Erat in nāvī Argonautārum fīlius quīdam rēgis Aeētae, nōmine Absyrtus, quem, ut suprā dēmōnstrāvimus, Mēdēa ex urbe fugiēns sēcum abdūxerat. Hunc puerum Mēdēa cōnstituit interficere eō cōnsiliō ut membrīs ēius in mare cōniectīs cursum Colchōrum impedīret; prō certō enim 10 sciēbat Aeētem, cum membra fīlī vīdisset, nōn longius prōsecūtūrum esse, neque opīniō eam fefellit; omnia enim ita ēvēnērunt ut Mēdēa spērāverat. Aeētēs, ubi prīmum membra vīdit, ad ea conligenda nāvem statuī iussit; dum tamen ea geruntur, Argonautae nōn inter- 15 mīssō rēmigandī labōre, mox, quod necesse fuit, ē cōnspectū hostium remōtī sunt neque prius fugere dēstitērunt quam ad flūmen Ēridanum pervēnērunt. At Aeētēs nihil sibi prōfutūrum esse arbitrātus, sī longius prōgressus esset, animō dēmīssō domum revertit, ut fīlī corpus ad 20 sepultūram daret.

20. The Bargain with Pelias.

Tandem post multa perīcula Iāsōn in eundem locum pervēnit unde ōlim profectus erat. Tum ē nāvī ēgressus

1 **minimum āfuit**: p. 6, l. 14.   15 **intermīssō**: p. 4, l. 2.
5 **cōnsilium cēpit**: p. 3, l. 8.   19 **prōfutūrum**: p. 10, l. 26.
7 **suprā**: *anteā.*   21 **sepultūram daret**: *sepe-*
10 **impedīret**: *morārētur.*   *līret.*

ad rēgem Peliam, quī rēgnum adhūc obtinēbat, statim sē
contulit et vellere aureō mōnstrātō ab eō postulāvit ut
rēgnum sibi trāderētur.; Peliās enim pollicitus erat, sī,
Iāsōn vellus rettulisset, sē rēgnum eī trāditūrum. Post-
5 quam Iāsōn ostendit quid fierī vellet Peliās prīmum nihil
respondit, sed diū in eādem trīstitiā tacitus permānsit ;
tandem ita locūtus est. " Vidēs mē aetāte iam esse cōnfectum neque dubium est quīn diēs suprēmus mihi adsit.
Liceat igitur mihi dum vīvam hōc rēgnum obtinēre ; tum,
10 postquam ego ē vītā discesserō, tū in meum locum
veniēs." Hāc ōrātiōne adductus Iāsōn respondit sē id
factūrum quod ille rogāsset.

21. Boiled Mutton.

Hīs rēbus cōgnitīs Mēdēa rem aegrē tulit et rēgnī
cupiditāte adducta cōnstituit mortem rēgī per dolum
15 īnferre. Hōc cōnstitūtō, ad fīliās rēgis vēnit atque ita
locūta est. " Vidētis patrem vestrum aetāte iam esse
cōnfectum neque ad labōrem rēgnandī perferendum satis
valēre. Voltisne eum rūrsus iuvenem fierī ? " Tum fīliae
rēgis hīs audītīs ita respondērunt. " Num hōc fierī potest ?
20 Quis enim umquam ē sene iuvenis factus est ? " At
Mēdēa respondit, " Scītis mē medicīnae summam habēre
scientiam. Nunc igitur vōbīs dēmōnstrābō quō modō
haec rēs fierī possit." Hīs dictīs, cum arietem aetāte
iam cōnfectum interfēcisset, membra ēius in vās aeneum
25 posuit et īgnī suppositō aquae herbās quāsdam īnfūdit.
Tum, dum aqua effervēsceret, carmen magicum cantābat.

---

7 cōnfectum : p. 10, l. 14.   13 aegrē tulit: *īrā commōtā est.*
9 obtinēre : *habēre, tenēre.*   22 scientiam : p. 8, l. 22.

Post breve tempus ariēs ē vāse exsiluit et vīribus refectīs
per agrōs currēbat.

22. A Dangerous Experiment.

Dum filiae rēgis hōc mīrāculum stupentēs intuentur,
Mēdēa ita locūta est. "Vidētis quantum valeat medicīna. Vōs igitur, sī voltis patrem vestrum in adulēscen- 5
tiam redūcere, id quod fēcī ipsae faciētis. Vōs patris
membra in vās cōnicite; ego herbās magicās praebēbō."
Hīs audītis filiae rēgis cōnsilium quod dederat Mēdēa
nōn omittendum putāvērunt. Patrem igitur Peliam necā-
vērunt et membra ēius in vās aeneum cōniēcērunt; nihil 10
enim dubitābant quīn hōc māximē eī prōfutūrum esset.
At rēs omnīnō aliter ēvēnit āc spērāverant, Mēdēa enim
nōn eāsdem herbās dedit quibus ipsa ūsa erat. Itaque,
postquam diū frūstrā exspectāvērunt, patrem suum rē vērā
mortuum esse intellēxērunt. Hīs rēbus gestīs, Mēdēa 15
spērābat sē cum coniuge suō rēgnum acceptūram esse;
at cīvēs, cum intellegerent quō modō Peliās periisset,
tantum scelus aegrē tulērunt itaque Iāsone et Mēdēā ē
rēgnō expulsīs Acastum rēgem creāvērunt.

23. A Fatal Gift.

Post haec Iāsōn et Mēdēa ē Thessaliā expulsī ad urbem 20
Corinthum vēnērunt, cūius urbis Creōn quīdam rēgnum
tum obtinēbat. Erat autem Creontī filia ūna, nōmine
Glaucē. Quam cum vīdisset, Iāsōn cōnstituit Mēdēam
uxōrem suam repudiāre eō cōnsiliō, ut Glaucēn in mātri-

---

3 intuentur: *vident.*
5 adulēscentiam: *iuventūtem.*
11 prōfutūrum: p. 13, l. 19.

12 āc: *quam.*
18 aegrē tulērunt: p. 14, l. 13.
22 obtinēbat: p. 14, l. 9.

mōnium dūceret. At Mēdēa, ubi intellēxit quae ille in
animō habēret, īrā graviter commōta, iūre iūrandō cōnfīrmāvit sē tantam iniūriam ultūram. Hōc igitur cōnsilium
cēpit. Vestem parāvit summā arte contextam et variīs
5 colōribus tīnctam. Hanc dīrō quōdam īnfēcit venēnō,
cūius vīs tālis erat ut sī quis eam vestem induisset
corpus ēius quasi īgnī ūrerētur. Hōc factō vestem ad
Glaucēn mīsit : illa autem nihil malī suspicāns dōnum
libenter accēpit et vestem novam mōre fēminārum
10 statim induit.

24. Flight of Medea and Death of Jason.

Vix vestem induerat Glaucē, cum dolōrem gravem per
omnia membra sēnsit et post paulum dīrō cruciātū adfecta
ē vītā excessit. Hīs rēbus gestīs, Mēdēa furōre atque
āmentiā impulsa filiōs suōs necāvit. Tum māgnum sibi
15 fore perīculum arbitrāta, sī in Thessaliā manēret, ex eā
regiōne fugere cōnstituit. Hōc cōnstitūtō Sōlem ōrāvit
ut in tantō perīculō auxilium sibi praebēret. Sōl autem
hīs precibus commōtus currum quendam mīsit, cuī dra-
cōnēs ālīs īnstrūctī iūnctī erant. Mēdēa nōn omittendam
20 tantam occāsiōnem arbitrāta currum cōnscendit itaque
per āera vēcta incolumis ad urbem Athēnās pervēnit.
Iāsōn autem post breve tempus mīrō modō occīsus est.
Ille enim, sīve cāsū sīve cōnsiliō deōrum, sub umbrā
nāvis suae, quae in lītus subducta erat, ōlim dormiēbat.
25 At nāvis, quae adhūc ērēcta steterat, in eam partem ubi
Iāsōn iacēbat subitō dēlapsa virum īnfēlīcem oppressit.

5 īnfēcit venēnō: p. 11, l. 18.   20 occāsiōnem : p. 8, l. 16.
13 ē vītā excessit : *mortua est.*   21 vēcta: p. 4, l. 19.
16 ōrāvit: *obsecrāvit*, p. 10, l. 25.   21 incolumis : p. 7, l. 20.

ULYSSES.

Ulysses, a celebrated Greek hero, took a prominent part in the long siege of Troy. After the fall of the city, he set out with his followers on his homeward voyage to Ithaca, an island of which he was king; but, being driven out of his course by northerly winds, he was compelled to touch at the country of the Lotus Eaters, who are supposed to have lived on the north coast of Libya (Africa). Some of his comrades were so delighted with the lotus fruit that they wished to remain in the country, but Ulysses compelled them to embark again, and continued his voyage. He next came to the island of Sicily, and fell into the hands of the giant Polyphemus, one of the Cyclopes. After several of his comrades had been killed by the monster, Ulysses made his escape by stratagem, and next reached the country of the Winds. Here he received the help of Æolus, king of the winds, and, having set sail again, arrived within sight of Ithaca; but, owing to the folly of his companions, the winds became suddenly adverse, and they were again driven back. They then touched at an island occupied by Circe, a powerful enchantress, who exercised her charms on the companions of Ulysses, and turned them into swine. By the help of the god Mercury, Ulysses himself not only escaped this fate, but forced Circe to restore her victims to human shape. After staying a year with Circe, Ulysses again set out, and eventually reached his home.

25. Homeward Bound.

Urbem Trōiam ā Graecīs decem annōs obsessam esse, satis cōnstat; dē hōc enim bellō Homērus, māximus poētārum Graecōrum, Īliadem, opus nōtissimum, scrīpsit.

2 **cōnstat**: *cōgnitum est.*

Trōiā tandem per īnsidiās captā, Graecī longō bellō fessī domum redīre mātūrāvērunt. Omnibus igitur ad profectiōnem parātīs nāvīs dēdūxērunt et tempestātem idōneam nactī māgnō cum gaudiō solvērunt. Erat inter prīmōs 5 Graecōrum Ulixēs quīdam, vir summae virtūtis āc prūdentiae, quem dīcunt nōnnūllī dolum istum excōgitāsse per quem Trōiam captam esse cōnstat. Hīc rēgnum īnsulae Ithacae obtinuerat et paulō antequam cum reliquīs Graecīs ad bellum profectus est, cum puellam fōrmōsissi-10 mam, nōmine Pēnelopēn, in mātrimōnium dūxisset. Nunc igitur cum iam decem annōs quasi in exsiliō cōnsūmpsisset, māgnā cupīdine patriae et uxōris videndae ārdēbat.

26. The Lotus Eaters.

Postquam tamen pauca mīllia passuum ā lītore Trōiae prōgressī sunt, tanta tempestās subitō coörta est ut nūlla 15 nāvium cursum tenēre posset, sed aliae aliās in partīs dīsicerentur. Nāvis autem quā ipse Ulixēs vehēbātur vī tempestātis ad merīdiem dēlāta, decimō diē ad lītus Libyae appulsa est. Ancorīs iactīs, Ulixēs cōnstituit nōnnūllōs ē sociīs in terram expōnere, quī aquam ad 20 nāvem referrent et quālis esset nātūra ēius regiōnis cōgnōscerent. Hī igitur ē nāvī ēgressī imperāta facere parābant. Dum tamen fontem quaerunt, quibusdam ex incolīs obviam factī ab iīs hospitiō acceptī sunt. Accidit autem ut vīctus eōrum hominum ē mīrō quōdam frūctū 25 quem lōtum appellābant paene omnīnō cōnstāret. Quem cum Graecī gustāssent, patriae et sociōrum statim oblītī

---

2 mātūrāvērunt: *contendē-*
runt, p. 12, l. 24.
12 ārdēbat: p. 12, l. 20.

16 dīsicerentur: *dispergerentur.*
18 appulsa: *admōta.*
25 cōnstāret: *cōnsisteret.*

cōnfīrmāvērunt sē semper in eā terrā mānsūrōs, ut dulcī illō cibō in aeternum vescerentur.

27. The Lotus Eaters — *continued.*

At Ulixēs, cum ab hōrā septimā ad vesperum exspec- tāsset, veritus nē sociī suī in perīculō versārentur, nōnnūllōs ē reliquīs mīsit, ut quae causa esset morae, 5 cōgnōscerent. Hī igitur in terram expositī, ad vīcum quī nōn longē āfuit sē contulērunt; quō cum vēnissent, sociōs suōs quasi vīnō ēbriōs reppererunt. Tum ubi causam veniendī docuērunt, iis persuādēre cōnābantur ut sēcum ad nāvem redīrent. Illī tamen resistere āc manū 10 sē dēfendere coepērunt, saepe clāmitantēs sē numquam ex eō locō abitūrōs. Quae cum ita essent, nūntiī rē īnfectā ad Ulixem rediērunt. Hīs rēbus cōgnitīs, Ulixēs ipse cum omnibus quī in nāvī relīctī sunt ad locum vēnit; et sociōs suōs frūstrā hortātus ut sponte suā redīrent, 15 manibus eōrum post terga vinctīs, invītōs ad nāvem reportāvit. Tum ancorīs sublātīs quam celerrimē ē portū solvit.

28. The One-eyed Giant.

Postrīdiē ēius diēī postquam tōtam noctem rēmīs con- tenderant, ad terram īgnōtam nāvem appulērunt. Tum, 20 quod nātūram ēius regiōnis īgnōrābat, ipse Ulixēs cum duodecim ē sociīs in terram ēgressus locum explōrāre cōnstituit. Paulum ā lītore prōgressī ad antrum ingēns

4 **versārentur**: *essent.*
6 **expositī**: *ēgressī*, p. 18, l. 21.
17 **ancorīs sublātīs**: cf. opp., p. 18, l. 18.

17 **quam celerrimē**: *summā celeritāte.*
19 **rēmīs contenderant**: p. 12, l. 23.

pervēnērunt, quod habitārī sēnsērunt; ēius enim introitum arte et manibus mūnītum esse animadvertērunt.
Mox, etsī intellegēbant sē nōn sine perīculō id factūrōs,
antrum intrāvērunt, quod cum fēcissent, māgnam cōpiam
5 lactis invēnērunt in vāsīs ingentibus conditam. Dum
tamen mīrantur quis eam sēdem incoleret, sonitum terribilem audīvērunt et oculīs ad portam versīs mōnstrum
horribile vīdērunt, hūmānā quidem speciē et figūrā sed
ingentī māgnitūdine corporis. Cum autem animadver-
10 tissent gigantem ūnum tantum oculum habēre in mediā
fronte positum, intellēxērunt hunc esse ūnum ē Cyclōpibus, dē quibus fāmam iam accēperant.

29. The Giant's Supper.

Cyclōpēs autem pāstōrēs erant quīdam, quī īnsulam
Siciliam et praecipuē montem Aetnam incolēbant; ibi
15 enim Volcānus, praeses fabrōrum et īgnis repertor, cūius
servī Cyclōpēs erant, officīnam suam habēbat.
Graecī igitur, simul āc mōnstrum vīdērunt, terrōre
paene exanimātī in interiōrem partem spēluncae refūgērunt et sē ibi cēlāre cōnābantur. Polyphēmus autem, ita
20 enim gigās appellātus est, pecora sua in spēluncam ēgit;
tum cum saxō ingentī portam obstrūxisset, īgnem in
mediō antrō accendit. Hōc factō, oculō omnia perlūstrābat et cum sēnsisset hominēs in interiōre parte antrī
cēlārī, māgnā vōce exclāmāvit. "Quī estis hominēs?
25 Mercātōrēs an latrōnēs?" Tum Ulixēs respondit sē
neque mercātōrēs esse neque praedandī causā vēnisse:

5 conditam: *positam.*   15 repertor: *inventor.*
12 accēperant: *audīverant.*   20 spēluncam: *antrum.*
22 perlūstrābat: *perspiciēbat.*

sed ē Trōiā redeuntīs vī tempestātum ā rēctō cursū dēpulsōs esse ; ōrāvit etiam ut sibi sine iniūriā abīre licēret.
Tum Polyphēmus quaesīvit ubi esset nāvis quā vēctī
essent ; Ulixēs autem, cum bene intellegeret sibi māximē
praecavendum esse, respondit nāvem suam in rūpīs 5
cōniectam et omnīnō perfrāctam esse. Polyphēmus autem
sine ūllō respōnsō duo ē sociīs manū corripuit et membrīs eōrum dīvolsīs carnem dēvorāre coepit.

30. No Way of Escape.

Dum haec geruntur, Graecōrum animōs tantus terror
occupāvit ut nē vōcem quidem ēdere possent, sed omnī 10
spē salūtis dēpositā mortem praesentem exspectārent.
At Polyphēmus, postquam famēs hāc tam horribilī cēnā
dēpulsa est, humī prōstrātus somnō sē dedit. Quod cum
vīdisset Ulixēs, tantam occāsiōnem reī bene gerendae
nōn omittendam arbitrātus, in eō erat ut pectus mōnstrī 15
gladiō trānsfīgeret. Cum tamen nihil temerē agèndum
exīstimāret, cōnstituit explōrāre, antequam hōc faceret,
quā ratiōne ex antrō ēvādere possent. At cum saxum
animadvertisset, quō introitus obstrūctus erat, nihil
sibi prōfutūrum intellēxit sī Polyphēmum interfēcisset. 20
Tanta enim erat ēius saxī māgnitūdō ut nē ā decem
quidem hominibus āmovērī posset. Quae cum ita essent,
Ulixēs hōc dēstitit cōnātū et ad sociōs rediit ; quī, cum
intellēxissent quō in locō rēs essent, nūllā spē salūtis
oblātā, dē fōrtūnīs suīs dēspērāre coepērunt. Ille tamen, 25

---

1 **dēpulsōs:** *dēlātōs,* p. 18,
l. 17.
   5 **praecavendum:** *cavendum,*
p. 2, l. 21.

7 **corripuit :** *prehendit.*
   8 **dīvolsīs :** *dīvīsīs.*
   15 **in eō erat ut :** *minimum
āfuit quīn,* p. 13, l. 1.

nē animōs dēmitterent, vehementer hortātus est ; dēmōnstrāvit sē iam anteā ē multīs et māgnīs perīculīs ēvāsisse,
neque dubium esse quīn in tantō discrīmine diī auxilium
adlātūrī essent.

31. A Plan for Vengeance.

5 Ortā lūce Polyphēmus iam ē somnō excitātus idem
quod hēsternō diē fēcit ; correptīs enim duōbus ē reliquīs
virīs, carnem eōrum sine morā dēvorāvit. Tum, cum
saxum āmōvisset, ipse cum pecore suō ex antrō prōgressus est. Quod cum vidērent Graecī, māgnam in spem
10 vēnērunt sē post paulum ēvāsūrōs. Mox tamen ab hāc
spē repulsī sunt ; nam Polyphēmus, postquam omnēs
ovēs exiērunt, saxum in locum restituit. Reliquī omnī
spē salūtis dēpositā lāmentīs lacrimīsque sē dēdidērunt :
Ulixēs vērō quī, ut suprā dēmōnstrāvimus, vir māgnī
15 fuit cōnsilī, etsī bene intellegēbat rem in discrīmine esse,
nōndum omnīnō dēspērābat. Tandem postquam diū tōtō
animō cōgitāvit, hōc cēpit cōnsilium. Ē lignīs quae in
antrō reposita sunt, pālum māgnum dēlēgit, quem summā
cum dīligentiā praeacūtum fēcit ; tum postquam sociīs quid
20 fierī vellet ostendit, reditum Polyphēmī exspectābat.

32. A Glass too Much.

Sub vesperum Polyphēmus ad antrum rediit et eōdem
modō quō anteā cēnāvit. Tum Ulixēs ūtrem vīnī prōmpsit, quem fōrte, ut in tālibus rēbus accidere cōnsuēvit,
sēcum attulerat, et postquam māgnam crātēram vīnō

---

1 animōs dēmitterent : *ani-*
mōs dēspondērent.
6 hēsternō diē : *herī.*
7 sine morā : *statim.*
15 discrīmine : *perīculō.*
22 ūtrem : *pellem.*
22 prōmpsit : *prōtulit.*

replēvit, gigantem ad bibendum prōvocāvit. Polyphēmus, quī numquam anteā vīnum gustāverat, tōtam crātēram statim hausit ; quod cum fēcisset, tantam voluptātem percēpit ut iterum et tertium crātēram replērī iusserit. Tum cum quaesīvisset quō nōmine Ulixēs appellārētur, ille 5 respondit sē Nēminem appellārī. Quod cum audīvisset, Polyphēmus ita locūtus est : " Hanc tibi grātiam prō tantō beneficiō referam ; tē ūltimum omnium dēvorābō." Hīs dictīs cibō vīnōque gravātus recubuit et post breve tempus somnō oppressus est. Tum Ulixēs sociīs convocātīs, 10 " Habēmus," inquit, " quam petiimus facultātem ; nē igitur tantam occāsiōnem reī bene gerendae omittāmus."

33. Noman.

Hīs dictīs postquam extrēmum pālum īgnī calefēcit, oculum Polyphēmī dum dormit flagrante līgnō trānsfōdit; quō factō, omnēs in dīversās spēluncae partīs sē abdidē- 15 runt. At ille subitō illō dolōre, quod necesse fuit, ē somnō excitātus, clāmōrem terribilem sustulit et dum per spēluncam errat, Ulixī manum inicere cōnābātur ; cum tamen iam omnīnō caecus esset, nūllō modō hōc efficere potuit. Intereā reliquī Cyclōpēs clāmōre audītō undique 20 ad spēluncam convēnērunt et ad introitum adstantēs quid Polyphēmus ageret quaesīvērunt et quam ob causam tantum clāmōrem sustulisset. Ille respondit sē graviter volnerātum esse et māgnō dolōre adficī. Cum tamen cēterī quaesīvissent quis eī vim intulisset, respondit ille 25 Nēminem id fēcisse. Quibus audītīs, ūnus ē Cyclōpibus,

2 gustāverat : cf. p. 19, l. 2.   14 trānsfōdit : *trānsfīxit*, p.
3 percēpit : p. 5, l. 9.   21, l. 16.
8 referam : *reddam*.   21 introitum : p. 21, l. 19 ;
11 facultātem : *occāsiōnem*.   *aditum.*

"At sī nēmō," inquit, "tē volnerāvit, haud dubium est quīn cōnsiliō deōrum, quibus resistere nec possumus nec volumus, hōc suppliciō adficiāris." Hīs dictīs abiērunt Cyclōpēs eum in īnsāniam incidisse arbitrātī.

34. Escape.

5 At Polyphēmus, ubi sociōs suōs abiisse sēnsit, furōre atque āmentiā impulsus Ulixem iterum quaerere coepit; tandem cum portam invēnisset, saxum quō obstrūcta erat āmōvit, ut pecus ad agrōs exīret. Tum ipse in introitū sēdit et ut quaeque ovis ad locum vēnerat tergum ēius
10 manibus tractābat, nē virī inter ovīs exīre possent. Quod cum animadvertisset Ulixēs, hōc iniit cōnsilium ; bene enim intellēxit omnem spem salūtis in dolō magis quam in virtūte pōnī. Prīmum trēs quās vīdit pinguissimās ex ovibus dēlēgit. Quibus inter sē vīminibus cōnexīs, ūnum
15 sociōrum ventribus eārum ita subiēcit ut omnīnō latēret : deinde ovīs hominem sēcum ferentīs ad portam ēgit. Id accidit quod fore suspicātus erat. Polyphēmus enim, postquam manūs tergīs eārum imposuit, ovīs praeterīre passus est. Ulixēs, ubi rem ita fēlīciter ēvēnisse vīdit,
20 omnīs suōs sociōs ex ōrdine eōdem modō ēmīsit ; quō factō, ipse ūltimus ēvāsit.

35. Out of Danger.

Hīs rēbus ita cōnfectīs, Ulixēs cum sociīs māximē veritus nē Polyphēmus fraudem sentīret, quam celerrimē ad litus contendit. Quō cum vēnissent, ab iīs quī nāvī

---

6 **āmentiā impulsus:** p. 16, l. 14. **15 latēret:** *cēlārētur*, p. 20,
11 iniit cōnsilium: *cēpit cōn-* l. 19.
silium, p. 22, l. 17. **23 fraudem:** *dolum*, l. 12.

praesidiō relīctī erant, māgnā cum laetitiā acceptī sunt.
Hī enim, cum animīs anxiīs iam trēs diēs reditum eōrum
in hōrās exspectāvissent, eōs in perīculum grave incidisse,
id quod erat, suspicātī, ipsī auxiliandī causā ēgredī parābant. Tum Ulixēs nōn satis tūtum esse arbitrātus sī in 5
eō locō manēret, quam celerrimē proficīscī cōnstituit.
Iussit igitur omnīs nāvem cōnscendere et ancorīs sublātīs
paulum ā lītore in altum prōvēctus est. Tum māgnā
vōce exclāmāvit, "Tū, Polyphēme, quī iūra hospitī
spernis, iūstam et dēbitam poenam immānitātis tuae 10
solvistī." Hāc vōce audītā Polyphēmus īrā vehementer
commōtus ad mare sē contulit et ubi intellēxit nāvem
paulum ā lītore remōtam esse saxum ingēns manū cor-
reptum in eam partem cōniēcit, unde vōcem venīre sēnsit.
Graecī autem, etsī minimum āfuit quīn submergerentur, 15
nūllō acceptō damnō cursum tenuērunt.

36. The Country of the Winds.

Pauca mīllia passuum ab eō locō prōgressus Ulixēs
ad īnsulam quandam, nōmine Aeoliam, nāvem appulit.
Haec patria erat Ventōrum.

> "Hīc vāstō rēx Aeolus antrō 20
> Lūctantēs ventōs tempestātēsque sonōrās
> Imperiō premit āc vinclīs et carcere frēnat."

Ibi rēx ipse Graecōs hospitiō accēpit atque iīs persuāsit
ut ad recuperandās vīrīs paucōs diēs in eā regiōne
commorārentur. Septimō diē cum sociī ē labōribus sē 25

1 **laetitiā**: *gaudiō,* p. 12, l. 11;
opp. *dolōre.*
10 **immānitātis**: *crūdēlitātis.*
15 **minimum āfuit quīn**: p. 13,
l. 1 ; *prope.*

21 **lūctantēs**: *inter sē pūgnan-*
tēs, p. 10, l. 12.
25 commorārentur : *manē-*
rent, l. 6.

recēpissent, Ulixēs, nē annī tempore ā nāvigātiōne exclūderētur, sibi sine morā proficīscendum statuit.   Tum
Aeolus, qui bene sciēbat eum māximē cupidum esse patriae
videndae, Ulixī iam profectūrō māgnum dedit saccum ē
5 coriō cōnfectum, in quō ventōs omnīs praeter ūnum
inclūserat.   Zephyrum tantum praetermīserat, quod illum
ventum ad Ithacam nāvigandō idōneum esse sciēbat.
Ulixēs hōc dōnum libenter accēpit et grātiīs prō tantō
beneficiō relātīs saccum ad mālum ligāvit.   Tum omnibus
10 ad profectiōnem parātīs merīdiānō fere tempore ē portū
solvit.

37. The Wind-Bag.

Novem diēs ventō secundissimō cursum tenuērunt,
iamque in cōnspectum patriae suae vēnerant, cum Ulixēs
lassitūdine cōnfectus, ipse enim manū suā gubernābat,
15 ad quiētem capiendam recubuit.   At sociī, quī iamdūdum
mīrābantur quid in illō saccō inclūsum esset, cum vidērent
ducem somnō oppressum esse, tantam occāsiōnem nōn
omittendam arbitrātī sunt, crēdēbant enim aurum et
argentum ibi cēlārī.   Itaque spē lucrī adductī saccum
20 sine morā solvērunt :   quō factō, ventī

"Velut āgmine factō
Quā data porta ruunt et terrās turbine perflant."

Extemplō tanta tempestās subitō coörta est ut illī cursum
tenēre nōn possent, sed in eandem partem unde erant

2 **statuit :** *cōnstituit,* p. 21,
l. 17.
6 **praetermīserat :** *omīserat,*
p. 23, l. 12.
8 **grātiīs** . . . **relātīs :** *grātiīs*
āctīs, p. 7, l. 24.

14 **lassitūdine :** p. 10, l. 1.
19 **cēlārī :** *latēre,* p. 24, l. 15.
19 **lucrī :** *pecūniae.*
21 **velut :** *sīcut.*
22 **data :** *aperta.*
23 **extemplō :** *statim,* p. 8, l. 3.

profectī referrentur. Ulixēs ē somnō excitātus, quō in
locō rēs esset, statim intellēxit. Saccum solūtum et
Ithacam post tergum relīctam vīdit. Tum vērō māximā
indīgnātiōne exārsit sociōsque obiurgābat, quod cupiditāte pecūniae adductī spem patriae videndae prōiēcissent. 5

38. Drawing Lots.

Brevī intermīssō spatiō, Graecī īnsulae cuīdam appro-
pīnquāvērunt quam Circē, fīlia Sōlis, incolēbat. Ibi cum
nāvem appulisset, Ulixēs in terram frūmentandī causā
ēgrediendum esse statuit ; cōgnōverat enim frūmentum
quod in nāvī habērent iam dēficere. Sociīs igitur ad sē 10
convocātīs, quō in locō rēs esset et quid fierī vellet
ostendit. Cum tamen omnēs in memoriā tenērent quam
crūdēlī morte occubuissent iī quī nūper in patriam Cyclō-
pum ēgressī essent, nēmō repertus est quī hōc negōtium
suscipere vellet. Quae cum ita essent, rēs ad contrōver- 15
siam dēducta est. Tandem Ulixēs cōnsēnsū omnium
sociōs in duās partīs dīvīsit, quārum alterī Eurylochus,
vir summae virtūtis, alterī ipse praeesset. Tum hī duo
inter sē sortītī sunt, uter in terram ēgrederētur. Hōc
factō, Eurylochō sorte ēvēnit ut cum duōbus et vīgintī 20
sociīs rem susciperet.

39. The House of the Enchantress.

Hīs rēbus ita cōnstitūtīs, iī quī sorte ductī erant in
interiōrem partem īnsulae profectī sunt. Tantus tamen
timor animōs eōrum occupāverat ut nihil dubitārent quīn

4 obiurgābat : *culpābat.*
10 dēficere : p. 5, l. 15, *deësse.*
13 occubuissent : *mortuī es-*
sent.

18 praeesset : *dux esset.*
20 ēvēnit : *accidit.*
24 occupāverat : *corripuerat,*
p. 21, l. 7.

mortī obviam īrent. Vix quidem poterant iī quī in nāvī
relictī erant lacrimās tenēre, crēdēbant enim sē sociōs
suōs numquam iterum vīsūrōs. Illī autem aliquantum
itineris prōgressī ad villam quandam pervēnērunt, summā
5 māgnificentiā aedificātam ; cūius ad ōstium cum adiissent,
carmen dulcissimum audīvērunt. Tanta autem fuit ēius
vōcis dulcēdō ut nūllō modō retinērī possent quīn iānuam
pulsārent. Hōc factō, ipsa Circē forās exiit et summā
cum benīgnitāte omnīs in hospitium invītāvit. Eurylochus
10 īnsidiās comparārī suspicātus forīs exspectāre cōnstituit,
at reliquī reī novitāte adductī intrāvērunt. Convīvium
māgnificum invēnērunt omnibus rēbus īnstrūctum et iūssū
dominae libentissimē accubuērunt. At Circē vīnum quod
servī apposuērunt medicāmentō quōdam miscuerat, quod
15 cum illī bibissent, gravī sopōre subitō oppressī sunt.

40. Men changed to Pigs.

Tum Circē, quae artis magicae summam scientiam
habēbat, baculō aureō quod gerēbat capita eōrum tetigit ;
quō factō omnēs in porcōs subitō conversī sunt. Intereā
Eurylochus īgnārus quid in aedibus agerētur ad ōstium
20 sedēbat ; postquam tamen ad sōlis occāsum anxiō animō
et sollicitō exspectāverat, sōlus ad nāvem regredī cōnstí-
tuit. Eō cum vēnisset, anxietāte āc timōre ita perturbā-
tus fuit ut quae vīdisset vix lūcidē nārrāre posset. At
Ulixēs satis intellēxit sociōs suōs in perīculō versārī et
25 gladiō correptō Eurylochō imperāvit ut sine morā viam
ad istam domum mōnstrāret. Ille tamen multīs cum

5 **ōstium**: *introitum*, p. 21,
l. 19.

7 **iānuam**: *portam.*

8 **forās**: *ē domō.*

12 **īnstrūctum**: *parātum.*

15 **sopōre**: *somnō.*

21 **regredī**: *redīre*, p. 2, l. 9.

24 **versārī**: *esse.*

lacrimīs Ulixem complexus obsecrāre coepit, nē in tantum
perīculum sē committeret : Sī quid gravius eī accidisset,
omnium salūtem in summō discrīmine futūram. Ulixēs
autem respondit sē nēminem invītum sēcum adductūrum ;
eī licēre, sī māllet, in nāvī manēre ; sē ipsum sine ūllō 5
auxiliō rem susceptūrum. Hōc cum māgnā vōce dīxisset,
ē nāvī dēsiluit et nūllō sequente sōlus in viam sē dedit.

41. The Counter Charm.

Aliquantum itineris prōgressus ad villam māgnificam
pervēnit, quam cum oculīs perlūstrāsset, statim intrāre
statuit, intellēxit enim hanc esse eandem dē quā Eury- 10
lochus mentiōnem fēcisset. At cum in eō esset ut līmen
trānsīret, subitō obviam eī stetit adulēscēns fōrmā pul-
cherrimā, aureum baculum manū gerēns. Hīc Ulixem
iam domum intrantem manū corripuit et "Quō ruis?"
inquit, "Nōnne scīs hanc esse Circēs domum? Hīc 15
inclūsī sunt amīcī tuī ex hūmānā speciē in porcōs conversī. Num vīs ipse in eandem calamitātem venīre?"
Ulixēs simul āc vōcem audīvit deum Mercurium āgnōvit,
nūllīs tamen precibus ab īnstitūtō cōnsiliō dēterrērī potuit.
Quod cum Mercurius sēnsisset, herbam quandam eī dedit, 20
quam contrā carmina māximē valēre dīcēbat. "Hanc
cape," inquit, "et ubi Circē tē baculō tetigerit, tū strictō
gladiō impetum in eam vidē ut faciās." Hīs dictīs
Mercurius

"Mortālēs vīsūs mediō sermōne relīquit, 25
Et procul in tenuem ex oculīs ēvanuit auram."

1 **obsecrāre**: *ōrāre.*
2 **gravius** : *trīstius.*
7 **in viam sē dedit**: *profectus est.*
8 **aliquantum itineris**: p. 28,
l. 3.

11 **in eō esset ut**: p. 21, l. 15.
13 **gerēns** : *ferēns.*
16 **speciē** : *figūrā.*
23 **vidē** : *cūrā.*
26 **procul** : *longē.*

42. The Enchantress Foiled.

Brevī intermīssō spatiō, Ulixēs ad omnia perīcula subeunda parātus ōstium pulsāvit et foribus patefactīs ab ipsā
Circē benīgnē exceptus est. Omnia eōdem modō atque
anteā facta sunt. Cēnam māgnificē īnstrūctam vīdit et
5 accumbere iūssus est. Mox, ubi famēs cibō dēpulsa est,
Circē pōculum aureum vīnō replētum Ulixī dedit. Ille,
etsī suspicātus est venēnum sibi parātum esse, pōculum
exhausit. Quō factō, Circē postquam caput ēius baculō
tetigit, ea verba locūta est quibus sociōs ēius anteā in
10 porcōs converterat. Rēs tamen omnīnō aliter ēvēnit
atque illa spērāverat. Tanta enim vīs erat ēius herbae
quam dederat Mercurius ut neque venēnum neque verba
quidquam efficere possent. Ulixēs autem, sīcut iusserat
Mercurius, gladiō strictō impetum in eam fēcit et mortem
15 minitābātur. Tum Circē, cum sēnsisset artem suam nihil
valēre, multīs cum lacrimīs eum obsecrāre coepit, nē
vītam adimeret.

43. Pigs changed to Men.

Ulixēs autem, ubi sēnsit eam timōre perterritam esse,
postulāvit ut sociōs sine morā in hūmānam speciem redū-
20 ceret, certior enim factus erat ā deō Mercuriō eōs in
porcōs conversōs esse : nisi id factum esset, ostendit sē
dēbitās poenās sūmptūrum. At Circē hīs rēbus graviter
commōta ad pedēs ēius sē prōiēcit et multīs cum lacrimīs
iūre iūrandō cōnfīrmāvit sē quae ille imperāsset omnia
25 factūram. Tum porcōs in ātrium immittī iussit. Illī datō

1 **spatiō**: *tempore.*	17 **adimeret**: *prīvāret.*
2 **ōstium**: *iānuam*, p. 28, l. 7.	23 **commōta**: *perterrita.*
3 **atque**: *ut*, as.	24 **iūre iūrandō cōnfīrmāvit**:
7 **venēnum**: p. 16, l. 5.	*iūrāvit.*

sīgnō inruērunt et cum ducem suum āgnōvissent, māgnō
dolōre adfectī sunt, quod nūllō modō potuērunt eum dē
rēbus suīs certiōrem facere. Circē tamen unguentō
quōdam corpora eōrum unxit ; quō factō omnēs post breve
tempus in speciem hūmānam redditī sunt. Māgnō cum 5
gaudiō Ulixēs amīcōs āgnōvit et nūntium ad lītus mīsit,
quī reliquīs Graecīs sociōs receptōs esse dīceret. Illī
autem hīs rēbus cōgnitīs statim ad domum Circaeam sē
contulērunt ; quō cum vēnissent, omnēs ūniversī laetitiae
sē dēdidērunt. 10

44. Afloat Again.

Postrīdiē ēius diēī Ulixēs in animō habēbat ex īnsulā
quam celerrimē discēdere. Circē tamen, cum haec cōgnōvisset, ex odiō ad amōrem conversa omnibus precibus
eum ōrāre et obtestārī coepit ut paucōs diēs apud sē
morārētur et hōc tandem impetrātō tanta beneficia in 15
eum contulit ut facile eī persuāsum sit ut diūtius manēret.
Postquam tamen tōtum annum apud Circēn cōnsūmp-
serat, Ulixēs māgnō dēsīderiō patriae suae videndae mōtus
est. Sociīs igitur ad sē convocātīs, quid in animō habēret
ostendit. Ubi tamen ad lītus dēscendit, nāvem suam 20
tempestātibus ita adflīctam invēnit ut ad nāvigandum
paene inūtilis esset. Hāc rē cōgnitā, omnia quae ad
nāvīs reficiendās ūsuī sunt comparārī iussit ; quā in rē
tantam dīligentiam omnēs praebēbant ut ante tertium
diem opus cōnfēcerint. At Circē, ubi vīdit omnia ad 25
profectiōnem parāta esse, rem aegrē ferēbat et Ulixem
vehementer obsecrābat ut eō cōnsiliō dēsisteret. Ille

2 dolōre adfectī sunt: *dolōrem*
percēpērunt, p. 5, l. 9.
   3 rēbus suīs : *calamitāte.*

16 contulit : *dedit.*
23 ūsuī : p. 3, l. 21.
26 aegrē ferēbat : p. 8, l. 19.

tamen, nē annī tempore ā nāvigātiōne exclūderētur, mātūrandum sibi exīstimāvit et tempestātem idōneam nactus
nāvem solvit.   Multa quidem perīcula Ulixī subeunda
erant antequam in patriam suam pervenīret, quae tamen
5 in hōc locō longum est perscrībere.

THE SEVEN KINGS OF ROME.

I. Romani Imperi Exordium.

Proca, rēx Albānōrum, Numitōrem et Amūlium fīliōs
habuit. Numitōrī, quī nātū māior erat, rēgnum relīquit ;
sed Amūlius pulsō frātre rēgnāvit et, ut eum subole prīvā-
ret, Rheam Silviam, ēius fīliam, Vestae sacerdōtem fēcit,
quae tamen Rōmulum et Remum geminōs ēdidit. Eā rē 5
cōgnitā Amūlius ipsam in vincula cōniēcit, parvulōs alveō
impositōs abiēcit in Tiberim, quī tunc fōrte super rīpās
erat effūsus ; sed relābente flūmine eōs aqua in siccō relīquit. Vāstae tum in eīs locīs sōlitūdinēs erant. Lupa,
ut fāmā trāditum est, ad vāgītum accurrit, īnfantīs linguā 10
lambit, ūbera eōrum ōrī admōvit mātremque sē gessit.

Cum lupa saepius ad parvulōs velutī ad catulōs rever-
terētur, Faustulus, pāstor rēgius, rē animadversā eōs tulit
in casam et Accae Lārentiae coniugī dedit ēducandōs.
Adultī deinde hī inter pāstōrēs prīmō lūdicrīs certāmini- 15
bus vīrēs auxēre, deinde vēnandō saltūs peragrāre et
latrōnēs ā rapīnā pecorum arcēre coepērunt. Quā rē
cum eīs īnsidiātī essent latrōnēs, Remus captus est,
Rōmulus vī sē dēfendit. Tum Faustulus necessitāte
compulsus indicāvit Rōmulō quis esset eōrum avus, quae 20
māter. Rōmulus statim armātīs pāstōribus Albam properāvit.

Intereā Remum latrōnēs ad Amūlium rēgem perdūxērunt, eum accūsantēs quasi Numitōris agrōs īnfestāre

3 subole: *prōgeniē.*
5 ēdidit : *peperit.*
8 relābente : *refluente.*

17 arcēre : *prohibēre.*
21 statim : *sine morā.*
24 īnfestāre : *vexāre.*

solitus esset ; itaque Remus ā rēge Numitōrī ad supplicium trāditus est ; at cum Numitor, adulēscentis voltum
cōnsīderāns, aetātem minimēque servīlem indolem comparāret, haud procul erat quīn nepōtem āgnōsceret. Nam
5 Remus ōris līneāmentīs erat mātrī simillimus aetāsque
expositiōnis temporibus congruēbat. Ea rēs dum Numitōris animum anxium tenet, repente Rōmulus supervenit,
frātrem līberat, interēmptō Amūliō avum Numitōrem in
rēgnum restituit.

10 Deinde Rōmulus et Remus urbem, in eīsdem locīs ubi
expositī ubique ēducātī erant, condidērunt ; sed ortā inter
eōs contentiōne uter nōmen novae urbī daret eamque
imperiō regeret, auspicia dēcrēvērunt adhibēre. Remus
prior sex voltūrēs, Rōmulus posteā duodecim vīdit. Sīc
15 Rōmulus, vīctor auguriō, urbem Rōmam vocāvit. Ad
novae urbis tūtēlam sufficere vāllum vidēbātur. Cūius
angustiās inrīdēns cum Remus saltū id trāiēcisset, eum
īrātus Rōmulus interfēcit hīs increpāns verbīs : " Sīc
deinde, quīcumque alius trānsiliet moenia mea." Ita
20 sōlus potītus est imperiō Rōmulus.

2. Romulus, Romanorum Rex Primus.

753-715 (?) B.C.

Rōmulus imāginem urbis magis quam urbem fēcerat ;
incolae deërant. Erat in proximō lūcus ; hunc asȳlum
fēcit. Et statim eō mīra vīs latrōnum pāstōrumque cōn-
fūgit. Cum vērō uxōrēs ipse populusque nōn habērent,
25 lēgātōs circā vīcīnās gentīs mīsit, quī societātem cōnū-

3 **indolem**: *nātūram.*	13 **adhibēre**: *ūtī.*
4 **haud**: *nōn.*	16 **tūtēlam**: *praesidium.*
6 **congruēbat**: *conveniēbat.*	22 **in proximō**: *prope.*
8 **interēmptō**: *interfectō.*	23 **vīs**: *numerus.*

biumque novō populō peterent. Nusquam benīgnē audīta
lēgātiō est ; lūdibrium etiam additum : "Cūr nōn fēminīs
quoque asȳlum aperuistis ? Id enim compār foret cōnūbium." Rōmulus aegritūdinem animī dissimulāns lūdōs
parat ; indīcī deinde fīnitimīs spectāculum iubet. Multī 5
convēnēre studiō etiam videndae novae urbis, māximē
Sabīnī cum līberīs et coniugibus. Ubi spectāculī tempus
vēnit eōque conversae mentēs cum oculīs erant, tum sīgnō
datō iuvenēs Rōmānī discurrunt, virginēs rapiunt.
Haec fuit statim causa bellī. Sabīnī enim ob virginēs 10
raptās bellum adversus Rōmānōs sūmpsērunt et, cum
Rōmae appropinquārent, Tarpēiam virginem nactī sunt,
quae aquam fōrte extrā moenia petītum ierat. Hūius
pater Rōmānae praeerat arcī. Titus Tatius, Sabīnōrum
dux, Tarpēiae optiōnem mūneris dedit, sī exercitum suum 15
in Capitōlium perdūxisset. Illa petiit quod Sabīnī in
sinistrīs manibus gererent, vidēlicet et ānulōs et armillās.
Quibus dolōsē prōmīssīs Tarpēia Sabīnōs in arcem per-
dūxit, ubi Tatius scūtīs eam obruī iussit ; nam et ea in
laevīs habuerant. Sīc impia prōditiō celerī poenā vindi- 20
cāta est.
Deinde Rōmulus ad certāmen prōcessit et in eō
locō ubi nunc Rōmānum Forum est, pūgnam cōnseruit.
Prīmō impetū vir inter Rōmānōs īnsīgnis, nōmine Hostīlius, fortissimē dīmicāns cecidit ; cūius interitū cōnster- 25
nātī Rōmānī fugere coepērunt. Iam Sabīnī clāmitābant :
"Vīcimus perfidōs hospitēs, imbellīs hostīs. Nunc sciunt
longē aliud esse virginēs rapere, aliud pūgnāre cum virīs."
Tunc Rōmulus arma ad caelum tollēns Iovī aedem vōvit,

---

11 **sūmpsērunt** : *suscēpērunt.*   17 vidēlicet : *id est.*
15 **mūneris** : *dōnī.*   23 cōnseruit : *commīsit.*
17 **sinistrīs** : *laevīs.*   25 interitū : *morte.*

et exercitus seu fōrte seu dīvīnitus restitit. Itaque proelium redintegrātur; sed raptae mulierēs crīnibus passīs
ausae sunt sē inter tēla volantia īnferre et hinc patrēs
hinc virōs ōrantēs, pācem conciliārunt.

5 Rōmulus foedere cum Tatiō ictō et Sabīnōs in urbem
recēpit et rēgnum cum Tatiō sociāvit. Vērum nōn ita
multō post occīsō Tatiō ad Rōmulum potentātus omnis
recidit. Centum deinde ex seniōribus ēlēgit, quōrum
cōnsiliō omnia ageret, quōs senātōrēs nōmināvit propter
10 senectūtem. Trēs equitum centuriās cōnstituit, populum
in trīgintā cūriās distribuit. Hīs ita ōrdinātīs cum ad
exercitum lūstrandum cōntiōnem in campō ad Caprae
palūdem habēret, subitō coörta est tempestās cum māgnō
fragōre tonitribusque et Rōmulus ē cōnspectū ablātus est.
15 Ad deōs trānsīsse volgō crēditus est; cui rei fidem fēcit
Iūlius Proculus, vir nōbilis. Ortā enim inter patrēs et
plēbem sēditiōne, in cōntiōnem prōcessit iūre iūrandō adfīrmāns vīsum ā sē Rōmulum augustiōre fōrmā, eun-
demque praecipere ut sēditiōnibus abstinērent et rem
20 mīlitārem colerent; futūrum ut omnium gentium domi-
nī exsisterent. Aedēs in colle Quirīnālī Rōmulō cōnstitūta, ipse prō deō cultus et Quirīnus est appellātus.

3. Numa Pompilius, Romanorum Rex Secundus.

715–673 (?) B.C.

Successit Rōmulō Numa Pompilius, vir inclutā iūstitiā
et religiōne. Is Curibus, ex oppidō Sabīnōrum, accītus
25 est. Quī cum Rōmam vēnisset, ut populum ferum religiōne mītigāret, sacra plūrima īnstituit. Āram Vestae

1 seu . . . seu: *vel . . . vel.*	23 inclutā : *clārā.*
8 recidit : *rediit.*	24 accītus est : *arcessītus est.*

cōnsecrāvit et īgnem in ārā perpetuō alendum virginibus dedit. Flāminem Iovis sacerdōtem creāvit eumque īnsīgnī veste et curūlī sellā adōrnāvit. Dīcitur quondam ipsum Iovem ē caelō ēlicuisse. Hīc ingentibus fulminibus in urbem dēmīssīs dēscendit in nemus Aventīnum, ubi 5 Numam docuit quibus sacrīs fulmina essent prōcūranda et praetereā imperī certa pīgnora populō Rōmānō datūrum sē esse prōmīsit. Numa laetus rem populō nūntiāvit. Postrīdiē omnēs ad aedīs rēgiās convēnērunt silentēsque exspectābant quid futūrum esset. Atque sōle ortō dēlā- 10 bitur ē caelō scissō scūtum, quod ancīle appellāvit Numa. Id nē fūrtō auferrī posset, Māmurium fabrum ūndecim scūta eādem fōrmā fabricāre iussit. Duodecim autem Saliōs Mārtis sacerdōtēs lēgit, quī ancīlia, sēcrēta illa imperī pīgnora, custōdīrent et Kalendīs Mārtiīs per urbem 15 canentēs et rīte saltantēs ferrent.

Annum in duodecim mēnsīs ad cursum lūnae dēscrīpsit; nefāstōs fāstōsque diēs fēcit ; portās Iānō geminō aedificāvit, ut esset index pācis et bellī ; nam apertus, in armīs esse cīvitātem, clausus, pācātōs circā omnīs 20 populōs, sīgnificābat.

Lēgēs quoque plūrimās et ūtilēs tulit Numa. Ut vērō māiōrem īnstitūtīs suīs auctōritātem conciliāret, simulāvit sibi cum deā Ēgeriā esse conloquia nocturna, ēiusque monitū sē omnia quae ageret facere. Lūcus erat, quem 25 medium fōns perennī rigābat aquā ; eō saepe Numa sine arbitrīs sē īnferēbat, velut ad congressum deae : ita omnium animōs eā pietāte imbuit ut fidēs āc iūs iūrandum nōn minus quam lēgum et poenārum metus cīvīs contineret. Bellum quidem nūllum gessit, sed nōn minus 30

---

4 **ēlicuisse**: *ēdūxisse.*
6 **prōcūranda**: *āvertenda.*
11 **scissō**: *dīvīsō.*

17 **dēscrīpsit**: *dīvīsit.*
27 **arbitrīs**: *testibus.*
27 **velut**: *velutī,* p. 33, l. 12.

cīvitātī prōfuit quam Rōmulus.   Morbō exstinctus in
Iāniculō monte sepultus est.   Ita duo deinceps rēgēs, ille
bellō, hīc pāce, cīvitātem auxērunt.   Rōmulus septem et
trīgintā rēgnāvit annōs, Numa trēs et quadrāgintā.

4. Tullus Hostilius, Romanorum Rex Tertius.

673-641 (?) B.C.

5   Mortuō Numā Tullus Hostīlius rēx creātus est.   Hīc
nōn sōlum proximō rēgī dissimilis, sed ferōcior etiam
Rōmulō fuit.   Eō rēgnante bellum inter Albānōs et
Rōmānōs exortum est.   Ducibus Hostīliō et Fūfetiō
placuit rem paucōrum certāmine fīnīrī.   Erant apud
10 Rōmānōs trigeminī frātrēs Horātiī, trēs apud Albānōs
Cūriātiī.   Cum eīs agunt rēgēs ut prō suā quisque patriā
dīmicent ferrō.   Foedus ictum est eā lēge, ut unde vīc-
tōria ibi imperium esset.

Ictō foedere trigeminī arma capiunt et in medium
15 inter duās aciēs prōcēdunt.   Cōnsēderant utrimque duo
exercitūs.   Datur sīgnum īnfestīsque armīs ternī iuvenēs,
māgnōrum exercituum animōs gerentēs, concurrunt.   Ut
prīmō concursū increpuēre arma micantēsque fulsēre
gladiī, horror ingēns spectantīs perstringit.   Cōnsertīs
20 deinde manibus statim duo Rōmānī alius super alium
exspīrantēs cecidērunt; trēs Albānī volnerātī.   Ad cā-
sum Rōmānōrum conclāmāvit gaudiō exercitus Albānus.
Rōmānōs iam spēs tōta dēserēbat.   Ūnum Horātium
trēs Cūriātiī circumsteterant.   Fōrte is integer fuit; sed

---

1 **exstinctus** : *mortuus.*
6 **ferōcior** : *bellicōsior.*
9 **certāmine** : *pūgnā.*
12 **lēge** : *conditiōne.*
16 **īnfestīs** : *inimīcīs.*

17 **gerentēs** : *habentēs.*
17 **ut** : *cum.*
18 **increpuēre** : *resonāvērunt.*
19 **perstringit** : *corripit.*
24 **integer** : *involnerātus.*

quia tribus impār erat, ut distraheret hostīs, fugam capes-
sīvit, siagulōs per intervāllā secūtūrōs esse ratus. Iam
aliquantum spatī ex eō locō ubi pūgnātum est aufūgerat,
cum respiciēns videt ūnum ē Cūriātiīs haud procul ab
sēsē abesse. In eum māgnō impetū redit et, dum Albā- 5
nus exercitus inclāmat Cūriātiīs ut opem ferant frātrī,
iam Horātius eum occīderat. Alterum deinde, priusquam
tertius posset cōnsequī, interfēcit.

Iam singulī supererant, sed nec spē nec vīribus parēs.
Alter erat intāctus ferrō et gemināta victōriā ferōx ; 10
alter fessum volnere fessum cursū trahēbat corpus. Nec
illud proelium fuit. Rōmānus exsultāns male sustinentem arma Cūriātium cōnficit, iacentem spoliat. Rōmānī
ovantēs āc grātulantēs Horātium accipiunt et domum
dēdūcunt. Prīnceps ībat Horātius trium frātrum spolia 15
prae sē gerēns. Cui obvia fuit soror, quae dēspōnsa
fuerat ūnī ex Cūriātiīs, vīsōque super umerōs frātris palū-
dāmentō spōnsī, quod ipsa cōnfēcerat, flēre et crīnīs solvere coepit. Movet ferōcis iuvenis animum complōrātiō
sorōris in tantō gaudiō pūblicō ; itaque strictō gladiō 20
trānsfīgit puellam, simul eam verbīs increpāns : "Abī
hinc cum immātūrō amōre ad spōnsum, oblīta frātrum,
oblīta patriae. Sīc eat quaecumque Rōmāna lugēbit
hostem."

Atrōx id vīsum est facinus patribus plēbīque ; quā rē 25
raptus est in iūs Horātius et apud iūdicēs condemnātus.
Iam accesserat līctor iniciēbatque laqueum. Tum Horātius ad populum prōvocāvit. Intereā pater Horātī senex
prōclāmābat fīliam suam iūre caesam esse ; et iuvenem

---

2 ratus : *exīstimāns.*
12 male : *vix.*
13 cōnficit : *interficit.*

19 complōrātiō : *lūctus.*
21 increpāns : *culpāns.*
26 iūs : *iūdicium.*

amplexus spoliaque Cūriātiōrum ostentāns ōrābat populum nē sē, quem paulō ante cùm ēgregiā stirpe cōnspēxis-
sent, orbum līberīs faceret. Nōn tulit populus patris
lacrimās iuvenemque absolvit admīrātiōne magis virtūtis
5 quam iūre causae. Ut tamen caedēs manifesta expiārētur,
pater quibusdam sacrificiīs perāctīs trānsmīsit per viam
tigillum et filium capite adopertō velut sub iugum mīsit ;
quod tigillum sorōrium appellātum est.

Nōn diū pāx Albāna mānsit ; nam Mettius Fūfetius,
10 dux Albānōrum, cum sē invidiōsum apud cīvīs vidēret,
quod bellum ūnō paucōrum certāmine fīnisset, ut rem
corrigeret, Vēientēs Fīdēnātēsque adversus Rōmānōs
concitāvit. Ipse ā Tullō in auxilium arcessītus aciem
in collem subdūxit, ut fōrtūnam bellī exspectāret et
15 sequerētur. Quā rē Tullus intellēctā māgnā vōce ait
suō illud iūssū Mettium facere, ut hostēs ā tergō cir-
cumvenīrentur. Quō audītō hostēs territī et vīctī sunt.
Posterō diē Mettius cum ad grātulandum Tullō vēnisset,
iūssū illīus quadrīgīs religātus et in dīversa distractus
20 est. Deinde Tullus Albam propter ducis perfidiam dīruit
et Albānōs Rōmam trānsīre iussit.

Rōma interim crēvit Albae ruīnīs ; duplicātus est
cīvium numerus ; mōns Caelius urbī additus et, quō
frequentius habitārētur, eam sēdem Tullus rēgiae cēpit
25 ibique deinde habitāvit. Auctārum vīrium fīdūciā ēlātus
bellum Sabīnīs indīxit : pestilentia īnsecūta est ; nūlla
tamen ab armīs quiēs dabātur. Crēdēbat enim rēx bellicōsus salūbriōra mīlitiae quam domī esse iuvenum cor-

2 **stirpe** : *prōgeniē.*	10 **invidiōsum** : *invīsum.*
6 **perāctīs** : *perfectīs.*	20 **dīruit** : *dēlēvit.*
7 **adopertō** : *tēctō.*	25 **fīdūciā** : *fidē.*
9 **mānsit** : *dūrāvit.*	28 **salūbriōra** : *validiōra.*

pora, sed ipse quoque diūturnō morbō est implicātus.
Tunc vērō adeō frāctī simul cum corpore sunt spīritūs
illī ferōcēs ut nūllī reī posthāc nisi sacrīs operam daret.
Memorant Tullum fulmine ictum cum domō cōnflagrāsse.
Tullus māgnā glōriā bellī rēgnāvit annōs duōs et trīgintā. 5

5. Ancus Marcius, Romanorum Rex Quartus.

641–616 (?) B.C.

Tullō mortuō Ancum Mārcium rēgem populus creāvit.
Numae Pompilī nepōs Ancus Mārcius erat, aequitāte et
religiōne avō similis. Tunc Latīnī, cum quibus Tullō
rēgnante ictum foedus erat, sustulerant animōs et incur-
siōnem in agrum Rōmānum fēcērunt. Ancus, priusquam 10
eīs bellum indīceret, lēgātum mīsit, quī rēs repeteret,
eumque mōrem posterī accēpērunt. Id autem hōc modō
fīēbat. Lēgātus, ubi ad fīnīs eōrum vēnit ā quibus
rēs repetuntur, capite vēlātō, "Audī, Iuppiter," inquit,
"audīte, fīnēs hūius populī. Ego sum pūblicus nūntius 15
populī Rōmānī : verbīs meīs fidēs sit." Deinde peragit
postulāta. Sī nōn dēduntur rēs quās exposcit, hastam
in fīnīs hostium ēmittit bellumque ita indīcit. Lēgātus
quī eā dē rē mittitur fētiālis, rītusque bellī indīcendī iūs
fētiāle appellātur. 20
Lēgātō Rōmānō rēs repetentī superbē respōnsum est
ā Latīnīs : quā rē bellum hōc modō eīs indictum est.
Ancus exercitū cōnscrīptō profectus Latīnōs fūdit et
complūribus oppidīs dēlētīs cīvīs Rōmam trādūxit. Cum

1 implicātus : *adflīctus.*	16 peragit : *explicat.*
4 memorant : *nārrant.*	17 exposcit : *postulat.*
9 sustulerant : *ērēxerant.*	23 fūdit : *fugāvit.*
14 vēlātō : *adopertō,* p. 40, l. 7.	24 dēlētīs : *dīrutīs.*

autem in tantā hominum multitūdine facinora clandes-
tīna fierent, Ancus carcerem in mediā urbe ad terrōrem
incrēscentis audāciae aedificāvit.   Īdem nova moenia
urbī circumdedit, Iāniculum montem ponte sublicīō in
5 Tiberī factō urbī coniūnxit, in ōre Tiberis Ōstiam urbem
condidit.   Plūribus aliīs rēbus intrā paucōs annōs cōnfectīs immātūrā morte praereptus obiit.

6. Lucius Tarquinius Priscus, Romanorum Rex Quintus.

616–578 (?) B.C.

Ancō rēgnante Lūcius Tarquinius, Tarquiniīs ex Etrū-
riae urbe profectus, cum coniuge et fōrtūnīs omnibus
10 Rōmam commigrāvit.   Additur haec fābula: advenientī
aquila pilleum sustulit et super carpentum, cuī Tarquinius
īnsidēbat, cum māgnō clangōre volitāns rūrsus capitī aptē
reposuit ; inde sublīmis abiit.   Tanaquil coniūnx, caeles-
tium prōdigiōrum perīta, rēgnum eī portendī intellēxit ;
15 itaque, virum complexa, excelsa et alta spērāre eum iussit.
Hās spēs cōgitātiōnēsque sēcum portantēs urbem ingressī
sunt, domicilīōque ibi comparātō Tarquinius pecūniā et
industriā dīgnitātem atque etiam Ancī rēgis familiāritā-
tem cōnsecūtus est ; ā quō tūtor līberīs relīctus rēgnum
20 intercēpit et ita administrāvit, quasi iūre adeptus esset.
Tarquinius Prīscus Latīnōs bellō domuit ;   Circum
Māximum aedificāvit ; dē Sabīnīs triumphāvit ; mūrum
lapideum urbī circumdedit.   Equitum centuriās duplicā-
vit, nōmina mūtāre nōn potuit, dēterritus, ut ferunt, Attī
25 Nāvī auctōritāte.   Attus enim, eā tempestāte augur

7 **immātūrā** : *praemātūrā.*   20 **intercēpit** : *ūsūrpāvit.*
15 **virum** ˙ *coniugem.*   20 **adeptus** : *cōnsecūtus,* l. 19.
15 **excelsa** : *ēgregia,* p. 40, l. 2.   25 **tempestāte** : *tempore.*

inclutus, id fieri posse negābat, nisi avēs addīxissent; īrātus
rēx in experīmentum artis eum interrogāvit fierīne posset
quod ipse mente concēpisset; Attus auguriō āctō fieri
posse respondit. "Atquī hōc," inquit rēx, "agitābam,
num cōtem illam secāre novāculā possem." "Potes   5
ergo," inquit augur, et rēx secuisse dīcitur. Tarquinius
fīlium tredecim annōrum, quod in proeliō hostem percussisset, praetextā bullāque dōnāvit; unde haec ingenuōrum
puerōrum īnsīgnia esse coepērunt.

Supererant duo Ancī fīliī, quī aegrē ferentēs sē paternō   10
rēgnō fraudātōs esse rēgī īnsidiās parāvērunt. Ex pāstōribus duōs ferōcissimōs dēligunt ad patrandum facinus.
Eī simulātā rixā in vestibulō rēgiae tumultuantur. Quōrum clāmor cum penitus in rēgiam pervēnisset, vocātī
ad rēgem pergunt. Prīmō uterque vōciferārī coepit et 15
certātim alter alterī obstrepere. Cum vērō iūssī essent
invicem dīcere, ūnus ex compositō rem ōrdītur; dumque
intentus in eum sē rēx tōtus āvertit, alter ēlātam secūrim
in ēius caput dēiēcit, et relīctō in volnere tēlō ambō forās
sē prōripiunt.   20

7. Servius Tullius, Romanorum Rex Sextus.

578-534 (?) B.C.

Post hunc Servius Tullius suscēpit imperium genitus
ex nōbilī fēminā, captīvā tamen et famulā. Quī cum in
domō Tarquinī Prīscī ēducārētur, ferunt prōdigium vīsū
ēventūque mīrābile accidisse. Flammae speciēs puerī
dormientis caput amplexa est. Hōc vīsū Tanaquil sum- 25

---

1 inclutus: p. 36, l. 23.   7 percussisset: *interfēcisset.*
1 addīxissent: *secundae fuis-*   22 famulā: *servā.*
sent.   23 ferunt: *dīcunt.*

mam eī dignitātem portendī intellēxit coniugīque suāsit
ut eum haud secus āc suōs līberōs ēducāret.   Is postquam adolēvit, et fortitūdine et cōnsiliō īnsīgnis fuit.   In
proeliō quōdam, in quō rēx Tarquinius adversus Sabīnōs
5 cōnflīxit, mīlitibus sēgnius dīmicantibus, raptum sīgnum
in hostem mīsit.   Cūius recipiendī grātiā Rōmānī tam
ācriter pūgnāvērunt ut et sīgnum et vīctōriam referrent.
Quā rē ā Tarquiniō gener adsūmptus est; et cum Tarquinius occīsus esset, Tanaquil, Tarquinī uxor, mortem
10 ēius cēlāvit populumque ex superiōre parte aedium ad-
locūta, ait rēgem grave quidem, sed nōn lētāle volnus
accēpisse eumque petere ut interim, dum convalēsceret,
Serviō Tulliō dictō audientēs essent.   Sīc Servius Tullius
rēgnāre coepit, sed rēctē imperium administrāvit.   Sabī-
15 nōs subēgit; montīs trēs, Quirīnālem, Vīminālem, Esquilī-
num urbī adiūnxit; fossās circā mūrum dūxit.   Īdem
cēnsum ōrdināvit et populum in classīs et centuriās distribuit.
      Servius Tullius aliquod urbī decus addere volēbat.
20 Iam tum inclutum erat Diānae Ephesiae fānum.   Id commūniter ā cīvitātibus Asiae factum fāma ferēbat.   Itaque
Latīnōrum populīs suāsit ut et ipsī fānum Diānae cum
populō Rōmānō Rōmae in Aventīnō monte aedificārent.
Quō factō bōs mīrae māgnitūdinis cuīdam Latīnō nāta
25 dīcitur et respōnsum somniō datum, eum populum summam imperī habitūrum cūius cīvis bovem illam Diānae
immolāsset.   Latīnus bovem ad fānum Diānae ēgit et
causam sacerdōtī Rōmānō exposuit.   Ille callidus dīxit

---

2 secus : *aliter.*   11 lētāle : *mortiferum.*
2 āc : *quam.*   19 decus : *ōrnāmentum.*
5 sēgnius : *īgnāvius.*   25 respōnsum : *ōrāculum.*
10 aedium : *domūs.*   27 immolāsset : *sacrificāsset.*

prius eum vīvō flūmine manūs abluere dēbēre. Latīnus
dum ad Tiberim dēscendit, sacerdōs bovem immolāvit.
Ita imperium cīvibus sibique glōriam adquīsīvit.

Servius Tullius filiam altèram ferōcem, mītem alteram
habēns, cum Tarquinī fīliōs parī esse animō vidēret, ferō- 5
cem mītī, mītem ferōcī in mātrimōnium dedit, nē duo
violenta ingenia mātrimōniō iungerentur. Sed mītēs seu
fōrte seu fraude periērunt; ferōcīs mōrum similitūdō
coniūnxit. Statim Tarquinius ā Tulliā incitātus advocātō
senātū rēgnum paternum repetere coepit. Quā rē audītā 10
Servius dum ad cūriam contendit, iūssū Tarquinī per
gradūs dēiectus et domum refugiēns interfectus est.
Tullia carpentō vēcta in Forum properāvit et coniugem ē
cūriā ēvocātum prīma rēgem salūtāvit; cūius iūssū cum
ē turbā āc tumultū dēcessisset domumque redīret, vīsō 15
patris corpore mūliōnem cunctantem et frēna inhibentem
super ipsum corpus carpentum agere iussit. Unde vīcus
ille scelerātus dictus est. Servius Tullius rēgnāvit annōs
quattuor et quadrāgintā.

8. Tarquinius Superbus, Romanorum Rex Septimus et Ultimus.

534-510 (?) B.C.

Tarquinius Superbus rēgnum scelestē occupāvit. Ta- 20
men bellō strēnuus Latīnōs Sabīnōsque domuit. Urbem
Gabiōs in potestātem redēgit fraude Sextī fīlī. Is cum
indīgnē ferret eam urbem ā patre expūgnārī nōn posse,
ad Gabīnōs sē contulit, patris saevitiam in sē conquerēns.

---

3 adquīsīvit: *cōnsecūtus est*,
p. 42, l. 19.
5 parī: *similī*.
16 cunctantem: *dubitantem*.

16 inhibentem: *retinentem*.
20 scelestē: *nefāriē*.
23 indīgnē: *aegrē*, p. 43, l. 10.
24 saevitiam: *crūdēlitātem*.

Benīgnē ā Gabīnīs exceptus paulātim eōrum benevolentiam cōnsequitur, fictīs blanditiīs ita eōs adliciēns ut apud
omnīs plūrimum posset et ad postrēmum dux bellī ēligerē-
tur.   Tum ē suīs ūnum ad patrem mittit scīscitātum quid-
5 nam sē facere vellet.   Pater nūntiō fīlī nihil respondit,
sed velut dēlīberābundus in hortum trānsiit ibique inam-
bulāns sequente nūntiō altissima papāverum capita baculō
dēcussit.   Nūntius fessus exspectandō rediit Gabiōs.
Sextus cōgnitō silentiō patris et factō intellēxit quid vellet
10 pater.   Prīmōrēs cīvitātis interēmit patrīque urbem sine
ūllā dimicātiōne trādidit.

Posteā rēx Ardeam urbem obsidēbat.   Ibi cum in
castrīs essent, Tarquinius Collātīnus, sorōre rēgis nātus,
fōrte cēnābat apud Sextum Tarquinium cum iuvenibus
15 rēgiīs.   Incidit dē uxōribus mentiō : cum suam ūnus
quisque laudāret, placuit experīrī.   Itaque citātīs equīs
Rōmam āvolant; rēgiās nurūs in convīviō et lūxū dēprehendunt.   Pergunt inde Collātiam; Lucrētiam, Collātīnī
uxōrem, inter ancillās lānae dēditam inveniunt.   Ea ergō
20 cēterīs praestāre iūdicātur.   Paucīs interiectīs diēbus
Sextus Collātiam rediit et Lucrētiae vim attulit.   Illa
posterō diē advocātīs patre et coniuge rem exposuit et sē
cultrō, quem sub veste abditum habēbat, occīdit.   Con-
clāmant vir paterque et in exitium rēgum coniūrant.
25 Tarquiniō Rōmam redeuntī clausae sunt urbis portae et
exsilium indictum.

In antīquīs annālibus memoriae haec sunt prōdita.
Anus hospita atque incōgnita ad Tarquinium quondam

4 scīscitātum: *rogātum.*   17 dēprehendunt : *inveniunt.*
10 prīmōrēs : *prīncipēs.*   21 attulit : *fēcit, intulit.*
11 dīmicātiōne : *certāmine.*   ` 24 exitium : *interitum,* p. 35,
15 incidit : *accidit.*   l. 25.

Superbum rēgem adiit, novem librōs ferēns, quōs esse dicēbat dīvīna ōrācula : eōs sē velle vēnum dare. Tarquinius pretium percontātus est : mulier nimium atque immēnsum poposcit. Rēx, quasi anus aetāte dēsiperet, dērīsit. Tum illa foculum cum īgnī appōnit et trēs 5 librōs ex novem deūrit ; et, ecquid reliquōs sex eōdem pretiō emere vellet, rēgem interrogāvit. Sed Tarquinius id multō rīsit magis dīxitque anum iam procul dubiō dēlīrāre. Mulier ibīdem statim trēs aliōs librōs exussit ; atque id ipsum dēnuō placidē rogat, ut trēs reliquōs 10 eōdem illō pretiō emat. Tarquinius ōre iam sēriō atque attentiōre animō fit ; eam cōnstantiam cōnfīdentiamque nōn neglegendam intellegit ; librōs trēs reliquōs mercātur nihilō minōre pretiō quam quod erat petītum prō omnibus. Sed eam mulierem tunc ā Tarquiniō dīgressam posteā 15 nusquam locī vīsam cōnstitit. Librī trēs in sacrāriō conditī Sibyllīnīque appellātī. Ad eōs, quasi ad ōrāculum, Quīndecim virī adeunt, cum diī immortālēs pūblicē cōnsulendī sunt.

3 **percontātus** : cf. p. 46, l. 4.   10 **dēnuō** : *rūrsus*, p. 42, l. 12.
4 **dēsiperet** : *stulta esset.*   11 **ōre** : *voltū.*
8 **dēlīrāre** : *īnsānam esse.*   13 **mercātur** : *emit.*

FABLES.

1. Haedus et Lupus.

Haedus, stāns in tēctō domūs, lupō praetereuntī male-
dīxit. Cuī lupus, "Nōn tū," inquit, "sed tēctum mihi
maledīcit."
Saepe locus et tempus hominēs timidōs audācīs reddit.

2. Grus et Pavo.

5 Pāvō cōram grue pennās suās explicāns, "Quanta est,"
inquit, "fōrmōsitās mea et tua dēfōrmitās !" At grūs ēvo-
lāns, "Et quanta est," inquit, "levitās mea et tua tarditās !"
Monet haec fābula nē, ob aliquod bonum quod nōbīs
nātūra tribuit, aliōs contemnāmus quibus nātūra alia et
10 fōrtasse māiōra dedit.

3. Pavo.

Pāvō graviter conquerēbātur apud Iūnōnem, dominam
suam, quod vōcis suāvitās sibi negāta esset, dum luscinia,
avis tam parum decōra, cantū excellat. Cuī Iūnō, "Et
meritō," inquit; "nōn enim omnia bona in ūnum cōnferrī
15 oportuit."

4. Capra et Lupus.

Lupus capram in altā rūpe stantem cōnspicātus, "Cūr
nōn," inquit, "relinquis nūda illa et sterilia loca, et hūc

5 cōram : *prō.*
5 explicāns : *ostentāns.*
6 fōrmōsitās : *pulchritūdō.*
9 tribuit: *dat.*

11 apud : *cōram*, 1. 5.
13 decōra : *pulchra.*
14 cōnferrī : *tribuī*, 1. 9.
16 cōnspicātus : *vidēns.*

dēscendis in herbidōs campōs, quī tibi laetum pābulum
offerunt?" Cuī respondit capra, "Mihi nōn est in animō
dulcia tūtīs praepōnere."

5. Canis et Boves.

Canis iacēbat in praesaepī bovēsque lātrandō ā pā-
bulō arcēbat. Cuī ūnus boum, "Quanta ista," inquit, 5
"invidia est, quod nōn pateris ut eō cibō vescāmur
quem tū ipse capere nec velīs nec possīs!"
Haec fābula invidiae indolem dēclārat.

6. Volpes et Leo.

Volpēs, quae numquam leōnem vīderat, cum eī fōrte
occurrisset, ita est perterrita ut paene morerētur formi- 10
dine. Eundem cōnspicāta iterum, timuit quidem, sed nēquāquam ut anteā. Tertiō illī obviam facta, ausa est
etiam propius accēdere eumque adloquī.

7. Cancri.

Cancer dīcēbat filiō, "Mī filī, nē sīc oblīquīs semper
gressibus incēde, sed rēctā viā perge." Cuī ille, "Mī 15
pater," respondit, "libenter tuīs praeceptīs obsequar, sī
tē prius idem facientem vīderō."
Docet haec fābula adulēscentiam nūllā rē magis quam
exemplīs īnstruī.

1 laetum: *abundāns.*	8 dēclārat: *expōnit.*
3 tūtīs: *salvīs.*	10 formīdine: *timōre.*
3 praepōnere: *mālle.*	15 perge: *prōgredere.*
5 arcēbat: *prohibēbat.*	16 obsequar: *pārēbō.*
8 indolem: *nātūram.*	19 īnstruī: *docērī.*

8. Boves.

In eōdem prātō pāscēbantur trēs bovēs in māximā concordiā et sīc ab omnī ferārum incursiōne tūtī erant. Sed dissidiō inter illōs ortō, singulī ā ferīs petītī et laniātī sunt.

5 Fābula docet quantum bonī sit in concordiā.

9. Asinus.

Asinus pelle leōnis indūtus territābat hominēs et bēstiās, tamquam leō esset. Sed fōrte, dum sē celerius movet, aurēs ēminēbant ; unde āgnitus in pīstrīnum abductus est, ubi poenās petulantiae dedit.

10 Haec fābula stolidōs notat quī immeritīs honōribus superbiunt.

10. Mulier et Gallina.

Mulier quaedam habēbat gallīnam, quae eī cottīdiē ōvum pariēbat aureum. Hinc suspicārī coepit illam aurī massam intus cēlāre et gallīnam occīdit. Sed nihil in eā 15 repperit nisi quod in aliīs gallīnīs reperīrī solet. Itaque dum māiōribus dīvitiīs inhiat, etiam minōrēs perdidit.

11. Tubicen.

Tubicen ab hostibus captus, "Nē mē," inquit, "interficite ; nam inermis sum, neque quidquam habeō praeter hanc tubam." At hostēs, " Propter hōc ipsum," inquiunt, 20 " tē interimēmus, quod, cum ipse pūgnandī sīs imperītus, aliōs ad pūgnam incitāre solēs."

2 **incursiōne**: *impetū*.	15 **nisi**: *praeter.*
3 **dissidiō**: *dissēnsiōne.*	16 **inhiat**: *cupit.*
7 **tamquam**: *quasi.*	20 **interimēmus** : *interficiē-*
9 **petulantiae**: *impudentiae.*	*mus.*

Fābula docet nōn sōlum maleficōs esse pūniendōs, sed etiam eōs quī aliōs ad male faciendum inrītent.

12. Volpes et Uva.

Volpēs ūvam in vīte cōnspicāta ad illam subsiliit omnium vīrium suārum contentiōne, sī eam fōrte attingere posset. Tandem dēfatīgāta inānī labōre discēdēns dīxit, 5 "At nunc etiam acerbae sunt, nec eās in viā repertās tollerem."

Haec fābula docet multōs ea contemnere quae sē adsequī posse dēspērent.

13. Mures.

Mūrēs aliquandō habuērunt cōnsilium, quō modo ā fēle 10 cavērent. Multīs aliīs prōpositīs, omnibus placuit ut eī tintinnābulum adnecterētur; sīc enim ipsōs sonitū admonitōs eam fugere posse. Sed cum iam inter mūrīs quaererētur, quī fēlī tintinnābulum adnecteret, nēmō repertus est. 15

Fābula docet in suādendō plūrimōs esse audācīs, sed in ipsō perīculō timidōs.

14. Lupus et Grus.

In faucibus lupī os inhaeserat. Mercēde igitur condūcit gruem quī illud extrahat. Hōc grūs longitūdine collī facile effēcit. Cum autem mercēdem postulāret, 20 subrīdēns lupus et dentibus īnfrendēns, "Num tibi," inquit, "parva mercēs vidētur, quod caput incolume ex lupī faucibus extrāxistī?"

2 inrītent: *incitent.*
5 inānī: *inūtilī.*
8 adsequī: *cōnsequī.*

10 aliquandō: *ōlim.*
18 mercēde: *pretiō.*
22 incolume: *salvum.*

15. Agricola et Anguis.

Agricola anguem repperit frīgore paene exstinctum.
Misericordiā mōtus eum fōvit sinū et subter ālās recon-
didit.　Mox anguis recreātus vīrīs recēpit et agricolae
prō beneficiō lētāle volnus īnflīxit.
5　Haec fābula docet quālem mercēdem malī prō bene-
ficiīs reddere soleant.

16. Asinus et Equus.

Asinus equum beātum praedicābat, quī tam cōpiōsē
pāscerētur, cum sibi post molestissimōs labōrēs nē paleae
quidem satis praebērētur.　Fōrte autem bellō exortō equus
10　in proelium agitur, et circumventus ab hostibus, post in-
crēdibilīs labōrēs tandem multīs volneribus cōnfossus,
conlābitur.　Haec omnia asinus cōnspicātus, "O mē stolidum," inquit, "quī beātitūdinem ex praesentis temporis
fōrtūnā aestimāverim!"

17. Agricola et Filii.

15　Agricola senex, cum mortem sibi appropīnquāre sentīret, filiōs convocāvit, quōs, ut fierī solet, interdum discor-
dāre nōverat et fascem virgulārum adferrī iubet.　Quibus
adlātīs, filiōs hortātur ut hunc fascem frangerent.　Quod
cum facere nōn possent, distribuit singulās virgās, iīsque
20　celeriter frāctīs, docuit illōs quam firma rēs esset concordia quamque imbēcilla discordia.

1 exstinctum : *mortuum.*	9 praebērētur : *darētur.*
2 recondidit : *cēlāvit.*	12 conlābitur : *cadit.*
4 lētāle : *mortiferum.*	15 senex : *vetus.*
5 mercēdem : *grātiam.*	16 fierī : *accidere.*
7 beātum : *fēlīcem.*	21 imbēcilla : *īnfīrma.*

18. Equus et Asinus.

Asinus onustus sarcinīs equum rogāvit ut aliquā parte
oneris sē levāret, sī sē vīvum vidēre vellet. Sed ille asinī
precēs repudiāvit. Paulō post igitur asinus labōre cōn-
sūmptus in viā corruit et efflāvit animam. Tum agitātor
omnīs sarcinās quās asinus portāverat atque īnsuper 5
etiam pellem asinō dētractam in equum imposuit. Ibi
ille sērō priōrem superbiam dēplōrāns, "O mē miserum,"
inquit, "quī parvulum onus in mē recipere nōluerim, cum
nunc cōgar tantās sarcinās ferre ūnā cum pelle comitis
meī, cūius precēs tam superbē contempseram." 10

19. Mulier et Ancillae.

Mulier vidua, quae texendō vītam sustentābat, solēbat
ancillās suās dē nocte excitāre ad opus, cum prīmum gallī
cantum audīvisset. At illae diūturnō labōre fatīgātae
statuērunt gallum interficere. Quō factō, dēteriōre condiciōne quam prius esse coepērunt. Nam domina dē hōrā 15
noctis incerta nunc famulās saepe iam prīmā nocte exci-
tābat.

20. Senex et Mors.

Senex in silvā ligna cecīderat iīsque sublātis domum
redīre coepit. Cum aliquantum viae prōgressus esset, et
onere et viā dēfatīgātus fascem dēposuit et sēcum aetātis 20
et inopiae mala contemplātus mortem clārā vōce invo-
cāvit, quae ipsum ab omnibus hīs malīs līberāret. Tum

3 repudiāvit : *contempsit.*	14 statuērunt : *dēcrēvērunt.*
4 corruit : *conlābitur.*	14 dēteriōre : *pēiōre.*
6 ibi : *tum.*	16 famulās : *servās.*
11 sustentābat : *sustinēbat.*	20 aetātis : *senectūtis.*

mors senis precibus audītīs subitō adstitit et, quid vellet,
percontātur. At senex quem iam vōtōrum suōrum paenitēbat, "Nihil," inquit, "sed requīrō, quī onus paululum
adlevet, dum ego rūrsus subeō."

21. Corvus et Volpes.

5 Corvus alicunde cāseum rapuerat et cum illō in altam
arborem subvolārat. Volpēcula illum cāseum appetēns
corvum blandīs verbīs adoritur ; cumque prīmum fōrmam
ēius pennārumque nitōrem laudāsset, "Pol," inquit, "tē
avium rēgem esse dīcerem, sī cantus pulchritūdinī tuae
10 respondēret." Tum ille laudibus volpis īnflātus etiam
cantū sē valēre dēmōnstrāre voluit. Ita vērō ē rōstrō aper-
tō cāseus dēlapsus est, quem volpēs adreptum dēvorāvit.
    Haec fābula docet vītandās esse adūlātōrum vōcēs, quī
blanditiīs suīs nōbīs īnsidiantur.

22. Leo.

15 Societātem iūnxerant leō, iuvenca, capra, ovis. Praedā
autem, quam cēperant, in quattuor partīs aequālīs dīvīsā,
leō, "Prīma," ait, "mea est ; dēbētur enim haec prae-
stantiae meae. Tollam et secundam, quam merētur rōbur
meum. Tertiam vindicat sibi ēgregius labor meus.
20 Quartam quī sibi adrogāre voluerit, is sciat sē habitūrum
mē inimīcum sibi." Quid facerent imbēcillae bēstiae,
aut quae sibi leōnem īnfestum habēre vellet?

2 **percontātur**: *interrogat.*	8 **nitōrem** : *splendōrem.*
4 **adlevet** : *tollat.*	14 **blanditiīs** : *blandīs verbīs.*
5 **alicunde**: *ab aliquō locō.*	20 **adrogāre** : *vindicāre.*
6 **appetēns** : *cupiēns.*	21 **imbēcillae** : *īnfirmae.*
7 **adoritur** : *adloquitur.*	22 **īnfestum** : *inimīcum.*

23. Mus et Rusticus.

Mūs ā rūsticō in cāricārum acervō dēprehēnsus tam
ācrī morsū ēius digitōs volnerāvit ut ille eum dīmitteret
dīcēns, "Nihil, mehercule, tam pusillum est, quod dē salūte
dēspērāre dēbeat, modo sē dēfendere et vim dēpulsāre
velit." 5

24. Ranae et Iuppiter.

Rānae aliquandō rēgem sibi ā Iove petīvisse dīcuntur.
Quārum ille precibus exōrātus trabem ingentem in lacum
dēiēcit. Rānae sonitū perterritae prīmum refūgēre, deinde
vērō trabem in aquā nātantem cōnspicātae māgnō cum
contemptū in eā cōnsēdērunt aliumque sibi novīs clāmō- 10
ribus rēgem expetīvērunt. Tum Iuppiter eārum stultitiam
pūnītūrus hydrum illīs mīsit, ā quō cum plūrimae captae
perīrent, sērō eās stolidārum precum paenituit.

25. Puer Mendax.

Puer ovīs pāscēns crēbrō per lūsum māgnīs clāmōribus
opem rūsticōrum implōrāverat, lupōs gregem suum aggres- 15
sōs esse fingēns. Saepe autem frūstrātus eōs quī auxilium
lātūrī advēnerant, tandem lupō rē vērā inruente, multīs
cum lacrimīs vīcīnōs ōrāre coepit ut sibi et gregī subve-
nīrent. At illī eum pariter ut anteā lūdere exīstimantēs
precēs ēius et lacrimās neglēxērunt, ita ut lupus līberē in 20
ovīs grassārētur plūrimāsque eārum dīlaniāret.

3 pusillum : *parvulum.*
6 petīvisse : *rogāvisse.*
7 exōrātus : *adductus.*
11 expetīvērunt : *valdē petī-
vērunt.*

14 crēbrō : *saepe.*
16 fingēns : *simulāns.*
16 frūstrātus : *cum dēcēpisset.*
17 inruente : *aggrediente.*
21 grassārētur : *aggrederētur.*

26. Rusticus et Canis Fidelis.

Rūsticus in agrōs exiit ad opus suum. Fīliolum, quī in cūnīs iacēbat, relīquit canī fidēlī atque validō custō- diendum. Adrēpsit anguis immānis, quī puerulum ex- stinctūrus erat. Sed custōs fidēlis corripit eum dentibus 5 acūtīs, et, dum eum necāre studet, cūnās simul ēvertit super exstinctum anguem. Paulō post ex arvō rediit agricola ; cum cūnās ēversās cruentumque canis rictum vidēret, īrā accenditur. Temerē igitur custōdem fīliolī interfēcit ligōne, quem manibus tenēbat. Sed ubi cūnās 10 restituit, super anguem occīsum repperit puerum vīvum et incolumem. Paenitentia facinoris sēra fuit.

27. Cancer.

Mare cancer ōlim dēseruit, in lītore
Pāscendī cupidus. Volpēs hunc simul aspicit
Iēiūna, simul accurrit, et praedam capit.
15 " Nē," dīxit ille, " iūre plector, quī, salō
Cum fuerim nātus, voluerim solō ingredī ! "
Suus ūnīcuīque praefīnītus est locus,
Quem praeterīre sine perīclō nōn licet.

28. Culex et Taurus.

In cornū taurī parvulus quondam culex
20 Cōnsēdit ; sēque dīxit, mōle sī suā
Eum gravāret, āvolātūrum īlicō.
At ille, " Nec tē cōnsīdentem sēnseram."

12 ōlim : *aliquandō.*   15 plector : *pūnior.*
13 cupidus : *avidus.*   15 salō : *marī.*
            21 īlicō : *extemplō.*

29. De Vitiis Hominum.

Pērās imposuit Iuppiter nōbīs duās :
Propriīs replētam vitiīs post tergum dedit,
Aliēnīs ante pectus suspendit gravem.
Hāc rē vidēre nostra mala nōn possumus ;
Aliī simul dēlinquunt, cēnsōrēs sumus.   5

2 **propriīs :** *nostrīs.*   4 **hāc rē :** *unde.*
2 **replētam :** *plēnam.*   5 **dēlinquunt :** *peccant.*

GAIUS IULIUS CAESAR.

100–44 B.C.

C. Iūlius Caesar, nōbilissimā genitus familiā, annum
agēns sextum et decimum patrem āmīsit. Cornēliam,
Cinnae fīliam, dūxit uxōrem ; cūius pater cum esset Sullae
inimīcissimus, is Caesarem voluit compellere ut eam repu-
5 diāret ; neque id potuit efficere. Quā rē Caesar bonīs
spoliātus cum etiam ad necem quaererētur, mūtātā veste
nocte urbe ēlapsus est et quamquam tunc quartānae
morbō labōrābat, prope per singulās noctis latebrās com-
mūtāre cōgēbātur ; et comprehēnsus ā Sullae lībērtō, nē
10 ad Sullam perdūcerētur, vix datā pecūniā ēvāsit. Postrēmō per propīnquōs et adfīnīs suōs veniam impetrāvit.
Satis cōnstat, Sullam, cum dēprecantibus amīcissimīs et
ōrnātissimīs virīs aliquamdiū dēnegāsset atque illī pertināciter contenderent, expūgnātum tandem dīxisse eum,
15 quem incolumem tantō opere cuperent, aliquandō optimātium partibus, quās sēcum simul dēfendissent, exitiō
futūrum ; nam Caesarī multōs Mariōs inesse.
Mortuō Sullā Rhodum sēcēdere statuit, ut per ōtium
Apollōniō Molōnī, tunc clārissimō dīcendī magistrō,
20 operam daret. Hūc dum trāicit, ā praedōnibus captus est
mānsitque apud eōs prope quadrāgintā diēs. Per omne
autem illud spatium ita sē gessit ut pīrātīs pariter terrōrī

---

4 **compellere**: *cōgere.*   9 **comprehēnsus**: *dēprehēnsus.*
6 **necem**: *mortem.*   13 **dēnegāsset**: *recūsāvisset.*
8 **labōrābat**: *adflīgēbātur.*   14 **expūgnātum**: *victum.*
15 **incolumem**: *salvum.*

venerātiōnīque esset. Comitēs interim servōsque ad ex-
pediendās pecūniās quibus redimerētur dīmīsit. Vīgintī
talenta pīrātae postulāverant ; ille quīnquāgintā datūrum
sē spopondit. Quibus numerātīs cum expositus esset in
lītore, cōnfestim Mīlētum, quae urbs proximē aberat, pro- 5
perāvit ibique contractā classe, invēctus in eum locum in
quō ipsī praedōnēs erant, partem classis fugāvit, partem
mersit, aliquot nāvīs cēpit pīrātāsque in potestātem re-
dāctōs eō suppliciō, quod illīs saepe minātus inter iocum
erat, adfēcit crucīque suffīxit. 10

Caesar quaestor factus in Hispāniam profectus est.
Quō profectus cum Alpīs trānsiret et ad cōnspectum
pauperis cūiusdam vīcī comitēs per iocum inter sē dispu-
tārent, num illīc etiam esset ambitiōnī locus, sēriō dīxit
Caesar, mālle sē ibi prīmum esse, quam Rōmae secundum. 15
Dominātiōnis avidus ā prīmā aetāte rēgnum concupīscē-
bat semperque in ōre habēbat hōs Eurīpidis, Graecī poētae,
versūs :

> Nam sī violandum est iūs, rēgnandī grātiā
> Violandum est, aliīs rēbus pietātem colās. 20

Cumque Gādēs, quod est Hispāniae oppidum, vēnisset,
animadversā apud Herculis templum māgnī Alexandrī
imāgine ingemuit et lacrimās fūdit. Causam quaerentibus
amīcīs, " Nōnne," inquit, " idōnea dolendī causa est quod
nihildum memorābile gess'erim in eā aetāte, quā iam Alex- 25
ander orbem terrārum subēgerat ? "

Aedīlis praeter Comitium āc Forum etiam Capitōlium
ōrnāvit porticibus. Vēnātiōnēs autem lūdōsque et cum

conlēgā M. Bibulō et sēparātim ēdidit. Hīs autem rēbus
patrimōnium effūdit tantumque cōnflāvit aes aliēnum ut
ipse dīceret sibi opus esse mīliēns sēstertium, ut habēret
nihil.

5   Cōnsul deinde creātus cum M. Bibulō, societātem cum
Gnaeō Pompēiō et Mārcō Crassō iūnxit Caesar, nē quid
agerētur in rē pūblicā, quod displicuisset ūllī ex tribus.
Deinde lēgem tulit ut ager Campānus plēbī dīviderētur.
Cuī lēgī cum senātus repūgnāret, rem ad populum dētulit.
10 Bibulus conlēga in Forum vēnit, ut lēgī obsisteret, sed
tanta in eum commōta est sēditiō ut in caput ēius cophinus stercore plēnus effunderētur fascēsque eī frange-
rentur atque adeō ipse armīs Forō expellerētur. Quā rē
cum Bibulus per reliquum annī tempus domō abditus cūriā
15 abstinēret, ūnus ex eō tempore Caesar omnia in rē pūblicā ad arbitrium administrābat, ut nōnnūllī urbānōrum,
sī quid testandī grātiā sīgnārent, per iocum nōn, ut mōs
erat, "cōnsulibus Caesare et Bibulō" āctum scrīberent,
sed "Iūliō et Caesare," ūnum cōnsulem nōmine et cōg-
20 nōmine prō duōbus appellantēs.

Fūnctus cōnsulātū Caesar Galliam prōvinciam accēpit. Gessit autem novem annīs, quibus in imperiō fuit,
haec ferē: Galliam in prōvinciae fōrmam redēgit; Ger-
mānōs, quī trāns Rhēnum incolunt, prīmus Rōmānōrum
25 ponte fabricātō aggressus māximīs adfēcit clādibus.
Aggressus est Britannōs, īgnōtōs anteā, superātīsque
pecūniās et obsidēs imperāvit. Hīc cum multa Rōmānōrum mīlitum īnsīgnia nārrantur, tum illud ēgregium ipsīus

---

1 **ēdidit**: *exhibuit.*
2 **cōnflāvit**: *contrāxit.*
9 **repūgnāret**: *resisteret.*
9 **dētulit**: *rettulit.*

11 **sēditiō**: *tumultus.*
15 **ūnus**: *sōlus.*
16 **arbitrium**: *voluntātem.*
16 **urbānōrum**: *facētōrum.*

Caesaris, quod nūtante in fugam exercitū, raptō fugientis
ē manū scūtō, in prīmam volitāns aciem proelium restituit. Īdem aliō proeliō legiōnis aquiliferum ineundae
fugae causā iam conversum faucibus comprehēnsum
in contrāriam partem dētrāxit dextramque ad hostem 5
tendēns, "Quōrsum tū," inquit, "abīs? Illīc sunt, cum
quibus dīmicāmus." Quā adhortātiōne omnium legiō-
num trepidātiōnem corrēxit vincīque parātās vincere
docuit.

Interfectō intereā apud Parthōs Crassō et dēfūnctā 10
Iūliā, Caesaris fīliā, quae, nūpta Pompēiō, generī soce-
rīque concordiam tenēbat, statim aemulātiō ērūpit. Iam
prīdem Pompēiō suspectae Caesaris opēs et Caesarī
Pompēiāna dīgnitās gravis, nec hīc ferēbat parem, nec
ille superiōrem. Itaque cum Caesar in Galliā dētinērētur, 15
et, nē imperfectō bellō discēderet, postulāsset ut sibi
licēret quamvīs absentī alterum cōnsulātum petere, ā
senātū suādentibus Pompēiō ēiusque amīcīs negātum eī
est. Hanc iniūriam acceptam vindicātūrus in Ītaliam
rediit et bellandum ratus cum exercitū Rubicōnem flūmen, 20
quī prōvinciae ēius fīnis erat, trānsiit. Hōc ad flūmen
paulum cōnstitisse fertur āc reputāns, quantum mōlīrētur,
conversus ad proximōs, "Etiam nunc," inquit, "regredī
possumus ; quod sī ponticulum trānsierimus, omnia armīs
agenda erunt." Postrēmō autem, "Iacta ālea estō!" 25
exclāmāns, exercitum trāicī iussit plūrimīsque urbibus
occupātīs Brundisium contendit, quō Pompēius cōnsu-
lēsque cōnfūgerant.

1 nūtante: *cēdente.*
3 ineundae: *incipiendae.*
6 quōrsum: *quō.*
10 dēfūnctā : *mortuā.*

20 ratus : *exīstimāns.*
22 mōlīrētur : *susciperet.*
26 trāicī : *trādūcī.*
27 contendit : *properāvit.*

Quī cum inde in Ēpīrum trāiēcissent, Caesar eōs
secūtus ā Brundisiō Dyrrhachium inter oppositās classīs
gravissimā hieme trānsmīsit; cōpiīsque quās subsequī
iusserat diūtius cessantibus cum ad eās arcessendās frū-
5 strā mīsisset, mīrae audāciae facinus ēdidit. Morae enim
impatiēns castrīs noctū ēgreditur, clam nāviculam cōnscendit, obvolūtō capite, nē āgnōscerētur, et quamquam
mare saevā tempestāte intumēscēbat, in altum tamen prōtinus dīrigī nāvigium iubet et gubernātōre trepidante,
10 "Quid timēs?" inquit, "Caesarem vehis!" neque prius
gubernātōrem cēdere adversae tempestātī passus est,
quam paene obrutus esset fluctibus.

Deinde Caesar in Ēpīrum profectus Pompēium Phar-
sālicō proeliō fūdit, et fugientem persecūtus, ut occīsum
15 cōgnōvit, Ptolemaeō rēgī, Pompēī interfectōrī, ā quō sibi
quoque īnsidiās tendī vidēret, bellum intulit; quō vīctō
in Pontum trānsiit Pharnacemque, Mithridātis fīlium, re-
bellantem et multiplicī successū praeferōcem intrā quīn-
tum ab adventū diem, quattuor quibus in cōnspectum
20 vēnit hōrīs ūnā prōflīgāvit aciē, mōre fulminis, quod ūnō
eōdemque mōmentō vēnit, percussit, abscessit. Nec vāna
dē sē praedicātiō est Caesaris, ante vīctum hostem esse
quam vīsum. Ponticō posteā triumphō trium verbōrum
praetulit titulum: "Vēnī, vīdī, vīcī." Deinde Scīpiōnem
25 et Iubam, Numidiae rēgem, reliquiās Pompēiānārum par-
tium in Āfricā refoventīs, dēvīcit et omnium vīctor, re-
gressus in urbem omnibus quī contrā sē arma tulerant
īgnōvit et quīnquiēns triumphāvit.

1 trāiēcissent : *trānsiissent.*		8 altum : *mare.*	
3 hieme : *tempestāte.*		20 prōflīgāvit : *superāvit.*	
5 ēdidit : *fēcit.*		24 titulum : *īnscrīptiōnem.*	
7 obvolūtō : *adopertō.*		26 refoventīs : *renovantīs.*	

Bellis civilibus confectis, conversus iam ad ordinandum rei publicae statum, fastos correxit annumque ad cursum solis accommodavit, ut trecentorum sexaginta quinque dierum esset et intercalario mense sublato unus dies quarto quoque anno intercalaretur. Ius laboriosissime ac severissime dixit. Repetundarum convictos etiam ordine senatorio movit. Peregrinarum mercium portoria instituit; legem praecipue sumptuariam exercuit. De ornanda instruendaque urbe, item de tuendo ampliandoque imperio plura ac maiora in dies destinabat; imprimis ius civile ad certum modum redigere atque ex immensa legum copia optima quaeque et necessaria in paucissimos conferre libros; bibliothecas Graecas et Latinas, quas maximas posset, publicare, siccare Pomptinas paludes; viam munire a Mari Supero per Appennini dorsum ad Tiberim usque; Dacos qui se in Pontum effuderant, coërcere; mox Parthis bellum inferre per Armeniam.

Haec et alia agentem et meditantem mors praevenit. Dictator enim in perpetuum creatus agere insolentius coepit; senatum ad se venientem sedens excepit et quendam ut adsurgeret monentem irato voltu respexit. Cum Antonius, Caesaris in omnibus bellis comes et tunc consulatus conlega, capiti eius in sella aurea sedentis pro rostris diadema, insigne regium, imposuisset, id ita ab eo est repulsum ut non offensus videretur. Qua re coniuratum in eum est a sexaginta amplius viris, Cassio et Bruto ducibus, decretumque eum Idibus Martiis in senatu confodere.

5

10

15

20

25

---

1 confectis: *finitis.*
7 movit: *sustulit,* p.42, l. 11.
8 exercuit: *exsecutus est.*

9 tuendo: *defendendo.*
15 munire: *facere.*
28 decretum: *constitutum.*

Plūrima indicia futūrī perīculī obtulerant diī immortālēs. Uxor Calpurnia, territa nocturnō vīsū, ut Īdibus
Mārtiīs domī subsisteret ōrābat, et Spūrinna harūspex
praedīxerat ut proximōs diēs trīgintā quasi fātālīs ca-
5 vēret, quōrum ūltimus erat Īdūs Mārtiae.   Hōc igitur
diē Caesar Spūrinnae, "Ecquid scīs," inquit, "Īdūs
Mārtiās iam vēnisse?" et is, "Ecquid scīs, illās nōndum
praeterīsse?" Atque cum Caesar eō diē in senātum
vēnisset, adsīdentem coniūrātī speciē officī circumste-
10 tērunt īlicōque ūnus, quasi aliquid rogātūrus, propius ac-
cessit renuentīque ab utrōque umerō togam apprehendit.
Deinde clāmantem, "Ista quidem vīs est," Casca, ūnus
ē coniūrātīs, adversum volnerat paulum īnfrā iugulum.
Caesar Cascae brāchium adreptum graphiō trāiēcit cōnā-
15 tusque prōsilīre aliō volnere tardātus est.   Dein ut ani-
madvertit undique sē strictīs pūgiōnibus petī, togā caput
obvolvit et ita tribus et vīgintī plāgīs cōnfossus est.   Cum
Mārcum Brūtum, quem fīlī locō habēbat, in sē inruentem
vīdisset, dīxisse fertur: "Tū quoque, mī fīlī!"
20   Fuisse trāditur excelsā statūrā, ōre paulō plēniōre,
nigrīs vegetīsque oculīs, capite calvō; quam calvitī dē-
fōrmitātem, quod saepe obtrectātōrum iocīs obnoxia erat,
aegrē ferēbat.   Ideō ex omnibus dēcrētīs sibi ā senātū
populōque honōribus nōn alium aut recēpit aut ūsūrpāvit
25 libentius quam iūs laureae perpetuō gestandae.   Vīnī
parcissimum eum fuisse nē inimīcī quidem negāvērunt.
Verbum Catōnis est, ūnum ex omnibus Caesarem ad
ēvertendam rem pūblicam sōbrium accessisse.   Armōrum

3 subsisteret : *remanēret.*	20 excelsā : *altā.*
10 īlicō : *repente.*	21 vegetīs : *vīvidīs.*
11 renuentī : *recūsantī.*	22 obtrectātōrum : *dētractō-*
14 trāiēcit : *cōnfōdit.*	*rum.*
17 obvolvit : *tēxit.*	25 perpetuō : *semper.*

et equitandī perītissimus, labōris ūltrā fidem patiēns ; in
āgmine nōnnumquam equō, saepius pedibus anteībat,
capite dētēctō, seu sōl, seu imber erat. Longissimās viās
incrēdibilī celeritāte cōnficiēbat, ut persaepe nūntiōs dē
sē praevenīret ; neque eum morābantur flūmina, quae vel 5
nandō vel innīxus īnflātīs ūtribus trāiciēbat.

3 **dētēctō** : *nūdō.*   6 trāiciēbat : *trānsībat.*

ALCIBIADES.

450(?)-404 B.C.

Alcibiadēs, Clīniae fīlius, Athēniēnsis. In hōc quid
nātūra efficere possit vidētur experta. Cōnstat enim inter
omnīs quī dē eō memoriae prōdidērunt, nihil illō fuisse
excellentius vel in vitiīs vel in virtūtibus. Nātus in
5 amplissimā cīvitāte summō genere, omnium aetātis suae
multō fōrmōsissimus, ad omnīs rēs aptus cōnsilīque
plēnus, namque imperātor fuit summus et marī et terrā,
disertus ut in prīmīs dīcendō valēret, quod tanta erat
commendātiō ōris atque ōrātiōnis ut nēmō eī posset resis-
10 tere ; dīves ; cum tempus posceret, labōriōsus, patiēns ;
līberālis, splendidus nōn minus in vītā quam vīctū ; adfābilis, blandus, temporibus callidissimē serviēns : īdem,
simul āc sē remīserat neque causa suberat quā rē animī
labōrem perferret, lūxuriōsus, dissolūtus, libīdinōsus, in-
15 temperāns, reperiēbātur, ut omnēs admīrārentur in ūnō
homine tantam esse dissimilitūdinem tamque dīversam
nātūram.

Ēducātus est in domō Periclī (prīvīgnus enim ēius
fuisse dīcitur), ērudītus ā Sōcrate. Socerum habuit Hip-
20 ponīcum, omnium Graecā linguā loquentium dītissimum,
ut, sī ipse fingere vellet, neque plūra bona comminīscī

2 cōnstat inter omnīs : *omnēs cōnsentiunt.*

3 memoriae prōdidērunt :
scrīpsērunt.

4 excellentius : *clārius, magis ēgregium.*

5 amplissimā : *splendidissimā,* p. 7 5, l. 7.

6 fōrmōsissimus : *pulcherri-
mus.*

8 disertus : *ēloquēns.*

9 ōris : *vōcis.*

13 sē remīserat : *sē relaxā-
verat.*

21 comminīscī : *excōgitāre.*

neque māiōra posset cōnsequī quam vel nātūra vel fōrtūna tribueret.

Bellō Peloponnēsiō hūius cōnsiliō atque auctōritāte
Athēniēnsēs bellum Syrācūsānīs indīxērunt; ad quod
gerendum ipse dux dēlēctus est, duo praetereā conlēgae 5
datī, Nīcias et Lamachus. Id cum apparārētur, prius
quam classis exīret, accidit ut ūnā nocte omnēs hermae
quī in oppidō erant Athēnīs dēicerentur praeter ūnum,
quī ante iānuam erat Andocidī. Itaque ille posteā Mercurius Andocidī vocitātus est. Hōc cum appārēret nōn 10
sine māgnā multōrum cōnsēnsiōne esse factum, quae nōn
ad prīvātam, sed ad pūblicam rem pertinēret, māgnus mul-
titūdinī timor est iniectus, nē qua repentīna vīs in cīvitāte exsisteret, quae lībērtātem opprimeret populī. Hōc
māximē convenīre in Alcibiadem vidēbātur, quod et 15
potentior et māior quam prīvātus exīstimābātur: multōs
enim līberālitāte dēvinxerat, plūrīs etiam operā forēnsī
suōs reddiderat. Quā rē fīēbat ut omnium oculōs, quotiēnscumque in pūblicum prōdīsset, ad sē converteret
neque eī pār quisquam in cīvitāte pōnerētur. Itaque nōn 20
sōlum spem in eō habēbant māximam, sed etiam timōrem,
quod et obesse plūrimum et prōdesse poterat. Aspergē-
bātur etiam īnfāmiā, quod in domō suā facere mystēria
dīcēbātur, quod nefās erat mōre Athēniēnsium, idque nōn
ad religiōnem sed ad coniūrātiōnem pertinēre exīstimā- 25
bātur.

Hōc crīmine in cōntiōne ab inimīcīs compellābātur.
Sed īnstābat tempus ad bellum proficīscendī. Id ille

10 **vocitātus**: *nōminātus.*   20 **pōnerētur**: *exīstimārētur.*
10 **appārēret**: *vidērētur.*   22 **obesse**: *nocēre.*
14 **exsisteret**: *orerētur.*   27 **compellābātur**: *accūsābātur.*
15 **convenīre**: *congruere.*   28 **īnstābat**: *aderat.*

intuēns neque ignōrāns cīvium suōrum cōnsuētūdinem
postulābat, sī quid dē sē agī vellent, potius dē praesente
quaestiō habērētur quam absēns invidiae crīmine accūsā-
rētur.   Inimīcī vērō ēius quiēscendum in praesentī, quia
5 nocērī eī nōn posse intellegēbant, et illud tempus exspectandum dēcrēvērunt quō exīsset, ut absentem aggrederen-
tur, itaque fēcērunt.   Nam postquam in Siciliam eum
pervēnisse crēdidērunt, absentem quod sacra violāsset,
reum fēcērunt.   Quā dē rē cum eī nūntius ā magistrātū
10 in Siciliam mīssus esset, ut domum ad causam dīcendam
redīret, essetque in māgnā spē prōvinciae bene admini-
strandae, nōn pārēre nōluit et in trirēmem quae ad
eum erat dēportandum mīssa ascendit.   Hāc Thūriōs in
Ītaliam pervēctus, multa sēcum reputāns dē immoderātā
15 cīvium suōrum licentiā crūdēlitāteque ergā nōbilīs, ūtilis-
simum ratus impendentem ēvitāre tempestātem, clam
sē ab custōdibus subdūxit et inde prīmum Ēlidem, dein
Thēbās vēnit.   Postquam autem sē capitis damnātum
bonīs pūblicātīs audīvit, et (id quod ūsū vēnerat) Eumol-
20 pidās sacerdōtēs ā populō coāctōs ut sē dēvovērent,
ēiusque dēvōtiōnis quō testātior esset memoria, exemplum
in pīlā lapideā incīsum esse positum in pūblicō, Lacedae-
monem dēmigrāvit.   Ibi, ut ipse praedicāre cōnsuērat,
nōn adversus patriam sed inimīcōs suōs bellum gessit,
25 quod iīdem hostēs essent cīvitātī: nam cum intellegerent
sē plūrimum prōdesse posse reī pūblicae, ex eā ēiēcisse
plūsque īrae suae quam ūtilitātī commūnī pāruisse.

1 intuēns: cōgitāns.
2 agī: fierī.
9 reum fēcērunt: accūsāvē-
runt.
11 prōvinciae: officī.
14 reputāns: cōgitāns.
16 ratus: exīstimāns.
17 dein: deinde, tum.
19 ūsū vēnerat: acciderat.
23 praedicāre: cōnfirmāre.
27 pāruisse: serviisse, p. 66,
l. 12.

Itaque hūius cōnsiliō Lacedaemoniī cum Persē rēge
amīcitiam fēcērunt, dein Decelēam in Atticā mūniērunt
praesidiōque ibi perpetuō positō in obsidiōne Athēnās
tenuērunt. Ēiusdem operā Iōniam ā societāte āvertē-
runt Athēniēnsium. Quō factō multō superiōrēs bellō 5
esse coepērunt.

Neque vērō hīs rēbus tam amīcī Alcibiadī sunt factī
quam timōre ab eō aliēnātī. Nam cum ācerrimī virī
praestantem prūdentiam in omnibus rēbus cōgnōscerent,
pertimuērunt, nē cāritāte patriae ductus aliquandō ab 10
ipsīs dēscīsceret et cum suīs in grātiam redīret. Itaque
tempus ēius interficiendī quaerere īnstituērunt. Id Alcibiadēs diūtius cēlārī nōn potuit ; erat enim eā sagācitāte
ut dēcipī nōn posset, praesertim cum animum attendisset
ad cavendum. Itaque ad Tissaphernem, praefectum 15
rēgis Dārēī, sē contulit. Cūius cum in intimam amīcitiam pervēnisset et Athēniēnsium male gestīs in Siciliā
rēbus opēs senēscere, contrā Lacedaemoniōrum crēscere
vidēret, initiō cum Pīsandrō praetōre, quī apud Samum
exercitum habēbat, per internūntiōs conloquitur et dē re- 20
ditū suō facit mentiōnem. Erat enim eōdem quō Alcibiadēs sēnsū, populī potentiae nōn amīcus et optimātium
fautor. Ab hōc dēstitūtus prīmum per Thrasybūlum,
Lycī fīlium, ab exercitū recipitur praetorque fit apud
Samum ; post suffrāgante Thērāmene populī scītō restitui- 25
tur parīque absēns imperiō praeficitur simul cum Thrasy-
būlō et Thērāmene. Hōrum in imperiō tanta commūtātiō

3 **perpetuō** : *continuō.*
9 **praestantem** : *excellentem,*
66, 4.
10 **cāritāte** : *amōre.*
11 **dēscīsceret** : *dēsereret.*

18 **senēscere** : *dēficere.*
22 **sēnsū** : *mente.*
22 **optimātium** : *nōbilium,* p.
68, l. 15.
25 **suffrāgante** : *favente.*
26 **simul cum** : *ūnā cum.*

rērum facta est ut Lacedaemoniī, quī paulō ante vīctōrēs
viguerant, perterritī pācem peterent. Vīctī enim erant
quīnque proeliīs terrestribus, tribus nāvālibus, in quibus
ducentās nāvīs trirēmīs āmīserant, quae captae in hos-
5 tium vēnerant potestātem. Alcibiadēs simul cum conlēgīs
recēperat Iōniam, Hellēspontum, multās praetereā urbīs
Graecās, quae in ōrā sitae sunt Thrāciae, quārum expūg-
nārant complūrīs, in hīs Byzantium, neque minus multās
cōnsiliō ad amīcitiam adiūnxerant, quod in captōs clēmen-
10 tiā fuerant ūsī. Ita praedā onustī locuplētātō exercitū
māximīs rēbus gestīs Athēnās vēnērunt.

His cum obviam ūniversa cīvitās in Pīraeum dēscendis-
set, tanta fuit omnium exspectātiō vīsendī Alcibiadis ut
ad ēius trirēmem volgus cōnflueret proinde āc sī sōlus ad-
15 vēnisset. Sīc enim populō erat persuāsum et adversās
superiōrēs et praesentīs secundās rēs accidisse ēius operā.
Itaque et Siciliam āmīssam et Lacedaemoniōrum vīctōriās
culpae suae tribuēbant, quod tālem virum ē cīvitāte expulissent. Neque id sine causā arbitrārī vidēbantur.
20 Nam postquam exercituī praeesse coeperat, neque terrā
neque marī hostēs parēs esse potuerant. Hīc ut ē nāvī
ēgressus est, quamquam Thērāmenēs et Thrasybūlus
iīsdem rēbus praefuerant simulque vēnerant in Pīraeum,
tamen ūnum omnēs illum prōsequēbantur, et (id quod
25 numquam anteā ūsū vēnerat nisi Olympiae vīctōribus),
corōnīs laureīs taeniīsque volgō dōnābātur. Ille lacri-
māns tālem benevolentiam cīvium suōrum accipiēbat,
reminīscēns prīstinī temporis acerbitātem. Postquam in

---

2 viguerant : *flōruerant.*   14 volgus : *multitūdō.*
7 sitae : *positae.*   20 praeesse : *imperāre.*
9 in : *ergā,* p. 68, l. 15.   24 ūnum : *sōlum.*
13 vīsendī : *videndī.*   28 prīstinī : *superiōris.*

astū vēnit, cōntiōne advocātā sīc verba fēcit ut nēmō tam
ferus fuerit quīn ēius cāsuī inlacrimārit inimīcumque iīs
sē ostenderit quōrum operā patriā pulsus fuerat, proinde
āc sī alius populus, nōn ille ipse quī tum flēbat, eum sac-
rilegī damnāsset. Restitūta ergō huic sunt pūblicē bona, 5
iīdemque illī Eumolpidae sacerdōtēs rūrsus resacrāre sunt
coāctī quī eum dēvōverant, pīlaeque illae in quibus dēvōtiō fuerat scrīpta in mare praecipitātae.

Haec Alcibiadī laetitia nōn nimis fuit diūturna. Nam
cum eī omnēs essent honōrēs dēcrētī tōtaque rēs pūblica 10
domī bellīque trādita, ut ūnīus arbitriō gererētur, et ipse
postulāsset ut duo sibi conlēgae darentur, Thrasybūlus et
Adīmantus, neque id negātum esset, classe in Asiam profectus, quod apud Cȳmēn minus ex sententiā rem gesserat,
in invidiam recidit. Nihil enim eum nōn efficere posse 15
dūcēbant. Ex quō fīēbat ut omnia minus prōsperē gesta
culpae tribuerent, cum aut eum neglegenter aut malitiōsē
fēcisse loquerentur ; sīcut tum accidit : nam corruptum
ā rēge capere Cȳmēn nōluisse arguēbant. Itaque huic
māximē putāmus malō fuisse nimiam opīniōnem ingenī 20
atque virtūtis : timēbātur enim nōn minus quam dīligē-
bātur, nē secundā fōrtūnā māgnīsque opibus ēlātus tyran-
nidem concupīsceret. Quibus rēbus factum est ut absentī
magistrātum abrogārent et alium in ēius locum substi-
'tuerent. Id ille ut audīvit, domum revertī nōluit et sē 25
Pactyēn contulit ibique tria castella commūniit, Ornōs,
Bizanthēn, Neontīchos, manūque conlēctā prīmus Graecae
cīvitātis in Thrāciam introiit, glōriōsius exīstimāns bar-

1 **astū** : *urbem.*	16 **dūcēbant** : *exīstimābant.*
2 **ferus** : *crudēlis.*	17 **malitiōsē** : *dolōsē.*
5 **pūblicē** : *populī iūssū.*	19 **arguēbant** : *accūsābant.*
6 **resacrāre** : *dēvōtiōne solvere.*	21 **dīligēbātur** : *amābātur.*
15 **invidiam** : *odium.*	23 **concupīsceret** : *peteret.*

barōrum praedā locuplētārī quam Grāiōrum. Quā ex rē
crēverat cum fāmā tum opibus māgnamque amīcitiam sibi
cum quibusdam rēgibus Thrāciae pepererat.

Neque tamen ā cāritāte patriae potuit recēdere. Nam
5 cum apud Aegos flūmen Philoclēs, praetor Athēniēnsium,
classem cōnstituisset suam neque longē. abesset Lȳsander, praetor Lacedaemoniōrum, quī in eō erat occupātus
ut bellum quam diūtissimē dūceret, quod ipsīs pecūnia
ā rēge suppeditābātur, contrā Athēniēnsibus exhaustīs
10 praeter arma et nāvīs nihil erat super, Alcibiadēs ad exercitum vēnit Athēniēnsium ibique praesente volgō agere
coepit : sī vellent, sē coāctūrum Lȳsandrum dīmicāre aut
pācem petere spopondit ; Lacedaemoniōs eō nōlle classe
cōnflīgere, quod pedestribus cōpiīs plūs quam nāvibus
15 valērent; sibi autem esse facile Seuthem, rēgem Thrā-
cum, addūcere ut eum terrā dēpelleret; quō factō necessāriō aut classe cōnflictūrum aut bellum compositūrum.
Id etsī vērē dictum Philoclēs animadvertēbat, tamen
postulāta facere nōluit, quod sentiēbat sē Alcibiade re-
20 ceptō nūllius mōmentī apud exercitum futūrum et, sī quid
secundī ēvēnisset, nūllam in eā rē suam partem fore, contrā ea, sī quid adversī accidisset, sē ūnum ēius dēlictī
futūrum reum. Ab hōc discēdēns Alcibiadēs, " Quoniam,"
inquit, " vīctōriae patriae repūgnās, illud moneō, nē iūxtā
25 hostem castra habeās nautica ; perīculum est enim, nē
immodestiā mīlitum vestrōrum occāsiō dētur Lȳsandrō
vestrī opprimendī exercitūs." Neque ea rēs illum fefellit.

---

3 **pepererat:** *cōnsecūtus erat.*

9 **suppeditābātur :** *praebēbā-tur.*

10 **erat super:** *erat relīctum.*

11 **volgō :** *mīlitibus.*

18 **animadvertēbat :** *intelle-gēbat.*

20 **momentī :** *auctōritātis.*

24 **iūxtā :** *prope.*

26 **immodestiā :** *licentiā.*

Nam Lȳsander, cum per speculātōrēs comperisset volgum
Athēniēnsium in terram praedātum exīsse nāvīsque paene
inānīs relīctās, tempus reī gerendae nōn dīmīsit eōque
impetū bellum tōtum dēlēvit.

At Alcibiadēs, vīctīs Athēniēnsibus nōn satis tūta 5
eadem loca sibi arbitrāns, penitus in Thrāciam sē suprā
Propontidem abdidit, spērāns ibi facillimē suam fōrtūnam
occulī posse. Falsō. Nam Thrāces, postquam eum cum
māgnā pecūniā vēnisse sēnsērunt, īnsidiās fēcērunt eaque
quae apportārat, abstulērunt, ipsum capere nōn potuērunt. 10
Ille cernēns nūllum locum sibi tūtum in Graeciā propter
potentiam Lacedaemoniōrum ad Pharnabazum in Asiam
trānsiit : quem quidem adeō suā cēpit hūmānitāte ut eum
nēmō in amīcitiā antecēderet. Namque eī Grȳnium dederat, in Phrygiā castrum, ex quō quīnquāgēna talenta 15
vēctīgālis capiēbat. Quā fōrtūnā Alcibiadēs nōn erat
contentus neque Athēnās vīctās Lacedaemoniīs servīre
poterat patī. Itaque ad patriam līberandam omnī ferēbātur cōgitātiōne. Sed vidēbat id sine rēge Persē nōn
posse fierī, ideōque eum amīcum sibi cupiēbat adiungī 20
neque dubitābat facile sē cōnsecūtūrum, sī modo ēius conveniundī habuisset potestātem. Nam Cȳrum frātrem eī
bellum clam parāre Lacedaemoniīs adiuvantibus sciēbat :
id sī aperuisset, māgnam sē initūrum grātiam vidēbat.

Hōc cum mōlīrētur peteretque ā Pharnabazō ut ad rē- 25
gem mitterētur, eōdem tempore Critiās cēterīque tyrannī
Athēniēnsium certōs hominēs ad Lȳsandrum in Asiam

1 comperisset : cōgnōvisset.   18 patī : perferre, p. 66, l. 14.
4 dēlēvit : cōnfēcit, fīnīvit.   21 cōnsecūtūrum : perfectūrum.
8 occulī : cēlārī, p. 69, l. 13.   22 potestātem : occāsiōnem.
13 cēpit : ad sē trāxit.   25 mōlīrētur : apparāret, p. 67,
13 hūmānitāte : cōmitāte.   l. 6.

mīserant, quī eum certiōrem facerent, nisi Alcibiadem sustulisset, nihil eārum rērum fore ratum quās ipse Athēnīs
cōnstituisset: quārē, sī suās rēs gestās manēre vellet, illum
persequerētur. Hīs Lacō rēbus commōtus statuit accū-
5 rātius sibi agendum cum Pharnabazō. Huic ergō renūntiat quae rēgī cum Lacedaemoniīs essent, nisi Alcibiadem
vīvum aut mortuum sibi trādidisset. Nōn tulit hunc
satrapēs et violāre clēmentiam quam rēgis opēs minuī
māluit. Itaque mīsit Susamithrēn et Bagaeum ad Alci-
10 biadem interficiendum, cum ille esset in Phrygiā iterque
ad rēgem comparāret. Mīssī clam vīcīnitātī in quā tum
Alcibiadēs erat dant negōtium ut eum interficiant. Illī
cum ferrō aggredī nōn audērent, noctū līgna contulērunt
circā casam in quā quiēscēbat eamque succendērunt, ut
15 incendiō cōnficerent quem manū superārī posse diffīdē-
bant. Ille autem ut sonitū flammae est excitātus, etsī
gladius eī erat subductus, familiāris suī subālāre tēlum
ēripuit. Namque erat cum eō quīdam ex Arcadiā hospes,
quī numquam discēdere voluerat. Hunc sequī sē iubet
20 et id quod in praesentiā vestīmentōrum fuit adripit. Hīs
in īgnem coniectīs flammae vim trānsiit. Quem ut bar-
barī incendium effūgisse vīdērunt, tēlīs ēminus mīssīs
interfēcērunt caputque ēius ad Pharnabazum rettulērunt.
At mulier quae cum eō vīvere cōnsuērat muliebrī suā
25 veste contēctum aedificī incendiō mortuum cremāvit,
quod ad vīvum interimendum erat comparātum. Sīc
Alcibiadēs annōs circiter quadrāgintā nātus diem obiit
suprēmum.

---

1 sustulisset : *interfēcisset.*   15 cōnficerent : *interficerent.*
2 fore ratum : *permānsūrum.*   26 interimendum : *interfici-*
4 accūrātius : *dīligentius.*   *endum.*
14 succendērunt : *incendērunt.*   28 suprēmum : *ūltimum.*

Hunc infāmātum ā plērīsque trēs gravissimī historicī summīs laudibus extulērunt : Thucȳdidēs, quī ēiusdem aetātis fuit, Theopompus, post aliquantō nātus, et Timaeus : quī quidem duo maledīcentissimī nēsciō quō modō in illō ūnō laudandō cōnsentiunt. Namque ea quae 5 suprā scrīpsimus dē eō praedicārunt atque hōc amplius : cum Athēnīs splendidissimā cīvitāte nātus esset, omnīs splendōre āc dīgnitāte superāsse vītae; postquam inde expulsus Thēbās vēnerit, adeō studiīs eōrum īnservīsse ut nēmō cum labōre corporisque vīribus posset aequiperāre 10 (omnēs enim Boeōtiī magis firmitātī corporis quam ingenī acūminī īnserviunt) ; eundem apud Lacedaemoniōs, quōrum mōribus summa virtūs in patientiā pōnēbātur, sīc dūritiae sē dedisse ut parsimōniā vīctūs atque cultūs omnīs Lacedaemoniōs vinceret ; vēnisse ad Persās, apud 15 quōs summa laus esset fortiter vēnārī, lūxuriōsē vīvere ; hōrum sīc imitātum cōnsuētūdinem ut illī ipsī eum in hīs māximē admīrārentur. Quibus rēbus effēcisse ut, apud quōscumque esset, prīnceps pōnerētur habērēturque cārissimus. 20

3 **aetātis** : *temporis.*
10 **aequiperāre** : *pār esse.*
11 **ingenī** : *animī.*

12 **īnserviunt** : *sē dant.*
14 **vīctūs** : *cibī.*
19 **pōnerētur** : *exīstimārētur.*

NOTES.

ιe grammatical references are to Allen and Greenough's Grammar, to Harkness' (H), and to the " First Latin Book " by Collar and Daniell (F).

THE ARGONAUTS.

2 1 **Thessaliā** : find Thessaly on a map of Greece, in the northern part.

2 **appellātus est** : understood with the first **alter** ; so often a verb belonging to two clauses will be found expressed in the second only. We usually express the verb in the first only, as here.

prīmum : here an adverb, not an adjective with **rēgnum**.

3 **obtinuerat** : this verb usually means *hold*, or *possess*. It is not the common Latin word for *obtain*.

6 **quīdam . . . ex amīcīs = quīdam amīcōrum** : **ē** or **ex** with the ablative is often used thus in place of the partitive genitive.

7 **cōnstituērunt** : compare in **animō habēbat**, l. 5.

9 **cum** : *when ;* but the words **cum . . . rediissent** can be well rendered *returning*, instead of *when they had returned.*

10 **cum . . . audīvisset** : *hearing of this.* See preceding note.

11 **speciem . . . praebuit** : *made a show of grief.* What literally?

12 **esset** : *was*, not *might be.* Observe, as you read, how often the subjunctive must be rendered by the indicative.

13 **cum** : *though.*

14 **nēsciō quam fābulam** : *some story or other.*

15 **veritus** : *fearing*, not *having feared.* 290, *b* ; H. 550, note 1.

16 **occupātum** : agrees with **rēgnum** ; translate by a clause. F. 353, 6, and *c* (2). Remember that the English uses the perfect participle much less than the Latin.

17 **Delphōs** : look for it in the central part of northern Greece.

2 17 **quī cōnsuleret**: translate by the infinitive.   317; H. 497, I;
F. 432, 1, and 433.

   18 **quam** . . . **vēnisset**: see **esset**, l. 12, and note.

   23 **conveniendī**: *for assembling.* Do not think that the genitive
must always be translated *of.*

3 2 **dum facit** . . . **āmīsit**: *while he was making the journey, he
lost.* This is a common construction, **dum** with a present
followed by a perfect or other past tense. In such cases
translate the present by a past tense, as here.

   alterum: **ūnum** was not used because *one of two* is meant.

   4 **cum**: *since.*

   5 **alterō**: it would be a natural but amusing mistake to render
alterō here *the other.* See l. 2 above, and note.

   quem: does not refer to **pede.**

   9 **obtinēbat**: see **obtinuerat**, p. 1, l. 3, and note.

   10 **illud**: *that famous.* 102, *b*; H. 450, 4; F. 100, *d.*

   11 **negōtium** . . . **potīrētur**: *to commission Jason to get.* What
literally?

   12 **rēs**: *the undertaking.*

   14 **igitur**: remember the common position of this word by seeing
it three times in this paragraph.

   vellet: see **esset**, p. 2, l. 12, and note.

   19 **quī** . . . **docērent**: see **quī cōnsuleret**, p. 2, l. 17, and note.

   20 **conveniendī**: see p. 2, l. 23, and note.

   21 **ūsuī**: *useful.* What literally?

   22 **negōtium** . . . **aedificāret**: see **negōtium** . . . **potīrētur**, l. 11,
and note.

4 4 **quibus** . . . **ūtī**: 249; H. 421, I; F. 361.

   5 **tōta**: agrees with **nāvis**; why not with **rōbore**? Translate
wholly.

   12 **quōs** . . . **eōs**: *whom he thought . . . those he chose; chose those
whom he thought.*

   14 **sociōs**: *as comrades*, in apposition with **eōs.**

   17 **solvit**: supply **nāvem**; literally, *loosed the ship.*

   18 **haud multum post**: compare **post breve tempus**, p. 2, l. 15.

5 4 **arbitrātī**: see **veritus**, p. 2, l. 15, and note.

   5 **pūgnātum est**: *they fought.* What literally?

   15 **iam dēficere**: *was now beginning to fail.*

5 17 fōrmā praestantissimā : 251 ; H. 419, II.

18 dum quaerit . . . sēcesserat: see dum facit . . . āmīsit, p. 3, l. 2, and note.

21 negāret . . . esse : *refused to do it.* What literally ?

24 dolōre adfectī : compare timōre adfectus est, p. 3, l. 6.

6 4 quis . . . obtinēret: on obtineō, see note on p. 2, l. 3 ; and on the translation of the subjunctive, p. 2, l. 12, and note.

7 cūius . . . genus: *whose punishment was of this sort.* What literally ? cūius supplicī may be " of which punishment."

9 speciē horribilī : see fōrmā praestantissimā, p. 5, l. 17, and note.

13 quae . . . essent: *since this was the state of things.* What literally ?

haud . . . morerētur : *it was not much distant but that Phineus should die of hunger;* in English, *Phineus was near dying of hunger.*

18 quantam . . . habērent: an indirect question, like esset, p. 2, l. 12 ; quam vēnisset, p. 2, l. 18 ; quid vellet, p. 3, l. 14 ; quis obtinēret, p. 6, l. 4 ; quantō . . . essent, l. 21.

23 sī repperissent: if *they should find,* not *should have found.* The pluperfect subjunctive represents a future perfect of direct discourse. Such a future perfect is commonly translated by the present, and when changed to a pluperfect subjunctive, by the auxiliary *should* or *would*, instead of *should have*, etc.

7 5 quod cum : translate cum first and quod as the object of sēnsissent. Cf. quem cum, p. 3, l. 5. How is the relative at the beginning of a sentence usually translated? 180, *f.*

11 ingentī māgnitūdine : see speciē horribilī, p. 6, l. 9, and note. eō cōnsiliō : explained by the following words.

12 nē quis : 105, *d* ; H. 455, 1.

15 doctus est : the subject is Iāsōn.

16 nāvem solvit : see p. 4, ll. 17 and 22.

8 1 brevī spatiō : compare post breve tempus, p. 2, l. 15.

7 negābat . . . esse : see negāret . . . esse, p. 5, l. 21, and note.

9 trāditūrum : notice the omission of esse, as often in compound forms of the infinitive.

10 perfēcisset : not *should have performed.* See repperissent, p. 6, l. 23, and note.

12 ostendit : the subject is Aeētēs.

8 15 serendī : what is to be supplied ?

21 eō ipsō cōnsiliō : *with this very purpose.* Compare eō cōnsiliō, p. 7, l. 11, and note.

quae . . . essent : the same phrase, p. 6, l. 13, where see note.

9 1 quod . . . aleret : *of such a kind as to nourish.* 319, 2 ; H. 500, I ; F. 432, 3, *b,* and 433. quod alēbat would mean, *which nourished.*

13 nihil . . . valēre : *could not withstand.* What literally ?

15 omnibus aspicientibus = in omnium cōnspectū.

10 1 sparsit : *had scattered ;* the perfect tense is very commonly used after postquam, ubi, and ut (all translated *when*), but most often it is to be rendered as a pluperfect.

4 rem ēvēnisse : depends on cōgnōvit.

ita . . . ut : *just as.*

10 cum : *since,* with vellet.

20 sī . . . mānsisset : *if she should remain.* Compare sī perfēcisset, p. 8, l. 10, and note.

11 4 āvēctūrum : esse omitted. Compare trāditūrum, p. 8, l. 9, and note.

9 quī . . . essent : *to serve.* What literally ? Compare quī cōnsuleret, p. 2, l. 17, and note.

praesidiō nāvī : *as a guard for the ship.* 233, *a* ; H. 390.

20 dum . . . dormit : compare dum facit, p. 3, l. 2, and note. So dum . . . geruntur, below, l. 23.

12 4 quae . . . essent : see the same phrase, p. 6, l. 13, and note ; also p. 8, l. 21.

mātūrandum sibi : *that they ought to hasten.* 232 ; H. 388 ; F. 465 and 466.

17 inimīcō . . . animō : *unfriendly towards them.* 251 ; H.419, II.

20 hōc dolōre : *with anger at this.*

13 1 minimum . . . caperentur : *it was a very little way off but that they should be captured;* in English, *they were within a very little of being captured.* Compare note on p. 6, l. 13.

2 longius . . . posset : *it was not longer between than whither a javelin could be thrown;* in English, *the interval was not greater than a javelin-cast.*

4 locō : not *place.*

9 eō cōnsiliō : compare p. 7, l. 11, and note.

13 13 ita ... ut: compare p. 10, l. 4, and note.

ubi prīmum: compare, in the same sense, simul atque, p. 6, l. 16.

17 prius ... quam: *until.* When priusquam is thus divided, translate the two parts with the last verb.

14 1 obtinēbat: see p. 2, l. 3, and note.

4 trāditūrum: what is to be supplied? See p. 8, l. 9, and note.

9 liceat ... vīvam: *let me, therefore, as long as I live.*

10 discesserō: *when I shall have departed,* would be clumsy English.

12 rogāsset: for rogāvisset.

13 aegrē tulit: where has aegrē ferēbat occurred?

16 aetāte ... cōnfectum: where has this phrase occurred?

17 neque: do not translate *nor.*

19 hīs audītīs = hīs rēbus audītīs.

15 5 vōs: subject of faciētis, and emphasized by ipsae in the next line.

13 quibus: with ūsa erat. 249; H. 421, I; F. 361.

14 postquam ... expectāvērunt: see postquam sparsit, p. 10, l. 1, and note.

23 cum vīdisset, Iāsōn cōnstituit: mark the difference between the Latin order and the English. We say, *when Jason saw (had seen), he determined;* the Latin puts the subject in the second clause and leaves it to be understood with the first. Compare doctus est ... Iāsōn solvit, p. 7, l. 15.

24 eō cōnsiliō, ut: find two previous instances.

16 3 ultūram: what is to be supplied? Find a similar instance.

13 ē vītā excessit: find ē vītā discesserō.

26 dēlapsa ... oppressit: *careened and crushed.* F. 353, 7, and *c* (3).

ULYSSES.

18 1 Trōiā ... captā: *when at last Troy was taken by stratagem.* F. 388, and *c.*

2 omnibus ... parātīs: *when all was ready;* omnibus is neuter.

4 solvērunt: find a sentence in which nāvem is expressed as object. What is the meaning of *loosed* the ship?

18 5 prūdentiae: the first meaning is *foresight.* What is the composition?

12 patriae . . . videndae: *to see his country and his wife.*

14 prōgressī sunt: *i.e.,* Ulysses and his companions.

15 aliae . . . partīs; *some in one way and some another.* What literally?

18 ancorīs iactīs: see the expression for the opposite, p. 7, l. 16.

19 quī . . . referrent: a purpose clause. See quī cōnsuleret, p. 2, l. 17, and note.

20 et: connects referrent and cōgnōscerent.

quālis . . . regiōnis: *what the character of that country was.* Compare quae causa esset, p. 2, l. 12, and note.

22 quibusdam . . . factī: *having met certain of the inhabitants.* What is the case of quibusdam? 228, *b.*

25 quem: refers to frūctū.

26 gustāssent: for gustāvissent. Compare rogāsset, p. 14, l. 12, and note.

19 1 mānsūrōs: find other examples of esse omitted.

3 cum . . . exspectāsset: *after waiting.* Do not think that a temporal clause with cum must always be translated in one way. Find other forms like exspectāsset.

4 veritus: is this to be translated *having feared?* See p. 2, l. 15, and note.

5 nōnnūllōs ē reliquīs = nōnnūllōs reliquōrum. Compare quibusdam ex incolīs, p. 18, l. 22.

12 rē īnfectā: *without accomplishing their object.*

16 invītōs: the opposite of sponte suā in the preceding line.

20 5 dum mīrantur: is this to be translated, *while they wonder?* Find other examples of dum and the present followed by the perfect or imperfect.

8 humānā speciē, etc.: ablative descriptive of mōnstrum. 251; H. 419, II.

21 4 sibi . . . praecavendum esse: *that he ought to be very guarded.* What literally? 232; H. 388; F. 465, 3, and 466.

12 hāc tam horribilī: do not translate, *this so horrible,* which is not English, but *so horrible a.*

15 arbitrātus: to be translated *having thought?* See veritus, p. 19, l. 4, and note.

22 15 in eŏ erat ut : *he was on the point of.*

19 nihil sibi prŏfutūrum : *that it would be of no use to them.*

20 sī interfēcisset : is this to be rendered, *if he should have killed ?*
Find other examples that have been commented on.

24 locŏ : see p. 13, l. 4, and note.

23 4 tertium : *a third time.*

11 quam petiimus facultātem = facultātem quam petiimus.
nē . . . omittāmus : *let us not lose.*

13 extrēmum pālum = extrēmam pālī partem.

16 quod necesse fuit : *necessarily.* Literally, *a thing which was
necessary.* The reference is to what follows. See p. 13, l. 16.

17 dum . . . errat : *groping his way.* What literally ? See p. 20,
l. 5, and note.

24 7 obstrūcta erat : the subject is to be drawn from **porta.**

9 ut . . . vēnerat : the mood shows that ut means *when.*

12 omnem spem . . . pōnī : *that all hope of safety depended on cunning rather than courage.*

18 postquam imposuit : is this to be translated, *when he placed ?*
See **postquam sparsit,** p. 10, l. 1, and note.

24 nāvī praesidiŏ : see p. 11, l. 9, and note.

25 3 in hŏrās : *hourly.*

4 id quod erat : *as was really true.*

15 etsī . . . submergerentur : *although they came near being
drowned.* What literally ? Find this idiom in two preceding
passages and the notes on them.

20 hīc : an adverb, *here.*
vāstŏ antrŏ = vāstŏ in antrŏ.

26 2 sibi proficīscendum : *that he must set out.*

4 iam profectūrō : *as he was just going to set out.*

6 Zephyrum : what would have been the effect if Aeolus had put
Zephyrus in with the other winds ? What if Zephyrus alone
had been put into the sack ? What if none had been shut up ?

9 omnibus . . . parātīs : see p. 18, l. 2, and note.

14 lassitūdine cŏnfectus : compare **aetāte cŏnfectus,** p. 14, l. 17.
For a different meaning of **cŏnfectus,** see p. 24, l. 22.

21 velut āgmine factŏ : *as if with battle line formed.*

22 quā data porta = quā data est porta : *where the gate was
opened.*

27 1 quō in locō rēs esset: *what the state of affairs was.* What
literally? Find two previous instances of locō thus used.

  9 ēgrediendum esse: *that they ought to disembark.*

  17 alterī: depends on praeesset to be supplied from the next line.

  19 uter: why not quis? What is the exact meaning of uter?

29 2 sī quid gravius eī accidisset: *if any misfortune should befall him*
(Ulysses); literally, *if anything heavier.* See note on p. 7, l. 12.

  5 eī licēre: *that he might,* that is, Eurylochus.

  7 in viam sē dedit: *set out.*

  8 aliquantum itineris: where before?

  14 iam intrantem: *as he was in the act of entering.*

  17 vīs: from volō.

  22 tetigerit: it would be clumsy English to translate *shall have
touched.*

  26 tenuem: with auram; such a straddle of the adjective and
noun is extremely common.

30 13 quidquam: *anything whatever;* aliquid, *anything.* Quidquam
is used after a negative; here after neque.

  24 sē ... factūram: take the words in this order: sē factūram
omnia quae ille imperāsset.

    imperāsset: *should command.* Point out other examples of
such contracted forms.

31 2 dē rēbus suīs: *about what had happened to them.*

  7 quī ... dīceret: not, *who said.* What kind of a relative clause?
Point out other instances.

  16 eī persuāsum sit: *he was persuaded;* literally, *it was persuaded
to him.*

32 3 subeunda erant: *had to be braved.*

  4 quae: object of perscrībere in the next line.

  5 longum est: *it would be tedious.*

ROMANI IMPERI EXORDIUM.

33 1 Albānōrum: find on the map Alba Longa, a short distance
southeast of Rome.

  2 Numitōrī: what is the effect of putting it first? Observe that,
as Numitōrī is followed by a clause enclosed by commas, it
must belong in construction with rēgnum relīquit.

83 2 **nātū māior** : *greater by birth = the elder.*

3 **pulsō frātre rēgnāvit** : *drove out his brother and reigned.*

4 **Vestae** : a goddess worshiped in every house as the guardian of the home, and also publicly as the guardian of the city.

5 **eā rē cōgnitā Amūlius** : *when Amulius learned of this.*

6 **ipsam** : *herself*, i.e., *the mother.*

alveō impositōs abiēcit : *he put into a tub and cast.* F. 353, 7, and *c* (3).

7 **fōrte** : *as it chanced.*

11 **ūbera . . . admōvit** : *applied her teats to their mouths.*

mātremque sē gessit : *and acted as a mother.*

12 **cum** : *since* ; in this sense followed by the subjunctive.

13 **rē animadversā** : *noticing the circumstance.* Observe now how the ablative absolute has been translated in lines 3, 5, and here. Avoid rendering it literally.

14 **ēducandōs** : agrees with **eōs**, *to be brought up.*

15 **adultī deinde hī** : *afterwards, when they had grown up.*

16 **auxēre** : for the more common form **auxērunt**.

17 **ā rapīnā pecorum** : *from seizing their flocks.*

quā rē cum : *when on this account.* Expect to find the imperfect and pluperfect tenses in the subjunctive in narration after **cum**, but render the subjunctive as if it were indicative.

20 **quis esset** : an indirect question. Often the subjunctive in an indirect question must be translated as if it were indicative.

eōrum : *their*, i.e., of Romulus and Remus.

21 **māter** : supply **esset**.

armātīs pāstōribus . . . properāvit : imitate the manner of translating **pulsō frātre rēgnāvit**, l. 3, and note.

Albam : see note on **Albānōrum**, l. 1.

24 **Numitōris agrōs** : from this it appears that Numitor, after being dethroned, had turned husbandman.

84 1 **Numitōrī** : do not mistake for an ablative.

supplicium : mark the derivation and primary meaning.

2 **cum . . . comparāret** : *when Numitor came to compare.* The looks of the youth made Numitor think of Remus, whom, we are to suppose, he had not seen since his babyhood ; his age corresponded, and he had the *manly bearing* (**minimē ser-**

34   vīlem indolem) that the fond grandfather imagined Remus
would have.

 4 haud procul erat quīn: *he was not far from;* literally, *it was
not far off but that he.*

 5 ōris līneāmentīs: *in his features;* literally, *in respect to the
lines of his face.*

 6 ea rēs dum: begin with dum.

 7 anxium tenet: *was troubling.*

   supervenit . . . līberat . . . restituit: the present for increased
vividness, just as in English.

 8 interēmptō Amūliō: see note on armātīs pāstōribus, p. 33, l. 21.

11 ortā . . . contentiōne: imitate the manner of translating eā rē
cōgnitā, p. 33, l. 5, note.

12 uter: why not quis?

13 auspicia: study the word carefully in the vocabulary. From
very early times men sought to know the will of the gods by
observing the flight of the larger lone-flying birds, as the
eagle, vulture, hawk.

16 cūius . . . cum: *when Remus, ridiculing its slenderness.* The
natural place for cum, as for the relative, is first in the
sentence; but cum has to give up the first place to the relative, when both are used.

18 sīc deinde: supply pereat; *so hereafter may he perish.*

ROMULUS, ROMANORUM REX PRIMUS.

22 in proximō: *near by,* that is, between the two summits of the
Capitoline Hill. The foundation of Rome was on the Pala-
tine Hill. See the relative positions of the Palatine and
Capitoline on the map of Rome.

   asȳlum: appositive to hunc (lūcum). We have borrowed the
word but changed its application. It meant a sacred place to
which fugitives from revenge or justice could flee, and be
protected by the sanctity of the place. The Jews had "cities
of refuge." See Numbers xxxv. 13–15.

24 uxōrēs: object of habērent, made emphatic by its position.
   ipse: Rōmulus. See ipsam, p. 33, l. 6, and note.

25 quī . . . peterent: *to ask for.* 317, 2; H. 497, I; F. 433.

PAGE

34 **25** cōnūbium : the right of intermarriage was made the subject of treaty between different tribes.

35 **2** additum : what is to be supplied?

4 aegritūdinem animī : *mortification.*

5 indīcī . . . iubet : *orders notice of the show to be proclaimed.* spectāculum : subject accusative of indīcī.

6 convēnēre : compare auxēre, p. 33, l. 16, and note.

studiō . . . urbis : *from eagerness to see the new city as well* (as the games).

videndae novae urbis = videndī novam urbem.

7 Sabīnī : see on the map of Italy where the Sabines dwelt.

8 eō : ad spectāculum.

9 discurrunt . . . rapiunt : on the tense, compare supervenit and līberat, p. 34, l. 7, and note.

13 petītum : supine to express purpose, 302 and R; H. 546; F. 476.

hūius : hūius virginis.

15 sī . . . perdūxisset : if *she would lead,* not *had led.*

18 quibus dolōsē prōmīssīs : translate by a clause denoting time.

25 cūius interitū : *by his fall.* Notice that a relative word at the beginning of a sentence must commonly be translated by a demonstrative or personal pronoun. How did you translate quibus, l. 18?

cōnsternātī : translate as a verb coupled with coepērunt by et. Compare impositōs abiēcit, p. 33, l. 6, and note.

28 longē aliud . . . aliud, *one thing . . . quite another.* We put the emphasis on the second aliud, the Romans on the first.

36 **2** crīnibus passīs : they had let down their hair as a sign of grief.

4 conciliārunt = conciliāvērunt.

5 et : best omitted in translating. The Latin uses et . . . et much oftener than we do *both . . . and.* A good way to translate is to suppress the first et and render the second by *and also.*

6 nōn . . . post : *not very long afterwards.*

7 occīsō Tatiō : do not translate, *Tatius having been killed,* but, *Tatius was killed and,* as on p. 33, l. 3.

8 quōrum cōnsiliō : *in order that by their advice.* Compare quī . . . peterent, p. 34, l. 25, and note ; also cūius interitū, p. 35, l. 25, and note.

11 cum : *while.*

PAGE

36 11 **ad**: *for the purpose of.*

12 **in campō**: in a plain which came to be called Campus Martius. It lay outside the ancient city. See map of Rome. It is now covered with buildings.

15 **cuī fēcit**: *to which thing Julius Proculus made belief;* in English, *a thing which Julius Proculus caused to be believed.*

18 **vīsum**: supply **esse** and take **Rōmulum** as subject-accusative. Note the emphasis on **vīsum** from its position, *actually seen.*

eundem: *and that he.*

fōrmā: 251 and *a*; H. 419, II.

20 **futūrum (esse)**: dependent on **adfīrmāns**, *that it would come to pass.*

21 **cōnstitūta . . . cultus**: what is to be supplied?

NUMA POMPILIUS, ROMANORUM REX SECUNDUS.

23 **vir . . . religiōne**: for the ablative compare **fōrmā**, p. 36, l. 18, and note.

24 **Curibus, ex oppidō**: *from Cures, a town.* See its position northeast of Rome.

25 **quī cum**: on the translation of **quī**, see note on p, 35, l. 25. On the position of **cum** see **cūius . . . cum**, p. 34, l. 16, and note.

ut . . . mītigāret: does not express the purpose of **vēnisset**, but of the clause **sacra plūrima īnstituit**. Nothing is commoner than for an ut-clause to precede the principal.

37 1 **īgnem . . . alendum**: like **eōs . . . ēducandōs** in construction, p. 33, l. 14.

perpetuō: do not render *perpetually*, but *constantly;* another example, like **asȳlum**, of a word changing its meaning in passing from one language to another. Be on your guard as to words identical, or nearly identical, in form in Latin and English.

3 **adōrnāvit**: not here *adorned;* see preceding note.

dīcitur: the subject remains the same, *i.e.,* **Numa.**

7 **et**: connects **docuit** and **prōmīsit.**

8 **sē**: subject-accusative of **datūrum esse.**

10 **dēlābitur**: on the tense, see **supervenit** and **līberat**, p. 34, l. 7, and note.

AGE

7 14 quī ... custōdīrent: *to guard.* Find two preceding examples of this construction.

15 Kalendīs Mārtiīs: as the year began with March and the Calends of March were the first day of the month, this was New Year's Day.

18 portās: there were two, one at each end of an arched passage-way.

Iānō geminō: Janus was represented with two faces turned in opposite directions, looking to the past and the future. From him January was named. He was the god of all beginnings, the guardian of gates, doors, entrances, and passages.

19 esset: namely, Janus.

apertus: in sense referring to **portās,** grammatically to **Iānō,** here identified with the passage-way.

20 clausus: this did not happen after Numa till the end of the first Punic War, B.C. 241, a period supposed to be about 400 years.

23 māiōrem ... auctōritātem: such inclusions of words and phrases between an adjective and a noun are very common; attention to this will often help you to see the sense more quickly.

24 ēius monitū: *by her advice.*

25 sē, etc.: the order is **sē facere omnia.**

quem medium: *the middle of which.*

26 perennī rigābat aquā: observe the order, and see note on l. 23, above.

27 īnferēbat: what is the force of the tense?

30 'quidem: do not translate '*indeed,*' a poor word.

!8 1 exstinctus: see note on **cōnsternātī,** p. 35, l. 25.

2 Iāniculō: see its position across the Tiber on the map of Rome.

TULLUS HOSTILIUS, ROMANORUM REX TERTIUS.

8 ducibus ... placuit: the Latin way of saying *the leaders resolved;* a common idiom.

11 prō ... patriā: in the English order, **quisque prō suā patriā.**

12 eā lēge: *on these terms;* points to the following clause.

16 ternī: how do **ternī** and **trēs** differ?

38 18 **increpuēre**: on the form of the perfect, see note on **auxēre**,
p. 33, l. 16. First they hurled their spears, which *clashed*
against the shields.

    arma: subject.

    micantēs . . . gladiī: on the order, compare **perennī rigābat
aquā**, p. 37, l. 26, and note on p. 37, l. 23.

20 **alius super alium**: better **alter super alterum**. Why?

21 **volnerātī**: **est** and **sunt** are often to be supplied. Compare
additum, p. 35, l. 2, and note.

23 **dēserēbat**: how does the force of the imperfect here differ from
that of **inferēbat**, p. 37, l. 27?

39 2 **ratus**: not, *having thought.* 290, *b* ; H. 550, note 1.

3 **ubi pūgnātum est**: *where the fight took place.*

5 **dum . . . inclāmat**: translate **inclāmat** as an imperfect.
Compare **dum . . . tenet**, p. 34, l. 6, and note.

9 **iam**: the two meanings of this word are perfectly illustrated in
l. 2 (*already*) and here (*at last*). The word does not mean
simply *now*, like **nunc**.

    singulī: *one on each side.*

    supererant: not from **superō**, but from **supersum**.

11 **fessum**, etc.: in English order, **trahēbat corpus fessum**.

12 **male sustinentem arma**: *who was hardly able to bear his arms.*
Justify this translation.

13 **cōnficit**: regularly means *make an end of;* the **con**, therefore,
means *completely.*

    iacentem spoliat: *strips him of his arms as he lies prostrate.*
The Latin expresses it in two words.

16 **cuī . . . soror**: *him his sister met.*

17 **vīsō**: translate as if it were **vidēns**.

18 **crīnīs solvere**: compare **crīnibus passīs**, p. 36, l. 2, and note.

19 **movet**: mark the emphasis on the verb by its unusual
position.

21 **increpāns**: mark the very different sense of this word on p. 38,
l. 18.

23 **sīc eat**: *thus perish;* **eat** is present subjunctive of **eō**.

    quaecumque Rōmāna = **omnis Rōmāna quae**.

25 **atrōx**: to feel the force of the order, translate as the words
stand: *awful seemed the deed to patricians and plebeians.*

39 27 līctor . . . laqueum: not to hang him, but to bind him to a stake preparatory to scourging and beheading. One function, then, of the *lictors* was to execute judgment; another was to precede high magistrates in public, serving as policemen, but instead of a club they carried on their shoulder a bundle of rods bound up with an axe. The king had twelve lictors.

28 ad populum prōvocāvit: not for pity, but to reverse the sentence, which the people had a right to do.

40 3 orbum līberīs faceret: *make him childless.* What literally? nōn tulit: *could not bear.*

8 tigillum sorōrium: *the "Sister's Beam."*

11 ut . . . corrigeret: expresses the purpose of concitāvit; see ut . . . mītigāret, p. 36, l. 25, and note.

15 quā rē Tullus intellēctā: *Tullus, understanding his purpose.* What literally?

16 suō . . . facere: in English order, Mettium facere illud suō iūssū; but the Latin order throws emphasis upon suō, which is the important word. Notice in suō illud iūssū the fondness of the Latin for thrusting a word between an adjective and a noun, as already remarked. See perennī rigābat aquā, p. 37, l. 26, and note. This is an extreme case.

19 in dīversa: *asunder.*

22 ruīnīs: *from the downfall;* primary meaning of ruīna.

28 mīlitiae quam domī: 258, 4, *d*; H. 426, 2.

41 2 frāctī . . . sunt: the subject is spīritūs.

ANCUS MARCIUS, ROMANORUM REX QUARTUS.

7 aequitāte et religiōne: *in justice and piety,* descriptive ablative.

11 quī . . . repeteret: see quī peterent, p. 34, l. 25, and note.

14 capite vēlātō: the Romans often covered the head in prayer and sacrifice. Mr. D'Ooge quotes from Conington's translation of Vergil, Aen. III., 405-407.

> "Ere yet you light your altars, spread
> A purple covering o'er your head,
> Lest, sudden bursting on your sight,
> Some hostile presence mar the rite."

41 16 **verbis meis fidēs sit** : *let my words be heeded ;* what literally?

21 **repetentī** : dative of the present participle agreeing with **lēgātō**. Translate *who demanded restitution* (**rēs**).

24 **cum** : *since.* On the mood following see p. 33, l. 12, and note.

42 2 **in mediā urbe** : *in the middle of the city.* Compare **quem medium**, p. 37, l. 25.

ad terrōrem : *to overawe ;* **ad** denoting purpose, as often. See **ad**, p. 36, l. 11, and note.

3 **īdem** : *he likewise.*

4 **Iāniculum montem** : *the hill Janiculum.* See its position on the map of Rome.

LUCIUS TARQUINIUS PRISCUS, ROMANORUM REX QUINTUS.

8 **Tarquiniīs . . . urbe** : like **Curibus, ex oppidō,** p. 36, l. 24, and note. For the position of **Tarquiniī**, northwest of Rome, in Etruria, see map of Italy.

10 **advenientī** : present participle; supply **eī**; *as he was coming, an eagle bore off his cap ;* literally, *for him.*

13 **sublīmis** : *on high.* Compare **laetus,** *joyfully,* p. 37, l. 8; also **silentēs,** *in silence,* p. 37, l. 9. So often a Latin adjective is best translated by an adverb or an adverbial phrase.

15 **excelsa et alta** : *an exalted and noble destiny.* The adjectives are in the neuter plural without any noun understood, but we are compelled in translation to add a noun.

19 **ā quō . . . intercēpit** : *and when left by him guardian to his children, he* (Tarquinius) *usurped the throne.*

20 **ita** : best omitted in translation.

adeptus esset : what is the object to be supplied?

43 1 **addīxissent** : *should be favorable,* not *had been.* See **sī . . . perdūxisset,** p. 35, l. 15, and note.

2 **in experīmentum** : *to make trial ;* **in** used to denote purpose, like **ad,** p. 36, l. 11.

fierīne posset : *whether that could be done.*

4 **atquī** : Professor Rolfe happily translates, " *Oh, but.*"

'AGE

l3 8 praetextā: an adjective, with *toga* understood and meaning
bordered toga. For an illustration of the **toga praetexta**, see
"First Latin Book," p. 191. The **praetexta** had a broad purple border. The next sentence implies that before this inci-
dent boys had been differently dressed.

bullā: a round golden ornament, hung about the neck.

ingenuōrum: emphatic, for similar ornaments, but made of
leather, were worn by children who were not born free.

13 simulātā rīxā: *pretending to quarrel.* What literally?

quōrum clāmor cum: on the translation of the relative, see note
on p. 35, l. 25 ; on the position of **cum**, see p. 34, l. 16, and note.

14 vocātī: on the way of translating, see **cōnsternātī**, p. 35, l. 25,
and note.

15 et certātim . . . obstrepere: *and to cry out against each other
vehemently.* What literally?

17 dum . . . āvertit: **dum** is regularly followed by the present
tense, though the time of the act belongs to the past. Several
examples have already occurred. Notice **dum āvertit, dēiēcit.**
Render **āvertit** as if it were **āvertēbat**; *while the king was
turning away wholly attentive to him.*

18 ēlātam . . . dēiēcit: another example of the participle best
rendered by a verb and coupled by **et** to the following verb ;
raised his axe and brought it down upon his head. What
literally?

SERVIUS TULLIUS, ROMANORUM REX SEXTUS.

22 nōbilī: *of noble birth,* the usual meaning ; not *noble* as we commonly use the word. See note on **perpetuō**, p. 37, l. 1.

quī cum: *while he.* See note on **quōrum**, etc., l. 13.

23 vīsū ēventūque: *in appearance and result.* The ablatives are
like **aequitāte et religiōne**, p. 41, l. 7.

25 summam eī dīgnitātem: do not be confused by words thrust
in between an adjective and a noun. See **suō illud iūssū**,
p. 40, l. 16, and note.

4 1 eī . . . portendī: compare p. 42, l. 14.

5 mīlitibus . . . dīmicantibus: *as the soldiers fought with too
little spirit.*

PAGE

44 **5 sīgnum**: see illustrations on p. 105 of the "First Latin Book."

11 grave quidem: *serious, it is true.* See p. 37, l. 30, and note.

13 dictō audientēs essent: *be obedient to.*

15 montīs: not *mountains*, but low hills.

16 īdem: see p. 42, l. 3, and note.

21 factum . . . ferēbat: *tradition said had been built.* What literally? With **factum** supply **esse**.

22 et ipsī: *they too.*

cum: *in common with.*

24 nāta: supply **esse**. It is extremely common to find **esse** omitted in the compound forms of the infinitive, both active and passive. Compare **factum**, for **factum esse**, l. 21; also, immediately following, **datum**, for **datum esse**: **habitūrum**, for **habitūrum esse**.

27 immolāsset: see **sī . . . perdūxisset**, p. 35, l. 15, and note.

45 **13 coniugem . . . salūtāvit**: *called her husband out of the senate, and was the first to greet him as king.* F. 353, 7 and 3 (*c*).

14 cūius iūssū: *at his order.*

16 cunctantem: *when he hesitated.*

TARQUINIUS SUPERBUS, ROMANORUM REX SEPTIMUS ET ULTIMUS.

22 Gabiōs: see its position nearly east of Rome.

46 **3 plūrimum posset**: *could very much; had great influence.*

"And they (the French) can well on horseback." — Ham. IV., 7, l. 83.

4 scīscitātum: see **petītum**, p. 35, l. 13, and note.

8 fessus exspectandō: *tired of waiting.*

12 Ardeam: see its position south of Rome.

13 sorōre . . . nātus: *son of the king's sister.* 244; H. 415, II.

15 cum . . . laudāret: *since each one praised his own wife.*

16 placuit: *they resolved.* What literally? See note on p. 38, l. 8.

18 Collātiam: see its position a little way from Rome to the east.

19 lānae dēditam: literally, *given up to wool; busily spinning.*

24 in exitium: *for the ruin;* **in** denoting purpose. Compare **in experīmentum**, p. 43, l. 2, and note.

AGE

‖7 2 **eōs** : object of **vēnum dare.**

sē velle : *that she wished,* dependent on **dīcēbat.**

3 **atque immēnsum** : *and in fact an excessive price.*

7 **et rēgem interrogāvit** : translate before the clause beginning **ecquid.**

10 **id ipsum** : explained by the following clause.

15 **sed . . . cōnstitit** : *but it is certain that that woman, after going away then from Tarquin, was not seen anywhere.*

16 **nusquam locī** : 216, 4; H. 397, 4.

vīsam : what is to be supplied?

18 **pūblicē** : not *publicly.* See note on **perpetuō,** p. 37, l. 1.

FABLES.

‖8 1 **praetereuntī** : present participle from **praetereō.** 141; H. 295; F. p. 237.

2 **inquit** : always placed after one or more of the words quoted.

4 **locus et tempus** : thought of as one thing and hence followed by the singular, **reddit.**

8 **nē . . . contemnāmus** : *not to despise.*

bonum : an adjective used as a noun, *advantage.*

9 **alia et fōrtasse māiōra** : supply **bona.**

11 **conquerēbātur** : do not confound **queror,** *complain,* with **quaerō,** *seek.*

12 **negāta esset** : *had been denied to her* (as she said). The indicative would have meant *had* (in fact) *been denied to her.* 321; H. 516.

14 **bona** : the subject-accusative of **cōnferrī.** See also note on **bonum,** l. 8.

‖9 2 **mihi . . . animō** : *to me it is not in mind ;* in English, *I do not intend.*

3 **dulcia tūtīs** : both adjectives in the neuter plural used as nouns. In English we have to say *sweet things to safe things ;* that is, *what is pleasant to what is safe.*

5 **arcēbat** : why is the imperfect used here and in the preceding line, rather than the perfect?

ista : *that (of yours),* 102 c ; F, 304, f.

6 **quod** : *in that.*

49 6 pateris : second person singular from **patior.**

9 eī : supply **leōnī;** translate *one.*

11 cōnspicāta : *when she had seen.*

quidem : *it is true,* or, *to be sure.*

12 tertiō illī obviam facta : *on meeting him a third time.*

ausa : perfect participle feminine from **audeō.**

14 nē . . . incēde : very well for a crab, but he should have said
nē . . . incēdās.

15 rēctā viā : not *by the right road,* but *in a straight line.*

16 respondit : placed like **inquit.** See note on **inquit,** p. 48, l. 2.

18 adulēscentiam : subject-accusative of **īnstruī.**

50 1 pāscēbantur : do not translate *fed,* but *used to feed.*

5 quantum bonī : *what great advantage.*

7 dum . . . movet : see note on **dum āvertit,** p. 43, l. 17.

celerius : *too quickly.* The comparative must sometimes be
rendered *too, quite,* or *rather.*

12 eī : *for her.*

13 ōvum pariēbat aureum : notice the order.

illam = **illam gallīnam** and is subject-accusative of **cēlāre.**

15 repperit : the present would be **reperit.**

16 quod'= id quod. dum . . . inhiat : see note on **dum movet,** l. 7.

minōrēs : supply the Latin noun in the proper form.

17 nē . . . interficite : better, **nē interficiātis.** See **nē incēde,**
p. 49, l. 14, and note.

18 quidquam : why not **aliquid? quidquam** means *anything at all,*
and is used after negatives.

19 propter hōc ipsum : *for this very reason.*

20 cum : *though.*

51 3 cōnspicāta : translate by the present participle. Compare **cōnspicāta,** p. 49, l. 11.

4 sī : *to see if.*

6 acerbae : as if **ūvae** had been used.

eās . . . repertās : *them found* = *if I had found them.*

8 quae sē : **quae** the object of **adsequī, sē** subject-accusative of
posse.

11 multīs aliīs prōpositīs : *after many other proposals had been made.*

omnibus placuit : *all resolved,* or, *it was unanimously resolved.*
What literally?

51 12 ipsōs : the subject-accusative of posse.

13 eam : fēlem.

14 quaererētur : *the question was raised.* The verb is used imper-
sonally.

18 condūcit : the present used for the perfect. What is the effect?
Give an example in English.

19 quī . . . extrahat : *to pull it out.* 317, 2 ; H. 497, I ; F. 432,
1 and 433.

21 subrīdēns : how different from rīdēns?

52 1 repperit : see note on repperit, p. 50, l. 15.

3 agricolae : *on the farmer,* depends on īnflīxit.

5 malī : *bad men,* or *the bad.*

7 praedicābat : what is the force of the imperfect?

quī . . . pāscerētur : *because* (as he, the ass, said) *he fed;*
pāscēbātur would mean, *he* (in fact) *fed.* Compare negāta
esset, p. 48, l. 12, and note.

8 cum : *while,* or *whereas.*

paleae : depends on satis, *straw enough.*

10 agitur : compare condūcit, p. 51, l. 18, and note. So conlābitur, l. 12, below.

12 O mē stolidum : *Oh, fool that I was!*

13 quī . . . aestimāverim : *because I judged,* or *to have judged.*
320, *e* ; H. 517 ; F. 432, 4 and *c.*

15 sibi : may be omitted in translation.

16 ut fierī solet : *as usually happens.* What literally?

18 quod cum, etc. : on the translation of the relative at the beginning of a sentence, see 180, *f.* H. 453.

20 esset : translate *is;* the imperfect is required in Latin on
account of the past tense docuit.

53 2 vīvum : about equal to vīvere.

8 quī . . . nōluerim : compare quī aestimāverim, p. 52, l. 13, and
note.

14 dēteriōre condiciōne : *in a worse state.*

What is the moral of this fable?

19 aliquantum viae : *some distance.* What literally?

et . . . et : *both . . . and.*

20 et sēcum . . . contemplātus : *and pondering on.* What literally?

PAGE

53 20 aetātis . . . mala: *the evils of old age and want.*

22 quae . . . līberāret: *to free him;* compare quī extrahat,
p. 51, l. 19, and note.

ipsum = sē, that is, senem.

54 2 quem . . . paenitēbat: *whom it repented;* in English, *who
repented.* What kind of a verb is paenitet?

3 nihil: supply volō.

quī: *some one to.*

What is the moral of this fable?

6 subvolārat: a shortened form for subvolāverat.

11 sē valēre: *that he excelled.*

12 adreptum dēvorāvit: *caught up and devoured.* 292, R.; F. 353,
7 and *c* (3).

15 praedā . . . dīvīsā: *when the booty had been divided.*

20 quī . . . voluerit, is sciat: *let him know who shall be disposed.*

sē habitūrum: supply esse.

21 facerent: *were to do.* Mark the force of the subjunctive.

55 3 quod: *that it.*

7 quārum . . . precibus: *by their prayers.*

8 refūgēre: for the more usual refūgērunt.

12 pūnitūrus: *in order to punish.*

ā quō cum: *and when by it.* What literally?

13 eās . . . paenituit: compare quem paenitēbat, p. 54, l. 2, and
note.

What is the moral of this fable?

15 lupōs, etc.: order, fingēns lupōs aggressōs esse suum gregem.

17 lātūrī: future participle of ferō.

19 eum pariter ut anteā, etc.: *thinking he was fooling just as
before;* eum is subject-accusative of lūdere.

56 2 canī: dative of agent with custōdiendum. Translate *left for
his dog to guard.* What literally?

5 dum . . . studet: compare dum movet, p. 50, l. 7, and note.

8 accenditur: compare condūcit, p. 51, l. 18, and note.

10 restituit: *had replaced.* After ubi, ut, and postquam, all meaning *when,* the perfect indicative is commonly used, but it is
often best rendered by the pluperfect.

56 10 occīsum : *which had been killed.* F. 353, 6 and *c* (2). Compare adreptum dēvorāvit, p. 54, l. 12, and note.

11 sēra : *too late.* Compare sērō, p. 55, l. 13.

13 simul . . . simul : *no sooner sees him . . . than.*

15 quī . . . voluerim : *for having wished, though I was born.*

17 suus : with locus.

20 sē : subject-accusative of āvolātūrum (esse).

22 tē cōnsīdentem : *that you were sitting there.*

57 1 duās : with pērās.

2 replētam : alteram pēram replētam.

3 aliēnīs, etc. : (alteram pēram) gravem aliēnīs (vitiīs).

4 hāc rē : *for this reason.*

5 simul = simul āc, *as soon as.*

GAIUS IULIUS CAESAR.

58 1 nōbilissimā . . . familiā : mark the fondness of the Latin for thrusting some word or words between an adjective and the noun with which it agrees.

3 dūxit uxōrem : *took to wife.* What literally?

cūius pater cum : *since her father.*

4 is : Sulla.

5 neque : do not translate *nor;* say *but . . . not.*

quā rē . . . cum : *when Caesar, robbed of his property on this account.*

8 prope per singulās : *almost every.*

9 nē . . . ēvāsit : *by giving a bribe he barely escaped being led to Sulla.* What literally?

12 Sullam . . . expūgnātum dīxisse : *that Sulla at length yielded and said.*

cum . . . contenderent : *when he had refused and they continued to press their point persistently.*

14 eum : refers to Caesar and is the subject-accusative of futūrum (esse), l. 17. *That he whom they so earnestly wished* (to be) *spared would sometime be the ruin of the aristocratic party which they* (the interceders) *had defended in company with him* (Sulla).

58 19 clārissimō . . . magistrō: compare nōbilissimā . . . familiā,
l. 1, and note.
59 2 quibus = ut eīs pecūniīs.
3 datūrum sē: sē the subject-accusative of datūrum (esse).
4 quibus: supply talentīs.
expositus esset: the subject of this verb and of all the following
except aberant and erant is Caesar.   In translating, it would
be well to break this long period into three; end the first
with properāvit, omit que of ibique, make another period at
cēpit, then continue, *Thus he got the pirates into his power and.*
8 pīrātās: object of adfēcit and suffīxit.
10 crucīque: que is explanatory, *that is.*
12 quō profectus: *on his way thither.*   What literally?
20 colās: *you ought to practice.*
23 causam . . . amīcīs: *to his friends, on their asking the reason.*
27 aedīlis: *when he was aedile.*   See the derivation of the word.
28 vēnātiōnēs: one of the shows in the amphitheatre was the
hunting of wild beasts.
60 1 hīs . . . rēbus: *in this way;* because as aedile he bore the
enormous expense of these shows.
3 mīliēns sēstertium: an abbreviated expression, centēna mīlia
being omitted.   Thus fully expressed, it would be mīliēns
centēna mīlia sēstertium; equal to between $4,000,000 and
$5,000,000.
ut habēret nihil: *to make him worth just nothing.*   He joked
about his debts because he counted on paying them, as he
afterwards did, through the plunder that he would get from
public office.
7 in rē pūblicā: *in public affairs.*
11 tanta . . . sēditiō: compare nōbilissimā . . . familiā,
p. 58, l. 1, and note.
17 sī . . . sīgnārent: *whenever they signed any document as
witnesses.*   What literally?
18 āctum (esse): like our *"given,"* in the sense of *drawn up* or
executed.
19 Iūliō et Caesare: the Romans were very witty and very fond of
jokes; cōnsulibus was often omitted, and the year indicated
only by the names of the consuls.

60 19 nōmine et cōgnōmine : observe the **praenōmen** and its abbreviation at the beginning of this Life.

    22 gessit : mark the emphatic position; *his achievements moreover.*

    24 prīmus : he was the first one of Roman commanders to build a bridge over the Rhine and attack the Germans in their own country.

    26 superātīsque : *defeated them and;* **superātīs** (Britannīs) is dative with **imperāvit.**

    27 cum . . . tum : suppress cum in translation and render **tum,** *and especially.*

61 1 quod : *I mean that.*

    3 aquiliferum . . . comprehēnsum : *the standard-bearer, who had already turned to flee, he seized by the throat and.* Make a word-for-word rendering without regard to the English, to see if the translation given can be justified.

    8 vincīque . . . docuit : *the to be conquered ready* (*legions*) *to conquer he taught.* What in English ?

    10 interfectō . . . Crassō : compare nōbilissimā . . . familiā, p. 58, l. 1, and note.

    11 generī socerīque : *between son-in-law and father-in-law.*

    13 Pompēiō suspectae (sunt) : 232, *a* ; H. 388, 1.

    14 gravis : *annoying;* predicate adjective with **erat** understood.

    16 nē . . . discēderet : *that he might not have to come away.*

    17 ā . . . eī est : *his request was refused by the senate through the advice of Pompey and his friends.* What literally ?

    20 Rubicōnem : look for this small stream northeast of Rome.

    27 Brundisium : look for it in southeastern Italy.

62 1 Ēpīrum : look for it on the eastern coast of the Adriatic.

    2 Dyrrachium : look for it nearly opposite Brundisium.

    10 prius . . . quam : translate with the last clause.

    14 ut . . . cōgnōvit : *when he learned that he had been killed.*

    17 Pontum : see on a map of Asia Minor.

    19 quattuor . . . hōrīs : *within four hours from the time when he came in sight of him.*

    22 ante . . . quam : *that the enemy was vanquished before he was seen.* Compare **prius . . . quam,** l. 10, and note.

    27 omnibus : limits īgnōvit.

PAGE

63 5 **quŏque**: from **quisque**, *each.*

6 **convīctŏs**: supply **eŏs**; *those who were convicted.*

12 **optima quaeque**: *all the best.* 93, *c*; H. 458, 1.

19 **agentem et meditantem**: agree with **eum (Caesarem)** understood, which is the object of **praevēnit.**

22 **quendam**, etc.: order, **quendam monentem (eum) ut adsurgeret īrātŏ voltū respēxit.**

27 **coniūrātum** . . . **est**: impersonal, *a conspiracy was formed.*
sexāgintā amplius = **amplius sexāgintā.**

64 2 **ut**, etc.: order, **ōrābat ut subsisteret.**

9 **adsīdentem**: that is, **eum** (C.) **adsīdentem**, following circum-
stetērunt.

11 **renuentī**: supply **eī**. *One, to him* (C.) *refusing, seizes the toga* =
on Caesar's refusal, one seizes his toga.

12 **clāmantem**: agrees with **Caesarem** understood, object of **volnerat.**
ista: *that (that you are doing).*

13 **adversum**: *in front,* an adjective agreeing with **Caesarem**
understood.

14 **adreptum** . . . **trāiēcit**: *seized and stabbed.* F. 353, *c* (3).

17 **obvolvit**:

"... then burst his mighty heart;
And, in his mantle muffling up his face,
Even at the base of Pompey's statua
Which all the while ran blood, great Caesar fell."

23 **omnibus**, etc.: order, **omnibus honōribus dēcrētīs sibi ā
senātū populŏque.**

27 **ūnum**: *alone.*

ALCIBIADES.

66 1 **In hōc** . . . **experta**: translate in this order: **nātūra vidētur
experta (esse) in hŏc (homine) quid possit efficere.**

3 **nihil** . . . **fuisse** = **nēminem fuisse**, depends on **cōnstat**, *it is
admitted.*
illŏ: *i.e.,* Alcibiade.

4 **nātus**: what form of **sum** is to be supplied?

5 **summŏ genere**: *of a very noble family.* 244, *a*; H. 415, II.

66 6 cōnsilī : the English word that most resembles a Latin word is very often not the one to choose in translation. Here *counsel* would not be the right word ; say *resources*, or *ability*. Compare **excellentius** in l. 4, which means, not *more excellent*, but *more conspicuous*. The clauses that follow, through **resistere**, illustrate the statement that *he was fitted for all activities and full of resources.*

7 summus : not to be translated as in l. 5, but *most able.*

8 disertus : *i.e.*, et tam disertus.

ut . . . valēret : literally, *that he was strong among the foremost in speaking.* Improve on this translation.

10 cum : *whenever.*

12 serviēns : *adapting himself.*

īdem : *at the same time*, literally, *the same man.*

19 ērudītus : study its composition.

21 vellet : *had wished.*

67 1 posset : *could have.*

2 tribueret : translate as if it were **tribuēbat**, which Nepos might have written.

3 hūius cōnsiliō : *through his advice.*

6 id cum apparārētur : *while preparations were making for this war.* What literally?

7 hermae : these were square pillars ending at the top in a carved head of Hermes (Mercury). They were set up in the streets at the entrances to houses.

9 ille : *i.e.*, herma.

10 hōc cum : begin with **cum**, as in the case of id cum, l. 6; hōc is the subjective-accusative of **factum esse.** *Since it appeared that this was not done.*

appārēret : do not confound **appāreō**, *appear*, with **apparō**, *make ready*, l. 6.

11 quae . . . ad pertinēret : *since it concerned.*

13 nē qua . . . vīs : *that some sedition.*

17 operā forēnsī : *aid in law suits.* What literally?

18 oculōs : object of **converteret**, *he turned.*

19 prōdīsset : pluperfect subjunctive of **prodeō.**

20 pār : predicate adjective with **pōnerētur**, *was thought.*

21 in eō : i.e., *Alcibiades ;* compare in hōc, p. 66, l. 1.

67 22 plūrimum : to be taken with both infinitives.

　24 dīcēbātur : *he was said;* not *it was said,* which would require
　　　eum to be expressed as the subject-accusative of facere.

　　　mōre : *according to the feelings,* or *in the eyes of.*

　　　id : facere mystēria.

　27 hōc crīmine : nearly equal to hāc causā, *on this ground.*

　28 tempus, etc. : order, tempus proficīscendī ad bellum.

68 1 neque īgnōrāns : *and not unacquainted with.*

　2 sī . . . vellent : *if they wished any action taken.* What literally?
　　　Don't forget that quid after sī is *anything.* Here quid is the
　　　subject-accusative of agī.

　　　dē praesente = dē sē praesente, *about him while he was present.*

　3 habērētur : as if ut had followed postulābat.

　　　invidiae crīmine : *a charge springing from hatred.* What
　　　literally?

　4 quiēscendum = quiēscendum esse sibi and to be taken with
　　　dēcrēvērunt, l. 6, *they decided that it was best to keep quiet.*

　5 nocērī . . . posse : *that he could not be injured.* What literally?
　　　On nocērī eī, see 230 ; H. 465, I. •

　　　exspectandum : what Latin words are to be mentally supplied?

　6 quō exīsset : *when he should have gone away;* more idiomati-
　　　cally, *till he should go away.*

　8 quod . . . violāsset : *because, as they charged, he had profaned.*
　　　321 ; B. 286, I.

　11 essetque : the conjunction connects esset with mīssus esset.
　　　In translation drop que and translate as if cum were repeated
　　　in the sense of *although.*

　　　prōvinciae : mark this use of prōvincia in its original sense.

　18 sē . . . pūblicātīs : *that he had been condemned to death and his
　　　property confiscated.* What literally?

　19 id quod ūsū vēnerat : *as had actually been done.* What literally?
　　　ūsū : for ūsuī, *to use, realization.*

　21 ēius : not *his,* but a demonstrative with dēvōtiōnis, which
　　　depends on exemplum.

　　　exemplum . . . pūblicō : this clause is connected by que in l. 21.
　　　to sacerdōtēs coāctōs (esse), and so is part of the object of
　　　audīvit.

　24 inimīcōs : how different from hostīs?

68 25 intellegerent : the subject is inimīcī.

26 sē : Alcibiades.

plūrimum prōdesse : compare p. 67, l. 22.

ēiēcisse : *that they (his enemies) had expelled him (Alcibiades).*
What Latin words must therefore be supplied as subject and
object of ēiēcisse ?

27 paruisse : "*had been guided by.*" What literally ?

69 5 quō factō : *in this way.* What literally ?

7 neque : *but — not.*

hīs rēbus : *in consequence of this.*

sunt factī : the subject is the same as of coepērunt.

9 prūdentiam : that is, of Alcibiades.

10 aliquandō : *at some time,* emphatic.

12 tempus . . . interficiendī : compare tempus proficīscendī, p. 67,
l. 28. Here tempus means *chance.*

id : accusative limiting cēlārī. *Alcibiades could not very long
be kept in the dark about this.* 239, *d;* H. 374, 2, N. 1.

13 eā = tālī, *such.*

17 pervēnisset et : et connects pervēnisset and vidēret.

male . . . crēscere : *that in consequence of the bad management of
Athenian interests in Sicily, their resources were waning, while,
on the contrary, those of the Lacedaemonians were increasing.*
Give a word-for-word rendering.

21 eōdem . . . sēnsū : order, eōdem sēnsū quō ; quō, *as.*

26 parīque . . . praeficitur : *in his absence is invested with equal
authority.* The word simul is unnecessary.

70 8 neque . . . multās : *and as many.*

12 hīs . . . obviam : *to meet these (commanders).*

15 sīc . . . persuāsum : *for thus it was persuaded to the people ;* in
English, *the people believed this, namely that.* For the construction compare nocērī posse, p. 68, l. 5, and note. The particle sīc
points forward to the words following et (*both*), through operā.

17 et Siciliam . . . vīctōriās : *both Sicily to have been lost,* āmīssam
(esse) *and the victories.* What in English ? Had the Athenians
ever ruled Sicily ?

18 suae : *their own,* that is, *the Athenians'.*

expulissent : *they had, as they said, banished.* Compare quod
violāsset, p. 68, l. 8, note and grammatical reference.

70 21 hīc ut: *when he.*

23 Pīraeum: what and where? See a map.

25 ūsū vēnerat: acciderat. See p. 68, l. 19, and note.

26 taeniīs: "the streamers of the bow that tied the ends of an honorary crown."

volgō: adverb.

71 2 quīn ... inlacrimārit: *as not to weep over.*

4 ille ipse: *that very one.*

5 pūblicē: see note on cōnsilī, p. 66, l. 6.

6 resacrāre: *to take off the curse;* notice the negative force of re-; what does it usually mean?

8 praecipitātae: what form of sum is to be supplied?

10 cum: *though;* repeat it in thought with postulāsset and negātum esset.

14 quod ... gesserat: gives the reason of the following clause.

15 reccidit: what is the meaning of re- here? Cf. l. 6, above.

nihil ... nōn: translate *everything.*

16 ex quō fīēbat: *the result of this was.* What literally?

omnia minus prōsperē gesta: *all failures.* But what literally?

17 culpae: culpae ēius.

18 corruptum: supply eum as subject-accusative of nōluisse.

20 opīniōnem: *i.e.,* that others had.

22 ēlātus: F. 353, c (3).

23 quibus rēbus factum est = ex quō fīēbat above, l. 16.

absentī: supply eī, *Alcibiades.*

27 prīmus: *was the first one to.*

28 glōriōsius ... Grāiōrum: order, exīstimāns locuplētārī (*to enrich himself*) praedā barbarōrum (esse) glōriōsius quam (praedā) Grāiōrum.

72 4 neque tamen: *and yet — not.*

7 quī ... dūceret: *who was bent on this, namely, to protract the war as long as possible.*

8 ipsīs: Lacedaemoniīs.

9 contrā: *while on the other hand.*

Athēniēnsibus: dative dependent on erat super = erat relīctum.

13 Lacedaemoniōs: *saying that the Lacedaemonians.*

eō: *for this reason,* explained by the clause beginning quod.

15 sibi: *i.e.,* Alcibiades.

72 16 eum : Lȳsandrum.

quō factō : *if this were done.*

17 cōnflictūrum (esse) : what must be supplied as the subject-accusative of this and the following infinitive ?

19 Alcibiade receptō : compare quō factō, l. 16, and note.

20 sī quid secundī : *if anything of favorable* = *if any success.*

21 contrā ea : the same as contrā, above, l. 9.

22 sē . . . reum : *he alone would be charged with this failure;* literally, *he alone would be the defendant of this failure.*

24 illud moneō, nē, etc. : *I give you this warning, not to,* etc.

27 vestrī . . . exercitūs : exercitūs depends on occāsiō. F. 474, *b.*

73 1 volgum : *the common soldiers,* subject-accusative of exīsse.

3 relīctās : supply esse.

tempus reī gerendae : *a chance for striking a blow.* What literally ?

5 vīctīs Athēniēnsibus : *now that the Athenians were vanquished.*

7 suam fōrtūnam : *his concerns,* i.e., *he and his fortunes.*

13 hūmānitāte : read again note on cōnsilī, p. 66, l. 6.

eum : Alcibiades.

15 quīnquāgēna : *i.e.,* annually. How so ?

17 Athēnās, etc. : *nor Athens vanquished to the Lacedaemonians to be subject was he able to endure.* What in English ?

18 omnī ferēbātur cōgitātiōne : *he bent all his thoughts.* But what literally ?

20 eum : subject-accusative of adiungī. The reference is to rēge Persē in the preceding line.

21 cōnsecūtūrum : fix the meaning of this common word in memory. See p. 67, l. 1.

ēius conveniundī : *of meeting him.* F. 474, *b.*

22 habuisset : not *had had,* but *should have.* How can such a translation of the pluperfect subjunctive be justified ? How can you tell when the pluperfect subjunctive is to be translated *should* and not *had?* In a future condition in direct discourse, the Latin often uses the future perfect; we very seldom. We usually employ the present. Thus, in Latin, id cōnsecūtus erō, sī habuerō potestātem, *I shall gain it, if I* HAVE *a chance.* Such a future perfect (habuerō) becomes a pluperfect subjunctive (habuisset) in indirect discourse, but

73   the same difference of idiom holds. As we translated *have,*
instead of *shall have,* we translate *should have,* in place of
should have had. To tell whether a pluperfect subjunctive
represents a future perfect, think what form a speaker's
words would take in direct discourse.

   nam . . . sciēbat: attack this sentence by taking the words
   as they stand. *For that Cyrus, his brother, for (against) him
   war secretly to be preparing, the Lacedaemonians aiding, he
   knew.* Then translate.

24 sī aperuisset: study again note on habuisset, l. 22, and make
   the application here.

27 certōs: see note on cōnsilī, p. 66, l. 6.

74 1 quī = ut iī.

   sustulisset: see again note on habuisset, p. 73, l. 22, and make
   the application here.

2 fore = futūrum esse.

3 cōnstituisset: *he had established;* cōnstituisset represents cōn-
   stituistī of direct discourse.

   suās rēs gestās: *his things done, what he had done.*

4 Lacō: Lysander.

   accūrātius sibi agendum: *that he must deal more decidedly.*

5 renūntiat: *gives notice that he will break off.*

6 quae . . . essent: *the relations existing between the Lacedaemonians and the king.* What literally?

7 trādidisset: read again note on habuisset, p. 74, l. 22, and make
   the application here.

   nōn tulit hunc: *did not hold out against him.* Some texts have
   hōc; then the meaning of tulit would be *could not bear.*

8 minuī: present passive infinitive.

11 mīssī: *the persons who were sent.*

   vīcīnitātī: depends on dant negōtium, and means *his,* Alcibiades', *neighbors.* We sometimes use *neighborhood* for
   neighbors, as here vīcīnitās for vīcīnī.

12 illī cum: *since they.*

17 eī: see absentī, p. 71, l. 23, and note.

   subālāre: sub, *under* and āla, *arm-pit.* The adjective suggests
   the notion *short* or *small,* like our prefix *hand.* Roberts
   compares *pocket,* as in *pocket-knife.*

74 20 id . . . vestīmentōrum: *such garments as were at hand.* On quod . . . vestīmentōrum, see 216, *a*, 3; H. 397, 3.

22 ēminus: examine its composition. Compare its opposite comminus, *hand to hand.*

25 contēctum . . . mortuum: (eum) mortuum contēctum, *covered his dead body and.* 292, R.; F. 353, 7 and *c.*

26 interimendum: probably Nepos meant *for burning him alive,* but he says *for killing him alive.*

27 nātus: *at the age of.* He was about forty-six.

diem obiit suprēmum: mark the order.

75 1 īnfāmātum: *though ill spoken of.*

4 quī quidem duo: *the two latter.*

nēsciō quō = aliquō modō, "*strange to say*" (Roberts).

8 superāsse: supply eum as subject-accusative, as with several following infinitives.

9 studiīs eōrum īnservīsse: *devoted himself to their pursuits.*

12 quōrum mōribus: *according to whose ideas; in whose view.* Compare mōre Athēniensium, p. 67, l. 24.

13 in patientiā: see note on cōnsilī, p. 66, l. 6. Mark the derivation of the word. The Lacedaemonians prided themselves as much on endurance of pain without making any sign of suffering as did the North American Indians. Here patientiā refers rather to endurance of privation and hardship than of seeming insensibility to pain.

18 quibus rēbus effēcisse ut: *hence; literally, by which means he brought it about that.*

VOCABULARY.

—••‡ ⁜ ‡••—

A

ā (ab), prep. w. abl., *from, away from*, 3. 1, 17; 6. 3, etc.; *by*, 4. 20; 5. 6, 14, etc.

abdō, 3, didī, ditus, *put from; hide, conceal*, 23. 15; 46. 23; 60. 14, etc.

abdūcō, 3, dūxī, ductus, *lead away; take away, carry off*, 13. 8; 50. 8.

abeō, īre, iī, itūrus, *go from; go away, depart*, 19. 12; 21. 2; 24. 3, etc.; *fly off*, 42. 13.

abiciō, 3, iēcī, iectus [iaciō, throw], *throw from; cast, throw, fling, hurl*, 33. 7; *throw* or *put down, lay aside*, 5. 8.

abluō, 3, luī, lūtus, *wash away; wash, bathe*, 45. 1.

abrogō, 1, *annul; depose from, remove from*, 71. 24.

abscēdō, 3, cessī, cessus, *give way; retire, withdraw, depart*, 62. 21.

absēns, entis, adj. [p. of absum], *absent, away from home*, 61. 17; 68. 3, 6, etc.

absolvō, 3, solvī, solūtus, *loose from; release, set free, discharge, acquit*, 40. 4.

abstineō, 2, tinuī, (tentus) [teneō], *keep back; keep oneself from, refrain, abstain*, 36. 19; 60. 15.

abstulī. See auferō.

absum, esse, āfuī, āfutūrus, *be from; be away, be distant*, 3. 18; 19. 7; 39. 5, etc.; *be away* or *absent;* haud multum (minimum) āfuit quīn, *came very near*, 6. 14; 13. 1; 25. 15.

Absyrtus, ī, M., brother of Medea, 10. 22.

abundāns, antis, adj. [p. of abundō, *overflow*], *overflowing; rich, plentiful, abundant.*

āc. See atque.

Acastus, ī, M., son of Pelias, king of the Colchi, 15. 19.

Acca, ae, F., *Acca Larentia*, wife of Faustulus, 33. 14.

accēdō, 3, cessī, cessūrus, *go to; draw near, approach*, 39. 27; 49. 13; 64. 10; *undertake, attempt*, 64. 28. Cf. appropīnquō, 7. 17, and adeō, 9. 18.

accendō, 3, cendī, cēnsus, *set on fire; kindle, light, make* (fire), 20. 22; *inflame*, 56. 8.

accidō, 3, cidī, — [cadō], *fall to;*

befall, happen, come to pass, 2.
22; **12.** 4; **18.** 23, etc. Cf.
ēveniō, **7.** 27.

✔ **acciō, 4,** cīvī, cītus, *call ; summon, send for, invite*, **36.** 24.
Cf. arcessō, **3.** 14.

accipiŏ, 3, cēpī, ceptus [capiō],
take to one ; receive, welcome,
9. 19; **15.** 16; **16.** 9, etc.; *inherit*, **41.** 12 ; *suffer, sustain*,
61. 19.

accommodŏ, 1, *fit ; arrange, adjust*, **63.** 3.

✔ **accumbŏ, 3,** cubuī, cubitum, *lay
oneself down ; recline at table*,
6. 12, 25; **28.** 13, etc. Cf.
Eng. "*fall to.*"

accūrātē, adv. [accūrātus, *carefully wrought*], *exactly, precisely, decidedly*, **74.** 4.

ᐠ **accurrŏ, 3,** currī or cucurrī, cursus, *run to ; hasten to, run up
to*, **33.** 10; **56.** 14.

accūsŏ, 1 [causa], *call to account ;
make complaint against, accuse,
charge*, w. acc. and gen., **33.** 24.

ācer, cris, cre, adj., *sharp ; keen*,
55. 2; *ardent, eager, zealous*,
69. 8.

✔ **acerbitās,** ātis, F. [acerbus], *bitterness, harshness*, **70.** 28.

✔ **acerbus,** a, um, adj., *harsh ;
bitter, unripe*, **51.** 6.

✔ **acervus,** ī, M., *mass of similar
objects ; heap, pile*, **55.** 1.

aciēs, ēī, F., *edge ; battle array,
army, line*, **38.** 15; **40.** 13; **61.**
2, etc. ; *battle*, **62.** 20.

ācriter, adv. [ācer], *sharply ;
fiercely, furiously, eagerly*, **5.**
5; **44.** 7.

acūmen, inis, N. [acuō], *point ;*

sharpness, keenness, acuteness,
75. 12.

✔ **acūtus,** a, um, adj. [p. of acuō,
sharpen], *sharpened ; sharp,
pointed*, **56.** 5.

ad, prep. w. acc., *to ; to, up to,
toward, at*, **2.** 9; **7.** 12, etc.;
to, for, **3.** 21 ; **4.** 2, 4, etc.; *at,
before*, **10.** 24; **30.** 23 ; *up to,
until*, **12.** 2 ; **19.** 3; **28.** 20 ;
near, **6.** 2 ; *according to*, **37.**
17; **60.** 16; **63.** 2.

adamŏ, 1, *feel love for ; fall in
love with*, **8.** 18.

✔ **addīcŏ, 3,** dīxī, dictus, *say yes to ;
be propitious, favor, consent*,
43. 1.

addŏ, 3, didī, ditus, *put to ; add,
join*, **35.** 2; **40.** 23; **44.** 19;
tell in addition, **42.** 10.

addūcŏ, 3, dūxī, ductus, *lead to ;
lead or take to* (a place), *conduct*, **29.** 4; *lead, prompt, induce, influence*, **2.** 4; **14.** 11,
14, etc.

adeŏ, īre, iī, itus, *go to, approach,
draw near*, **9.** 18; **28.** 5; **47.**
1, etc. Cf. accēdō, **39.** 27.

✔ **adeŏ,** adv., *to this ; to such an
extent, so far, so*, **41.** 2 ; **60.**
13; **73.** 13, etc.

✔ **adfābilis,** e, adj. [adfor, *address*],
*to be addressed ; approachable,
courteous, kind*, **66.** 11.

ᐟ **adferŏ,** ferre, tulī, lātus, *bear to ;
bring there*, **22.** 24; **52.** 17, 18;
bear, bring, give, **22.** 4; *bring
upon, cause to*, w. acc. and dat.,
6. 11 ; w. vim and dat., *do violence to, assault*, **46.** 21.

✔ **adficiŏ, 3,** fēcī, fectus [faciō], *do
to ; move, afflict, oppress, over-*

whelm, 3. 6; 5. 24; 16. 12, etc.; *punish, treat,* 6. 6; 59. 10.

✓ adfīnis, e, adj., *bordering on; as noun,* M. *and* F., *connection by marriage,* 58. 11.

adfīrmō, 1, *strengthen; maintain, assert,* 36. 17.

adflīgō, 3, flīxī, flīctus, *dash at; damage, shatter, injure,* 31. 21.

✓ adhibeō, 2, uī, itus [habeō], *hold toward; call to aid, employ, use, hold,* 34. 13.

adhortātiō, ōnis, F. [adhortor, *encourage*], *encouragement, exhortation,* 61. 7.

╱ adhūc, adv., *to this point; till then,* 16. 25; *yet, still,* 14. 1.

adiciō, 3, iēcī, iectus [iaciō], *throw to; throw, cast,* 13. 3.

Adimantus, ī, M., an Athenian general, 71. 13.

adimō, 3, ēmī, ēmptus [emō], *take to one; take away, deprive,* 30. 17.

adipīscor, 3, adeptus, *reach for; obtain, acquire, get, attain,* 42. 20.

ı· aditus, ūs, M. [adeō], *going to; approach, entrance.*

adiungō, 3, iūnxī, iūnctus, *fasten to; join with, annex, add to,* w. acc. and dat. or ad, 4. 14; 44. 16; 70. 9, etc.

ː adiuvō, 1, iūvī, iūtus, *help, assist, aid, support,* 73. 23.

adlātūrus. See adferō.

ː adlevō, 1, *lift to one; lift up, raise,* 54. 4.

ː adliciō, 3, lēxī, lectus, *allure, win over, persuade,* 46. 2.

adloquor, 3, cūtus, *speak to; address, exhort,* 44. 10; 49. 13.

administrō, 1, *manage, direct, execute, rule,* 42. 20; 44. 14; 60. 16, etc.

admīrātiō, ōnis, F. [admīror], *admiration, wonder,* 40. 4.

admīror, 1, *regard with wonder; wonder, be astonished,* 66. 15; *admire,* 75. 18.

admoneō, 2, uī, itus, *bring to mind; warn,* 51. 12.

admoveō, 2, mōvī, mōtus, *move to; apply, offer,* 33. 11.

adnectō, 3, nēxuī, nēxus, *tie to,* ╰ *fasten on, attach,* 51. 12, 14.

adolēscō, 3, olēvī, ultus, *grow; grow up, mature,* 33. 15; 44. 3.

adoperiō, 4, eruī, ertus, *cover, veil,* 40. 7.

adorior, 4, ortus, *arise against;* ╰ *approach, address, accost, attack,* 54. 7.

adōrnō, 1, *decorate; provide, furnish, fit out, equip,* 37. 3.

adquīrō, 3, quīsīvī, quīsītus ╰ [quaerō], *get in addition; gain, win, get besides,* 45. 3.

adrēpō, 3, rēpsī, —, *creep to, steal* ╰ *up,* 56. 3.

adripiō, 3, ripuī, reptus [rapiō], *snatch up, seize upon,* 54. 12; 64. 14; 74. 20.

adrogō, 1, *ask to one; claim, appropriate,* 54. 20.

adsequor, 3, secūtus, *follow to; reach, gain, attain,* 51. 8.

adsīdō, 3, sēdī, —, *take a seat,* ╰ *sit down, sit,* 64. 9.

adst = ast.

adsum, esse, fuī, futūrus, *be at; be at hand, come,* 14. 8.

adsūmō, 3, sūmpsī, sūmptus, *take to ; take, choose,* **44**. 8.

adsurgō, 3, surrēxī, surrēctus, *rise to ; stand, rise,* **63**. 22.

adūlātor, ōris, M., *flatterer,* **54**. 13.

adulēscēns, entis, adj. [p. of adolēscō], *growing ;* as noun, M., *youth, young man,* **29**. 12 ; **34**. 2.

adulēscentia, ae, F. [adulēscēns], *growing ; youth,* **15**. 5 ; **49**. 18.

adultī. See adolēscō.

adveniō, 4, vēnī, ventus, *come to ; come near, arrive, reach,* **42**. 9 ; **42**. 10 ; **55**. 17, etc.

adventus, ūs, M., *a coming to ; coming, approach, arrival,* **11**. 19 ; **62**. 19.

adversus, a, um, adj. [p. of advertō, *turn to*], *turned toward ; violent,* **62**. 11 ; *unfavorable,* **72**. 22 ; w. rēs, *misfortune, calamity,* **70**. 15.

adversus, prep. w. acc. [advertō, *turn to*], *turned towards ; in front,* **64**. 13 ; *against, upon,* **35**. 11 ; **40**. 12 ; **44**. 4, etc.

advocō, 1, *call to one ; call together, convoke, summon,* **45**. 9 ; **46**. 22 ; **71**. 1. Cf. arcessō, 3. 14.

aedificium, ī, N. [aedificō], *building, structure,* **74**. 25.

aedificō, 1 [aedis], *erect a building ; build, erect, construct,* 3. 23 ; **28**. 5 ; **37**. 19, etc.

aedīlis, is, M. [aedis], *aedile,* commissioner of buildings and public works, **59**. 27.

aedis (aedēs), is, F., *dwelling of*

the gods ; temple, **35**. 29 ; **36**. 21 ; pl. *house, dwelling, palace,* **28**. 19 ; **37**. 9 ; **44**. 10. Cf. templum ; domus, aedificium.

Aeētēs, ae, M., a mythical king of Colchis, **3**. 9.

Aegos-flūmen, inis, N., *Goat River* (*Aegospotami*), a river and town in the Thracian Chersonese, **72**. 5.

aegrē, adv. [aeger, *ill*], *painfully ;* w. ferō, *feel distress, bear ill, take to heart, be angry,* **8**. 19 ; **14**. 13 ; **15**. 18, etc.

aegritūdō, inis, F. [aeger, *ill*], *sickness ;* w. animī, *grief, chagrin, irritation,* **35**. 4.

aemulātiō, ōnis, F. [aemulor, *rival*], *rivalry, competition,* **61**. 12.

aēneus, a, um, adj. [aes], *of copper, bronze,* **14**. 24 ; **15**. 10.

Aeolia, ae, F., an island near Sicily, **25**. 18.

Aeolus, ī, M., the king of the winds, **25**. 20.

aequālis, e, adj. [aequō, *make equal*], *equal, like,* **54**. 16.

aequiperō, 1 [aequus, *equal*], *compare ; come up to, equal, rival,* **75**. 10.

aequitās, ātis, F. [aequus, *equal*], *evenness ; fairness, moderation, justice,* **41**. 7.

āēr, āeris, M., *air, sky,* **7**. 4 ; **16**. 21.

aes, aeris, N., *crude metal, copper ;* aes aliēnum, *another's money,* i.e., *debt,* **60**. 2.

Aesōn, onis, M., Jason's father, **1**. 1.

aestimō, 1, *determine the value*

of; value, esteem, rate, weigh, **52. 14.**

aetās, ātis, F. [for aevitās], *period of life,* **59.** 16; *age, years,* **14.** 7, 16, 23, etc.; *old age,* **47.** 4; **53.** 20; *time,* **75. 3.**

✔ **aeternus**, a, um, adj. [for aeviternus], *of an age;* in aeternum, *forever,* **19. 2.**

Aetna, ae, F., *Mt. Aetna* in Sicily, 20. 14.

Āfrica, ae, F., **62.** 26.

āfuī. See **absum.**

ager, agrī, M., *productive land; field, plain, land, country, territory,* **2.** 25; **8.** 14; **9.** 8, etc. Cf. arvum, fīnis.

aggredior, 3, gressus [gradior, *go*], *go to; fall upon, assail, attack,* **55.** 15; **60.** 25, 26, etc.

✔ **agitō**, 1, *set in violent motion; consider, ponder, meditate on,* **43. 4.**

✔ **agitātor**, ōris, M. [agitō], *driver,* **53. 4.**

āgmen, inis, N. [agō], *thing driven; line, army,* **26.** 21; in āgmine, *on the march,* **65. 2.**

āgnōscō, 3, nōvī, nitus, *recognize, identify, make out,* **5.** 3; **29.** 18; **31.** 1, etc.

✔ **agō**, 3, ēgī, āctus, *put in motion; drive,* **20.** 20; **24.** 16; **44.** 27; etc.; *do, perform, carry on,* **21.** 16; **28.** 19; **36.** 9, etc.; *treat, arrange,* **38.** 11; *negotiate,* **72.** 11; **74.** 5; *act,* **63.** 20; *take, make, hold,* **43.** 3; gratiās agō, *give thanks,* **7.** 25; *spend, live, pass,* annum agēns sextum et decimum, *in his sixteenth year,* **58. 2.**

agricola, ae, M. [ager, colō, *cultivate*], *cultivator of lands; farmer, rustic,* **52.** 1, 3, 15, etc.

āiō, defective verb [for agiō], *say, speak, cry,* **40.** 15; **44.** 11.

āla, ae, F., *driving thing; wing,* **7.** 4; **16.** 19; *armpit, arm,* **52. 2.**

Alba, ae, F., *Alba Longa,* the mother city of Rome, **33.** 21.

Albānus, a, um, adj. [Alba], *of Alba, Alban,* **39.** 5; as noun, M. pl., *the people of Alba, Albans,* **33.** 1.

Alcibiadēs, is, M., a celebrated Athenian general, **66.** 1.

alea, ae, F., *game with dice; die, chance, hazard,* **61.** 25.

Alexander, drī, M., *Alexander the Great,* king of Macedon [B. C. 356–323], **59.** 22.

alicunde, adv. [aliquis, unde], *from some source, from somewhere,* **54.** 5.

aliēnō, 1 [aliēnus], *make strange;* pass. w. abl., *have aversion for, shrink from, be estranged from,* **69.** 8.

aliēnus, a, um, adj. [alius], *of another; another's, other people's,* **57.** 3; aes aliēnum, *another's money,* i.e., *debt,* **60.** 2.

aliquamdiū or **aliquam diū**, *somewhat long; awhile, for some time,* **58.** 13.

aliquandō, adv., *at some time or other,* **58.** 15; **69.** 10; *once upon a time, at one time, once,* **51.** 10; **55.** 6.

aliquantō, adv., *by some little, somewhat, rather,* **75. 3.**

aliquantum, ī, N. [aliquantus,

some], *some, a little,* w. partit.
gen., **28**. 3; **29**. 8 ; **39**. 3, etc.

aliquī, qua, quod, indef. adj.,
some, any, 12. 4 ; **44**. 19 ; 48.
8, etc.

aliquis, qua, quid, indef. pron.,
some one, any one, something.

aliquot, indef. num. adj., indecl.,
some, several, a few, **59**. 8.

aliter, adv., *in another manner ;*
followed by āc or atque, *otherwise than, in a different way
from,* 15. 12; 30. 10.

alius, a, ud, gen. īus, pronom. adj.,
another, other, else, **2**. 25; 4.
11 ; 5. 6 ; **34**. 19 ; 48. 9 ; 57. 5,
etc.; alius . . . alius, *one . . . another,* 35. 28 ; **38**. 20 ; aliae aliās
in partīs, *some in one direction,
others in another,* 18. 15.

alō, 3, uī, altus or alitus, *feed ;
sustain, maintain, keep up,* 37.
1 ; *strengthen, harden,* 9. 1.

Alpēs, ium, F., *the Alps* mountains, **59**. 12.   ·

alter, era, erum, gen. ius, pronom. adj., *one of two,* 3. 2, 5;
a second, **39**. 7 ; **61**. 17 ; alter
. . . alter, *one . . . the other,* 2.
1, 2 ; **27**. 17, 18 ; 39. 10, 11, etc.

altus, a, um, adj., *grown ; high,
elevated, lofty,* **42**. 15 ; 48. 16 ;
54. 5; as noun, N., *sea, deep,*
25. 8; **62**. 8; superl. altissi-
mus, **46**. 7.

alveus, ī, M. [alvus, *belly*], *hollow ; tub, trough,* **33**. 6.

ambitiō, ōnis, F. [ambiō], *going
about; ambition, desire for
honor,* **59**. 14.

ambō, ae, ō, adj., *both, the two,*
43. 19.

āmentia, ae, F. [āmēns, *out of
one's senses*], *madness, frenzy,*
16. 14 ; **24**. 6.

amīcitia, ae, F. [amīcus], *friendship, alliance, league,* **69**. 2, 16 ;
70. 9, etc.

amīcus, a, um, adj., *loving,
friendly, favorable,* **69**. 7 ;
superl., **58**. 12.

amīcus, ī, M. [amīcus], *loved one ;
friend,* 2. 6, 16 ; **26**. 19, etc.

āmittō, 3, mīsī, mīssus, *send
away ; let slip, lose, be bereft of,*
2. 16 ; 3. 3, 4, etc.

amō, 1, *love ; like, be fond of.*

amor, ōris, M., *loving ; love, esteem, passion,* 31. 13 ; **39**. 22.

āmoveō, 2, mōvī, mōtus, *move
away ; take away, remove,
withdraw,* 21. 22 ; **22**. 8 ; **24**. 8.

amplector, 3, exus [plectō, *twist*],
twist around ; embrace, **40**. 1 ;
surround, play about, 43. 25.

ampliō, 1 [amplus], *widen ; increase, enlarge,* **63**. 9.

amplissimus, a, um, adj., superl.
of amplus, *of large extent ;
noble, distinguished, glorious,*
66. 5.

amplius, indecl. [N. comp. of
amplus], *more ;* as adv., *more,
further, in addition, besides,* **75**.
6; w. numerals, *more than,* **63**.
27.

Amūlius, ī, M., *son of Procas and
brother of Numitor,* **33**. 1.

an, conj., *in indir. question,
whether, if ; or,* **20**. 25.

ancīle, is, N., *curved thing ;
sacred shield, shield,* **37**. 11,
14.

ancilla, ae, F., dim. [ancula,

attendant], *handmaid, maid-servant,* 46. 19; 53. 12.

ancora, ae, F., *anchor,* 5. 12; 7. 16; 12. 15, etc.; in ancorīs, *at anchor,* 5. 13.

Ancus, ī, M., *Ancus Martius,* fourth king of Rome, 41. 6.

Andocidēs, is, M., an Athenian orator, 67. 9.

anguis, is, M. and F., *serpent, snake,* 52. 1, 3; 56. 3, etc.

angustiae, ārum, F. [angustus, *narrow*], *narrowness, small-ness,* 34. 17.

anima, ae, F., *air, breath; life, spirit;* w. efflō, *give up the ghost, die,* 53. 4.

animadvertō, 3, tī, sus, *direct the mind; observe, notice, per-ceive, see,* 20. 2, 9; 21. 19, etc.

animus, ī, M., *the rational soul* (cf. anima, *physical life*); *mind, heart,* 11. 24; 21. 9; 22. 17, etc.; *heart, sympathy, feel-ings, spirit,* 12. 18; 13. 20; 38. 17, etc.; *courage,* 22. 1; *nature, disposition,* 45. 5; in animō esse *or* habēre, *have a purpose, intend,* 2. 5; 16. 2; 31. 11, etc.

annālis, is, M. [annus], *record of events, chronicles,* 46. 27.

annus, ī, M., *that which goes round; year,* 2. 3, 21; 17. 1, etc.

ante, adv., *before; of time, before, previously,* 40. 2; 70. 1; 12. 17; as prep. w. acc., *before, in front of,* 57. 3; 67. 9; of time, 5. 13; 9. 16, etc.

anteā, adv., *before, formerly, pre-viously,* 22. 2, 22; 23. 2, etc.

antecēdō, 3, cessī, —, *go before;* *surpass, excel,* 73. 14. Cf. antecellō, 9. 5.

antecellō, 3, —, —, *be prominent; excel, surpass, be superior (to),* w. acc., 9. 5. Cf. antecēdō, 73. 14.

ante-eō, īre, īvī or iī, —, *go be-fore; march before, go ahead,* 65. 2.

antequam, or ante quam, adv., *sooner than, before,* 7. 21; 18. 8; 21. 17, etc.

antīquus, a, um, adj., *ancient, former, of old times,* 46. 27.

Antōnius, ī, M., *Marcus Antonius,* a distinguished Roman, 63. 23.

antrum, ī, N., *cavern, cave,* 19. 23; 20. 4, 22, etc.

ānulus, ī, M., dim. [ānus, *ring*], *little ring; finger ring, ring,* 35. 17.

anus, ūs, F., *old woman, sibyl,* 46. 28; 47. 4, 8.

anxietās, ātis, F. [anxius], *solici-tude, anxiety,* 28. 22.

anxius, a, um, adj., *choked; troubled, solicitous, anxious,* 11. 24; 25. 2; 28. 20, etc.

aperiō, 4, uī, pertus, *uncover, open, unclose; disclose, unfold,* 73. 24; *open, found, establish,* 35. 3; p. apertus, *opened, open,* 9. 11; 11. 19; 37. 19; 54. 11.

Apollōnius, ī, M., an orator at Rhodes in the time of Caesar, 58. 19.

appāreō, 2, uī, itūrus, *appear; be clear, plain,* or *evident,* 67. 10.

apparō, 1, *prepare, make ready,* 67. 6.

appellō, 3, pulī, pulsus, *drive to,* 18. 18; w. nāvem, *bring in, put in, land,* 6. 2, 16; 8. 3; 19. 20, etc.

appellō, 1, *address; call, name, term,* 2. 2; 4. 18; 6. 10, etc.

Apenninus, ī, M., *mountain summit; the Apennines,* 63. 15.

appetō, 3, īvī and iī, ītus, *seek for;* intr., *be at hand, draw near, approach,* 4. 6; *long for, desire,* 54. 6.

appōnō, 3, posuī, positus, *put to; set before, serve to,* w. dat., 6. 12, 25; 28. 14, etc.

apportō, 1, *carry to; bring along, bring,* 73. 10.

apprehendō, 3, dī, ēnsus, *seize; take hold of, seize, grasp,* 64. 11.

appropinquō, 1, *come near to; draw near, approach,* w. dat., and ad, 7. 17; 11. 18; 27. 6, etc. Cf. accēdō and adeō.

appulī. See appellō.

aptē, adv. [aptus], *fitly; rightly, properly,* 42. 12.

aptus, a, um, adj., *fitted; suited; ready, adapted,* 66. 6.

apud, prep. w. acc., *with; with, among, on the side of,* 3. 1; 38. 9, 10, etc.; *among, in the eyes of,* 40. 10; 72. 20; *in the presence of, before,* 39. 26; 48. 11; *at the house of,* 31. 14, 17; 46. 14, etc.; *at, near,* 59. 22; 69. 19, 24, etc.

aqua, ae, F., *water, waters, stream,* 5. 14, 16; 14. 25, etc.

aquila, ae, F., *eagle,* 42. 11.

aquilifer, erī, M. [aquila; ferō, *bear*], *eagle-bearer, standard-bearer,* 61. 3.

āra, ae, F., *raised place; altar,* 36. 26; 37. 1.

arbiter, trī, M., *he who is present; witness, hearer,* 37. 27.

arbitrium, ī, N. [arbiter], *judgment; authority, will, pleasure,* 60. 16; 71. 11.

arbitror, 1 [arbiter], *testify; be of an opinion, believe, consider, think,* 4. 12; 5. 4; 12. 16, etc.

arbor, oris, F., *thing grown; tree,* 11. 12, 15, 17, etc.

Arcadia, ae, F., a state of central Peloponnesus, 74. 18.

arceō, 2, uī, —, *shut in; keep off, hinder,* 33. 17; 49. 5.

arcessō, 3, īvī, ītus, causative [accēdō], *cause to come; summon, send for, call,* 3. 14; 40. 13; 62. 4. Cf. acciō, 36. 24, and advocō, 45. 9.

Ardea, ae, F., *heron;* chief city of the Rutuli, 46. 12.

ārdeō, 2, sī, sus, *be on fire; burn,* 18. 12. Cf. the trans. accendō, 20. 22.

argentum, ī, N., *shining thing; silver,* 26. 19.

Argō, ūs, acc. Argō, F., Jason's ship, 10. 23.

Argonautae, ārum, M. [nauta], *Argonauts,* crew of the Argo, 4. 18.

arguō, 3, uī, ūtus, *make clear; declare, prove, charge,* 71. 19.

Argus, ī, M., the builder of the Argo, 3. 22.

ariēs, ietis, M., *ram,* 14. 23; 15. 1.

arma, ōrum, N., *things fitted* (to any purpose); *arms, weapons, armor,* 5. 4, 7; 9. 3, etc.; *arms, fighting,* 40. 27.

Armenia, ae, F., a country of Asia Minor, 63. 17.

armilla, ae, F. [armus, *shoulder*], *bracelet, armlet*, 35. 17.

armō, 1 [arma], *furnish with weapons ; equip, arm, rouse to arms*, 3. 21 ; 9. 21, 24, etc.

arō, 1, *plough, till*, 8. 14 ; 9. 8, 15, etc.

✓ ars, artis, F., *skill in joining; art, skill, cunning*, 11. 14 ; 16. 4 ; 20. 2, etc.

arvum, ī, N. [N. of arvus, *ploughed*], *that has been ploughed; field*, 56. 6; pl., *fields, lands.* Cf. ager.

arx, arcis, F., *enclosing thing; citadel, stronghold*, 35. 14, 18.

ascendō, 3, dī, scēnsus [ad, scandō, *climb*], *climb upon ; go on board, embark*, 68. 13.

Asia, ae, F., *Asia Minor*, 44. 21.

asinus, ī, M., *ass*, 50. 6 ; 52. 7, 12, etc.

✓ aspergō, 3, ersī, ersus [ad, spargō, *scatter*], *stain, taint, cover*, 67. 22.

aspiciō, 3, ēxī, ectus, *look at; look on, behold, espy, see*, 9. 15; 56. 13.

astō, 1, itī, —, *stand at, take position near*, 23. 21 ; *be at hand*, 54. 1.

astū, N., indecl., *city*, 71. 1. Cf. urbs.

asȳlum, ī, N., *place of refuge, asylum, sanctuary*, 34. 22 ; 35. 3.

at, conj., *but* (introducing a contrast with what precedes), 2. 3; 4. 22; 6. 25, etc.

Athēnae, ārum, F., *Athens*, in Attica, 16. 21.

Athēniēnsis, e, adj. [Athēnae], *Athenian*, 66. 1.

atque or āc, conj., *and, also*, 9. 6; 14. 15; 16. 13, etc.; *than*, 15. 12; 30. 11 ; 44. 2 ; *as*, 30. 3 ; 70. 14; 71. 4 ; w. simul, *as soon as*, 6. 16, 25 ; 20. 17, etc.

atquī, conj., *but yet, however*, 43. 4.

ātrium, ī, N., *room which contains the hearth ; main hall, chief room*, 30. 25.

atrōx, ōcis, adj. [āter, *black*], *disagreeable to behold; cruel, savage, barbarous*, 39. 25.

attendō, 3, tendī, tentus, *stretch toward ;* w. animum, *give attention, consider, give heed*, 69. 14.

attentus, a, um, adj. [p. of attendō], *attentive, intent*, 47. 12.

Attica, ae, F., *a state of eastern Greece*, 69. 2.

attingō, 3, tigī, tāctus [tangō, *touch*], *touch upon ; arrive at, reach*, 4. 20 ; 5. 13; 51. 4.

attulī. See adferō.

Attus, ī, M., *Attus Navius*, a soothsayer in the reign of Tarquinius Priscus, 42. 24.

auctōritās, ātis, F. [auctor, *producer*], *production ; influence, weight, authority, power*, 37. 23; 42. 25; 67. 3.

auctus. See augeō.

audācia, ae, F. [audāx], *boldness, daring, audacity, insolence*, 42. 3; 62. 5.

audāx, ācis, adj., *daring ; bold, rash, presumptuous*, 48. 4 ; 51. 16.

audeō, 2, ausus sum, *dare, ven-*

ture, have the boldness, **36.** 3 ; **49.** 12 ; **74.** 13.

audiō, 4, *hear*, **2.** 10 ; **6.** 16 ; **8.** 5, etc. ; *listen to, regard, receive*, **35.** 1 ; w. dictō, foll. by dat., *obey*, **44.** 13.

✓ **auferō,** ferre, abstulī, ablātus, *bear away ; take away, remove, snatch*, **2.** 8 ; **5.** 22 ; **6.** 13 ; etc.; pass., *disappear*, **36.** 14; **37.** 12.

aufugiō, 3, fūgī, —, *flee away ; flee, run*, **7.** 6 ; **39.** 3.

augeō, 2, auxī, auctus, *cause to grow ; enlarge, increase, build up, add to*, **33.** 16; **38.** 3; **40.** 25.

augur, uris, M. and F. [avis], *observer of birds ; diviner, soothsayer, augur*, **42.** 25; **43.** 6.

augurium, ī, N. [augur], *observance of omens from birds ; divination, augury*, **34.** 15 ; **43.** 3.

.· **augustior,** ius, gen. ōris, adj., comp. of augustus, a, um, *increased ; (more) majestic, noble, venerable*, **36.** 18.

aura, ae, F., *air*, **29.** 26.

aureus, a, um, adj. [aurum], *of gold, golden*, **3.** 10 ; **8.** 5 ; **11.** 21, etc.

✓ **auris,** is, F., *hearing thing ; ear*, **50.** 8.

aurum, ī, N., *gold*, **26.** 18 ; **50.** 13.

auspicium, ī, N. [auspex, *one who divines by the flight of birds*],

examination of birds ; augury, auspices, **34.** 13.

aut, conj., *or*, **54.** 22; **72.** 12; **74.** 7, etc.; aut . . . **aut,** *either . . . or*, **4.** 8 ; **64.** 24 ; **71.** 17, etc.

autem, conj. (postpos.), *but, on the other hand, now, moreover*, **2.** 25; **4.** 9, etc. ; *however*, **3.** 15; **5.** 8, 19, etc.

auxērunt and **auxēre.** See augeō.

auxilior, 1 [auxilium], *give help, aid, assist, succor*, **25.** 4.

auxilium, ī, N., *increasing ; help, aid, assistance*, **6.** 19; **7.** 25, 26, etc.

āvehō, 3, vēxī, vēctus, *carry off,* ✓ *take away*, **11.** 4.

Aventīnus, a, um, adj., *of Mt. Aventine*, one of the seven hills of Rome, **37.** 5.

āvertō, 3, tī, sus, *turn from, cause to withdraw*, **69.** 4 ; *turn aside, ward off*; w. sē, *be off one's guard*, **43.** 18.

avidus, a, um, adj., *longing,* ✓ *greedy, eager*, **59.** 16.

avis, is, F., *bird*, **48.** 13 ; **54.** 9 ; hence *sign, omen*, **43.** 1.

āvolō, 1, āvī, ātūrus, *fly away ; hasten off, hurry*, **46.** 17 ; **56.** 21.

avus, ī, M., *grandfather*, **33.** 20 ; ✓ **34.** 8 ; **41.** 8.

B

baculum, ī, N., *walking-stick, staff, cane*, **28.** 17 ; **29.** 13, 22, etc.

Bagaeus, ī, M., brother of Pharnabazus, **74.** 9.

barbarus, a, um, adj., *of strange*

speech; as noun, M., *barbarian, foreigner,* **71.** 28 ; **74.** 21.

beātitūdō, inis, F. [beātus], *happiness,* **52.** 13.

beātus, a, um, adj. [p. of beō, *make happy*], *made happy; happy, fortunate,* **52.** 7.

bellicōsus, a, um, adj. [bellum], *full of war; given to fighting, warlike, valiant,* **40.** 27.

bellō, 1 [bellum], *wage war, carry on war, war,* **61.** 20.

bellum, ī, N. [for duellum], *contest between two; war,* **17.** 2 ; **18.** 1, 9, etc.; loc. bellī, *in the field, abroad,* **71.** 11.

bene, adv. [bonus], *well,* **2.** 13 ; **3.** 15; **7.** 22, etc.

beneficium,ī,N.[bene, facio], *welldoing; kindness, service, blessing,* **7.** 8 ; **23.** 8 ; **26.** 9, etc.

benevolentia, ae, F. [benevolēns, *well-wishing*], *favor, friendship,* **46.** 1 ; **70.** 27.

benīgnē, adv. [benīgnus, *kind*], *in a kindly manner; courteously, kindly, with friendliness,* **30.** 3 ; **35.** 1 ; **46.** 1.

benīgnitās, ātis, F. [benīgnus, *kind*], *kindness, friendliness, courtesy,* **28.** 9.

bēstia, ae, F., *beast, animal,* **50.** 6 ; **54.** 21.

bibliothēca, ae, F., *library, collection of books,* **63.** 13.

bibō, 3, bibī, —, *drink, swallow,* **23.** 1 ; **28.** 15.

Bibulus, ī, M., *Marcus Bibulus,*

Caesar's colleague in the consulship, **60.** 1.

Bizanthē, ēs, F., a town and fortress on the Chersonesus, **71.** 27.

blanditia, ae, F. [blandus], *a caressing; flattery,* **54.** 14 ; *pleasantry,* **46.** 2.

blandus, a, um, adj., *of smooth tongue; flattering, agreeable,* **54.** 7 ; **66.** 12.

Boeōtiī, ōrum, M., the people of Boeotia in Greece, *Boeotians,* **75.** 11.

bonus, a, um, *good;* as noun, N., *good thing* or *quality, good,* **48.** 8, 14; **50.** 5, etc., *property,* **58.** 5; **68.** 19; **71.** 5.

bōs, bovis, F., *cow;* pl., *cattle,* **44.** 24, 26, 27, etc.

bracchium (brāchium), ī, N., *forearm, lower arm, arm,* **64.** 14.

brevis, e, adj., *short, small, little,* **2.** 15; **8.** 1 ; **15.** 1, etc.

Britannī, ōrum, M., *people of Britain; Britons, British,* **60.** 26.

Brundisium, ī, N., a seaport in southeastern Italy, **61.** 27.

Brūtus, ī, M., *Marcus Brutus,* a friend of Caesar but a conspirator against him, **63.** 28.

bulla, ae, F., *medal, amulet* (worn by boys of free birth), **43.** 8.

Byzantium, ī, N., a Thracian city on the Bosporus, **70.** 8.

C

C., abbreviation for Gāius (Cāius).

cadō, 3, cecidī, cāsūrus, *fall down ; fall, fall dead, be slain,* 35. 25; 38. 21.

caecus, a, um, adj., *blind,* 6. 6; 23. 19.

caedēs, is, F., *a cutting ; slaughter, murder,* 40. 5.

caedō, 3, cecīdī, caesus, *cut ; cut, chop,* 53. 18; *kill, slay,* 39. 29.

caelestis, e, adj. [caelum], *of heaven ; of the skies, heavenly, divine,* 42. 13.

Caelius, ī, M., *Mt. Caelius,* one of the hills of Rome, 40. 23.

caelum, ī, N. [for cavilum], *hollow thing; heavens, sky,* 35. 29; 37. 4, 11.

Caesar, aris, M., *Caius Julius Caesar* [B.C. 100–44], 58. 1.

Cāius, ī, M., *Caius or Gaius.* See Caesar.

Calais, only nom., an Argonaut, son of the North Wind, 7. 3.

calamitās, ātis, F., *loss ; injury, disaster, misfortune,* 29. 17. Cf. cāsus, 12. 4.

calceus, ī, M., *covering ; shoe,* 2. 21; 3. 2, 4.

calefaciō, 3, fēcī, factus, *make warm ; heat, make hot,* 23. 13.

callidissimē, adv., superl. of callidē [callidus], *most skilfully, shrewdly, craftily,* 66. 12.

callidus, a, um, adj. [calleō, *know by experience*], *practiced ; shrewd, cunning, crafty,* 44. 28.

Calpurnia, ae, F., wife of Caesar at the time of his death, 64. 2.

calvitium, ī, N. [calvus], *baldness,* 64. 21.

calvus, a, um, adj., *hairless ; bald,* 64. 21.

Campānus, a, um, adj., *of Campania, Campanian,* 60. 8.

campus, ī, M., *digged place ; field, plain,* 36. 12 ; 49. 1. Cf. ager.

cancer, crī, M., *crab, sea-crab,* 49. 14 ; 56. 12.

canis, is, M. and F., *dog, hound,* 49. 4 ; 56. 2, 7.

canō, 3, cecinī, —, *utter musical* ✓ *sounds ; sing, chant,* 37. 16.

cantō, 1 [canō], *sing, chant,* 14. 26.

cantus, ūs, M., *singing, song,* 48. 13; 54. 9, 11 ; *crowing,* 53. 13.

capessō, 3, īvī (iī), ītūrus [capiō], ✓ *seize eagerly ;* w. fugam, *take to flight, begin to run,* 39. 1.

capiō, 3, cēpī, captus, *take ; take, get, receive, have,* 26. 15 ; 29. 22 ; 49. 7, etc. ; *take prisoner, seize, capture,* 13. 2 ; 18. 1, 7, etc.; *choose,* 40. 24 ; *take up, seize,* 38. 14 ; *take, form, conceive, make,* 13. 5 ; 16. 4 ; 22. 17 ; *gain over, win,* 73. 13 ; viam capiō, *make way, go,* 11. 10.

Capitōlium, ī, N., *Capitol,* the citadel of Rome, 35. 16; 59. 27.

capra, ae, F., *she-goat,* 48. 16; 49. 2 ; 54. 15; Caprae palūs, *Goat's Marsh,* 36. 12.

captīva, ae, F. [captīvus, *taken prisoner*], *captured woman ; female captive,* 43. 22.

captus, ī, M. [p. of capiō], *one taken ; captive, prisoner,* 70. 9.

caput, itis, N., *head,* 6. 9; 28. 17; 30. 8, etc.; gen. w. damnō, *to death,* 68. 18.

carcer, eris, M., *prison, jail,* 25. 22; 42. 2.

cărica, ae, F. [Cāria], *Carian fig, dried fig,* 55. 1.

cărissimus, a, um, adj., superl. of cārus, *dear; dearest, most beloved,* 75. 19.

cāritās, ātis, F. [cārus, *dear*], *affection, love,* 69. 10 ; 72. 4. Cf. amor, 31. 13.

carmen, inis, N., *singing; song, chant,* 14. 26 ; 28. 6 ; *charm, incantation,* 29. 21. Cf. cantus, 48. 13.

carō, carnis, F., *flesh,* 21. 8 ; 22. 7.

carpentum, ī, N., *covered chariot, carriage,* 42. 11 ; 45. 13, 17.

carpō, 3, psī, ptus, *pick; pluck, cull, gather,* 8. 25.

Casca, ae, M., one of the conspirators against Caesar, 64. 12.

casa, ae, F., *sheltering thing; small house, hut, cabin,* 33. 14 ; 74. 14.

cāseus, ī, M., *cheese,* 54. 5, 6, 12.

Cassius, ī, M., one of the conspirators against Caesar, 63. 27.

castellum, ī, N. [castrum], *castle ; fort, fortress, stronghold,* 71. 26.

Castor, oris, M., son of Tyndarus and Leda; twin brother of Pollux, 4. 10.

castrum, ī, N., *fortified place ; castle, fortress,* 73. 15 ; commonly pl., castra, ōrum, *mili-*

tary camp, camp, 46. 13 ; 62. 6 ; 72. 25.

cāsus, ūs, M., *a falling ; chance, happening, emergency,* 4. 15 ; cāsū, *by chance,* 16. 23 ; *misfortune, calamity, disaster,* 12. 4 ; 38. 21 ; 71. 2. Cf. calamitās.

Catō, ōnis, M., *Marcus Porcius Cato,* an enemy of Caesar, 64. 27.

catulus, ī, M., dim. [catus, *cat*], *small cat ; whelp, young,* 33. 12.

cauda, ae, F., *tail,* 7. 20.

causa, ae, F., *cause, motive, reason,* 2. 12, 18 ; 3. 19, etc. ; *cause, case, story,* 40. 5 ; 44. 28 ; 68. 10 ; causā as prep. w. gen., *on account of, for the purpose of,* 20. 26; 25. 4 ; 27. 8, etc.

caveō, 2, cāvī, cautus, *be on one's guard ; beware of, guard against,* w. acc., 2. 21 ; 51. 11 ; 64. 4, etc.

cēdō, 3, cessī, cessus, *go from ; withdraw, give way, leave the helm,* 62. 11.

celer, eris, ere, adj., *urged on ; swift, speedy, quick, prompt,* 35. 20.

celeritās, ātis, F. [celer], *swiftness, quickness, speed,* 7. 14, 23 ; 12. 25, etc.

celeriter, adv. [celer], *quickly, speedily, in haste, promptly,* 52. 20 ; compar. celerius, *rather quickly,* 50. 7 ; quam celerrimē, *as quickly as possible,* 2. 18 ; 10. 23 ; 11. 22, etc.

cēlō, 1, *hide from ; keep secret, cover, conceal,* 11. 8 ; 20. 19, 24, etc.

cēna, ae, F., *principal meal ; dinner,* 6. 25; 21. 12 ; 30. 4.

cēnāculum, ī, N. [cēna], *dining-room,* usually in upper story, 7. 1.

cēnō, 1 [cēna], *dine, take dinner,* 22. 22 ; 46. 14.

cēnseō, 2, uī, nsus, *estimate ; be of opinion, think, decide,* 9. 6; 12. 5.

cēnsor, ōris, M., title of a Roman magistrate who exercised general control over public morals; *critic, severe judge of morals,* 57. 5.

cēnsus, ūs, M. [cēnseō], *registering by censors ; list of citizens, census,* 44. 17.

Centaurus, ī, M., *Centaur,* a fabulous creature, half man, half horse, 3. 1.

centum, num. adj., indecl., *one hundred,* 36. 8.

centuria, ae, F. [centum], *division of a hundred ; century,* 36. 10 ; 42. 23; 44. 17.

cernō, 3, crēvī, certus, *separate ; perceive, understand, decide,* 73. 11.

certāmen, inis, N. [certō, contend], *decisive contest ; contest, competition, match,* 33. 15; 40. 11 ; *struggle, battle,* 35. 22 ; 38. 9.

certātim, adv. [certō, contend], *striving with one another ; in rivalry, vigorously, earnestly, eagerly,* 43. 16.

certus, a, um, adj. [p. of cernō], *separated ; certain, definite, unmistakable,* 37. 7 ; *certain, particular,* 73. 27 ; *fixed,* 2. 23 ;

3. 20; 63. 11 ; prō certō, *certainly,* 13. 10 ; certiōrem faciō, *inform,* 6. 4 ; 30. 20; 31. 3, etc.

cessō, 1, freq. [cēdō], *cease ; delay,* 62. 4.

cēterus, a, um, adj.; *the other ;* pl., *the others, the rest,* 23. 25 ; 46. 20 ; 73. 26.

cibus, ī, M., *food, nourishment,* 6. 12 ; 7. 1 ; 19. 2, etc.

Cinna, ae, M., father of Cornelia, Caesar's wife, 58. 3.

circā, prep. w. acc., *about, among, through,* 34. 25; *about, round,* 44. 16 ; 74. 14 ; as adv., *round about, in the vicinity,* 37. 20.

Circaeus, a, um, adj., *of Circe, Circe's,* 31. 8.

Circē, ae or ēs, F., an enchantress, daughter of the Sun, 27. 7.

circiter, adv. [circus], *about, not far from,* 3. 24 ; 74. 27.

circumdō, 1, dedī, datus, *place round ; surround, build round, encircle, enclose,* 42. 4, 23.

circumsistō, 3, stetī or stitī, —, *take a stand around ; stand around, surround,* 38. 24; 64. 9.

circumveniō, 4, vēnī, ventus, *come around ; surround, encompass,* 40. 16 ; 52. 10.

Circus, ī, M., *circular line ; racecourse,* especially the *Circus Maximus* (an oval track between the Palatine and Aventine hills, with room for 100,000 spectators), 42. 21.

cithāroedus, ī, M., *one who sings to the accompaniment of the cithara or lute, harpist,* 4. 10.

citō, 1, freq. [cieō, *stir*], *put into quick motion; urge, spur on,* 46. 16.

cīvīlis, e, adj. [cīvis], *of citizens; popular, civil,* 63. 1, 11.

cīvis, is, M. and F., *dweller; citizen, fellow-citizen,* 15. 17 ; 37. 29; 40. 10, etc.

cīvitās, ātis, F. [cīvis], *condition of a citizen; community, state,* 37. 20 ; 38. 1, 3, etc.

clādēs, is, F., *destruction, loss, defeat,* 60. 25.

clam, adv. and prep.: as adv., *secretly,* 62. 6 ; 68. 16 ; 73. 23, etc.; as prep. w. abl., *without the knowledge of, unknown to,* 8. 23.

clāmitō, 1, freq. [clāmō], *cry aloud; bawl, shout,* 19. 11 ; 35. 26.

clāmō, 1, *call, cry out, shout,* 64. 12.

clāmor, ōris, M., *calling; shouting, shouts, noise, shriek, cry,* 23. 17, 20, 23, etc.

clandestīnus, a, um, adj. [clam], *secret, hidden,* 42. 1.

clangor, ōris, M., *calling; noise, sound,* 42. 12.

clārus, a, um, adj., *clear, loud,* 53. 21 ; *distinguished, famous, eminent;* superl., 58. 19.

classis, is, F., *calling; class* (great division of people according to property), 44. 17 ; *fleet,* 59. 6, 7; 62. 2, etc.

claudō, 3, sī, sus, *shut; close, shut,* 37. 20 ; 46. 25.

clēmentia, ae, F. [clēmēns, *mild*], *mildness, moderation, mercy, kindness,* 70. 9 ; 74. 8.

Clīniās, ae, M., father of Alcibiades, 66. 1.

coāctus. See cōgō.

(coepiō), 3, coepī, coeptus [for coapiō], *lay hold of; make a beginning, begin, commence,* 9. 15; 10. 13; 12. 3, etc.

coerceō, 2, cuī, citus [arceō], *enclose together; keep back, restrain, check,* 63. 17.

cōgitātiō, ōnis, F. [cōgitō], *thinking; thought, resolution, project, plan,* 42. 16; 73. 19. Cf. cōnsilium.

cōgitō, 1 [agitō], *consider thoroughly; ponder, weigh, reflect upon,* 22. 17.

cōgnōmen, inis, N., *surname, second name,* 60. 19.

cōgnōscō, 3, gnōvī, gnitus, *become acquainted with; learn, ascertain, find out, know,* 5. 14, 27 ; 6. 5, etc.

cōgō, 3, ēgī, āctus [agō], *drive together; drive, urge, compel, force,* 53. 9; 58. 9; 68. 20, etc. Cf. compellō, 33. 20.

Colchī, ōrum, M., *inhabitants of Colchis, Colchians,* 8. 2.

Colchis, idis, F., a district east of the Black Sea, 3. 9.

Collātia, ae, F., a Sabine town near Rome, 46. 18.

Collātīnus, a, um, adj., *of Collatia.* See Tarquinius, 46. 13.

collis, is, M., *elevation; hill, mount,* 36. 21 ; 40. 14.

collum, ī, N., *neck,* 51. 20.

colō, 3, uī, cultus, *till; cultivate, devote oneself to, follow, practice,* 36. 20 ; 59. 20; *worship,* 36. 22 ; *dwell in, inhabit,* 5. 19.

color, ōris, M., *color, hue, tint,* 16. 5.

columba, ae, F., *dove,* 7. 18.

comes, itis, M. and F., *one who goes with ; companion, friend, associate, attendant,* 5. 18, 23; 53. 9, etc.

cōmitās, ātis, F. [cōmis, *courteous*], *courtesy, kindness, gentleness,* 59. 1.

Comitium, ī, N., *a coming together;* place for the assembly of the Romans when voting by curiae, 59. 27.

commendātiō, ōnis, F. [commendō, *commit*], *entrusting ; excellence, worth, attraction,* 66. 9.

commigrō, 1, *entirely remove ; remove* (*to*)*, enter,* 42. 10.

comminīscor, 3, mentus, *devise, invent, contrive,* 66. 21.

committō, 3, mīsī, mīssus, *bring together ; consign, deliver, entrust,* 3. 10 ; 29. 2.

commoror, 1, *delay, linger, wait,* 4. 14, 21 ; 25. 25.

commoveō, 2, mōvī, mōtus, *put in violent motion ; move, excite, disturb, provoke,* 8. 6 ; 10. 17 ; 16. 2, etc. ; *alarm,* 30. 23; 74. 4 ; *move, induce, influence, lead,* 16. 18.

commūniō, 4, *fortify on all sides, intrench, barricade,* 71. 26.

commūnis, e, adj., *common, general, public,* 68. 27.

commūniter, adv. [commūnis], *in common, jointly, together,* 44. 20.

commūtātiō, ōnis, F. [commūtō], *entire change, alteration,* 69. 27.

commūtō, 1, *wholly change ; change entirely,* 58. 8.

compār, paris, adj., *like ; equal, suitable, on equal terms,* 35. 3.

comparō, 1, *make ready, provide, prepare,* 4. 15; 31. 23; 74. 11, etc.; *establish, make,* 42. 17 ; *plot, contrive, devise,* 28. 10.

comparō, 1 [compār], *bring together as equal ; compare,* 34. 3.

compellō, 3, pulī, pulsus, *drive together; drive, force, constrain, compel,* 33. 20 ; 58. 4. Cf. cōgō, 53. 9.

compellō, 1, *accost ; accuse, arraign,* 67. 27.

comperiō, 4, perī, pertus, *obtain knowledge of ; find out, ascertain,* 73. 1.

complector, 3, plexus, *fold together ; embrace, enfold,* 29. 1 ; 42. 15.

complōrātiō, ōnis, F. [complōrō, *bewail*], *lamentation, loud crying, wailing,* 39. 19.

complūrēs, a or ia, *more together ; not a few, several, a number, many,* 41. 24 ; 70. 8.

compōnō, 3, posuī, positus, *bring together ; quiet, settle, bring to an end, lay aside,* 72. 17.

comportō, 1, *bring together ; collect, gather together,* 3. 21. Cf. conligō, 13. 14.

compositus, a, um, adj. [p. of compōnō], *well-placed ;* ex compositō, *by agreement, by a preconcerted plan,* 43. 17.

comprehendō, 3, dī, ēnsus, *bind together ; catch, seize, take prisoner,* 58. 9 ; 61. 4.

cŏnātus, ūs, m. [cōnor], *attempt,
enterprise, undertaking,* **21**. 23.

concĭliō, 1 [concilium, *meeting*],
*procure by consultation ; bring
about, acquire, obtain, win,* **36**.
4 ; **37**. 23.

concĭpiō, **3**, cēpī, ceptus [capiō],
*take together ; think of, con-
ceive,* **43**. 3.

concĭtō, 1, freq. [conciō, *stir up*],
*put in quick motion ; rouse,
impel, stir up, goad on,* **40**. 13.

conclāmō, 1, *cry out together ;
cry aloud, shout,* **38**. 22 ; **46**.
23.

concordia, ae, f. [concors, *of the
same mind*], *agreeing together ;
harmony, agreement,* **50**. 1, 5 ;
52. 20, etc.

concupīscō, **3**, īvī, ītus, inch.
[cupiō], *long for, be very desirous of, aspire to,* **59**. 16; **71**. 23.

✓ concurrō, **3**, rī or cucurrī, cursus,
run together, dash together, **7**.
14, 21 ; **10**. 10 ; *rush together
in battle, join battle, fight,* **38**.
17; *hurry, hasten,* **12**. 8.

✓ concursus, ūs, m. [concurrō],
*running together ; onset, en-
counter, shock,* **38**. 18.

condemnō, 1 [damnō], *condemn
entirely ; find guilty, condemn
to death, doom,* **39**. 26.

condĭciō, ōnis, f., *agreement,
terms ; condition, situation, circumstance,* **53**. 14.

✓ condō, **3**, didī, ditus, *put together ;
build, establish, found,* **34**. 11 ;
42. 6 ; *put away, lay up, store,*
20. 5 ; **47**. 16.

condūcō, **3**, dūxī, ductus, *draw
together ; induce, lead,* **51**. 18.

cŏnectō, **3**, —, nexus, *bind together, join, tie,* **24**. 14.

cŏnferō, ferre, tulī, lātus, *bring
together ; gather, collect, pile,
heap,* **63**. 13; **74**. 13 ; w. sē,
betake oneself, go, **2**. 18; **8**.
4 ; **9**. 9, etc.; *bestow, confer,*
31. 16 ; **48**. 14.

cŏnfestim, adv., *immediately,* ✓
without delay, at once, **59**. 5.

cŏnficiō, **3**, fēcī, fectus [faciō],
*make completely ; accomplish,
do,* **9**. 3, 17, 23 ; **10**. 17, etc. ;
make, work, **26**. 5 ; **39**. 18 ;
bring to an end, **63**. 1 ; *weaken,
exhaust, overcome,* **10**. 14 ; **14**.
7, 17, etc. ; *finish, kill,* **39**. 13 ;
74. 15.

cŏnfīdentia, ae, f. [cōnfīdēns,
trusting], *confidence, boldness,
assurance,* **47**. 12.

cŏnfīrmō, 1, *make firm ; make
steady,* **9**. 1 ; *affirm, assert,* **16**.
2 ; **19**. 1 ; **30**. 24.

cŏnflagrō, 1, *burn completely ;
burn, burn up, be destroyed by
fire,* **41**. 4.

cŏnflīgō, **3**, flīxī, flīctus, *strike together ; strike, dash together,*
7. 19 ; *contend, fight, be at war,*
44. 5 ; **72**. 14, 17.

cŏnflō, 1, *blow up ; bring about,* ✓
produce, cause, incur, **60**. 2.

cŏnfluō, **3**, flūxī, —, *flow together ;
flock together, assemble, be
gathered,* **70**. 14.

cŏnfodiō, **3**, fōdī, fossus, *dig up ;
transfix, stab, pierce,* **52**. 11 ;
63. 29; **64**. 17.

cŏnfugiō, **3**, fūgī, —, *flee, take
refuge, run for protection,* **34**.
23; **61**. 28.

congressus, ūs, M., *coming together; meeting, conference, in-
terview*, 37. 27.

congruō, 3, uī, —, *come together;
agree, coincide, correspond,*
34. 6.

cōniciō, 3, iēcī, iectus [iaciō],
*throw together; throw, hurl,
cast,* 10. 10; 13. 10; 15. 7, etc.

coniungō, 3, iūnxī, iūnctus,
*fasten together; join, unite,
connect,* w. acc. and dat., 42. 5;
45. 9.

coniūnx, ugis, M. and F., *one
joined with another; husband,*
15. 16; 44. 1; 45. 13, etc.;
wife, 33. 14; 35. 7; 42. 9, etc.
Cf. vir; uxor.

coniūrātiō, ōnis, F. [coniūrō],
*uniting in oath; conspiracy,
plot,* 67. 25.

coniūrātus, a, um, adj. [p. of
coniūrō], *bound together with
an oath;* as noun, M. pl., *conspirators,* 64. 9, 13.

coniūrō, 1, *swear together; con-
spire, plot, pledge oneself,* 46.
24; 63. 27.

conlābor, 3, lapsus, *fall together;
sink, fall,* 52. 12.

conlēga (collēga), ae, M., *partner
in office, colleague, associate,* 60.
1, 10; 63. 24, etc.

conligō, 3, lēgī, lēctus [legō,
gather], *gather together; get
together, pick up, collect,* 13. 14;
71. 27. Cf. comportō, 3. 21.

conloquium, ī, N. [conloquor],
*talking with; conference, con-
versation,* 37. 24.

conloquor, 3, cūtus, *talk, confer,
parley,* 69. 20.

cōnor, 1, *undertake; seek, try,
attempt,* 5. 20; 7. 1; 19. 9, etc.

conqueror, 3, questus, *lament,
deplore, complain (of), accuse,*
45. 24; 48. 11.

cōnscendō, 3, ndī, ēnsus
[scandō], *climb together;
mount,* 16. 20; *go on board,
embark on,* 12. 14; 25. 7; 62. 6.

cōnscrībō, 3, īpsī, īptus, *write together; enlist, enroll, levy,
raise,* 41. 23.

cōnsecrō, 1 [sacrō, *make sacred*],
consecrate, dedicate, devote,
37. 1.

cōnsecūtus. See cōnsequor.

cōnsēnsiō, ōnis, F. [cōnsentiō],
*agreeing together; combination,
plot, conspiracy,* 67. 11.

cōnsēnsus, ūs, M. [cōnsentiō],
agreement; abl. w. omnium,
*by common consent, unani-
mously,* 27. 16.

cōnsentiō, 4, sēnsī, sēnsus, *agree
together; agree, accord, unite,*
75. 5.

cōnsequor, 3, secūtus, *follow up;
overtake, catch up, reach,* 39. 8;
follow, succeed, 5. 11; *attain,
acquire, get,* 42. 19; 46. 2; 67.
1, etc.

cōnserō, 3, uī, sertus, *bind together; join, begin, fight,* 35.
23; w. manus, *fight hand to
hand, come to close quarters,*
38. 20.

cōnsīderō, 1, *look at closely, regard attentively, examine,* 34. 3.

cōnsīdō, 3, sēdī, sessus, *sit down
together; take a position, station
oneself, form,* 38. 15; 55. 10;
56. 20, etc.

cōnsilium, ī, N., *deliberation ; counsel, advice,* 10. 7 ; 36. 9 ; *design, purpose,* 7. 12 ; 8. 21 ; *plan, scheme,* 3. 8 ; 8. 23 ; 9. 7 ; 13. 5, etc.; *will, intention,* 16. 23 ; 24. 2 ; *sagacity, wisdom, foresight, ability,* 22. 15 ; 44. 3 ; 66. 6, etc. Cf. cōgitātiō.

cōnsistō, 3, stitī, stitus, *stand together ; stand still, halt, stop, hold,* 61. 22.

cōnspectus, ūs, M., *seeing ; sight, view,* 13. 16 ; 26. 13 ; 36. 13, etc.

cōnspiciō, 3, spēxī, spectus, *look at attentively ; see, perceive,* 12. 6 ; 40. 2.

cōnspicor, 1, *get sight of, descry, espy, see,* 48. 16 ; 49. 11 ; 51. 3, etc.

cōnstantia, ae, F. [cōnstāns, *standing together*], *firmness ; perseverance, steadiness, faithfulness,* 47. 12.

✓ cōnsternō, 1, *confound, terrify, alarm ;* pf. p., *panic-stricken,* 35. 25.

cōnstituō, 3, uī, ūtus, *put together ; set up, place, station,* 72. 6 ; *establish, make, constitute,* 36. 10 ; *rear, build, found, dedicate,* 36. 21 ; 74. 3 ; *arrange, determine on, appoint, fix,* 2. 24 ; 9. 9 ; 27. 22, etc.; *determine, decide, resolve,* 2. 7 ; 3. 11 ; 10. 21, etc.

cōnstō, 1, stitī, stātūrus, *stand with ; consist of,* 9. 6 ; 18. 25 ; cōnstat, impers., *it is agreed* or *known,* 17. 2 ; 18. 7 ; 47. 16, etc.

cōnsuēscō, 3, suēvī, suētus, *accus-* *tom ;* usually in perfect system, *be accustomed, be wont,* 4. 4 ; 22. 23 ; 68. 23, etc.

cōnsuētūdō, inis, F., *custom, habit, usage,* 68. 1 ; 75. 17. Cf. mōs.

cōnsul, ulis, M., *consul,* highest magistrate of the Roman people, 60. 5, 18, 19, etc.

cōnsulātus, ūs, M. [cōnsul], *office of consul, consulship, consulate,* 60. 21 ; 61. 17 ; 63. 24.

cōnsulō, 3, uī, ltus, *consider ; consult, inquire of, seek counsel,* 2. 17 ; 47. 18.

cōnsūmō, 3, psī, ptus, *take together ; spend, pass, consume,* 3. 24 ; 18. 11 ; 31. 17 ; *exhaust, overcome,* 53. 3.

contegō, 3, tēxī, tēctus, *cover up,* ✓ *conceal,* 74. 25.

contemnō, 3, tempsī, temptus, *value little, disdain, despise,* 48. 9 ; 51. 8 ; 53. 10.

contemplor, 1, *gaze at ; think over, consider, reflect on,* 53. 21. Cf. cōgitō, 22. 17.

contemptus, ūs, M., *despising ; contempt, scorn,* 55. 10.

contendō, 3, dī, tus, *strive ; strive, exert oneself,* 7. 23 ; 12. 24 ; 19. 19, etc. ; *hasten, hurry,* 11. 7 ; 24. 24 ; 45. 11, etc.; *ask, solicit, entreat,* 58. 14.

contentiō, ōnis, F., *straining together ; straining, exertion,* 51. 4 ; *dispute, quarrel, controversy,* 34. 12. Cf. contrōversia, 10. 12.

contentus, a, um, adj. [p. of contineō], *content, satisfied, pleased,* 73. 17.

contexō, 3, uī, tus, *weave, make,* ✓ 16. 4.

contineō, 2, uī, tentus [teneō], *hold together ; hold in check, restrain,* 37. 29.

continuus, a, um, adj., *holding together ; continuous, successive, in succession.*

contiō, ōnis, F. [for conventiō], *coming together; meeting, assembly,* 36. 12, 17 ; 67. 27, etc.

contrā, adv. and prep., *in opposition; on the other hand, while,* 69. 18 ; 72. 9, 21 ; as prep. w. acc., *against,* 9. 13 ; 29. 21 ; 62. 27.

contrahō, 3, āxī, actus, *draw together ; contract, assemble, collect, get together,* 59. 6.

contrārius, a, um, adj. [contrā], *lying over against ; opposite, contrary,* 61. 5.

contrōversia, ae, F. [contrōversus, *disputed*], *dispute, quarrel, contention,* 10. 12 ; 27. 15. Cf. contentiō, 34. 12.

contulī. See cōnferō.

cōnūbium, ī, N., *wedding together; marriage, alliance by marriage,* 34. 25 ; 35. 3.

convalēscō, 3, uī, — , inch., *grow wholly well ; recover, regain health,* 44. 12.

conveniō, 4, vēnī, ventus, *come together ; assemble, gather, flock together,* 2. 23, 25 ; 3. 20, etc. ; *meet,* 73. 21 ; *agree, accord, be suited* (*to*), 67. 15. Cf. congruō, 34. 6.

convertō, 3, ti, sus, *turn completely ; turn, direct, fix, draw,* 35. 8 ; 61. 4, 23, etc.; *change, transform,* 28. 18 ; 29. 16 ; 30. 10, etc.; pass., *turn oneself,* 63. 1.

convincō, 3, vīcī, vīctus, *overcome ; convict, expose,* 63. 6.

convīvium, ī, N., *living together ; feast, banquet,* 28. 11 ; 46. 17.

convocō, 1, *call together, summon, assemble,* 23. 10; 27. 11 ; 31. 19, etc.

coörior, 4, ortus, *come forth ; arise, appear, break, burst,* 4. 24 ; 18. 14 ; 26. 23, etc.

cophinus, ī, M., *basket,* 60. 11.

cōpia, ae, F. [ops], *abundance ; supply, amount,* 5. 14 ; 20. 4 ; pl., *forces, troops,* 62. 3; 72. 14 ; *number,* 63. 12.

cōpiōsē, adv. [cōpiōsus, *plentiful*], *in great abundance,* 52. 7.

cōram, adv. and prep. [ōs], *before the face;* as prep. w. abl., *before, in the presence of,* 48. 5.

Corinthus, ī, F., *Corinth,* 15. 21.

corium, ī, N., *skin, hide, leather,* 26. 5.

Cornēlia, ae, F., *wife of Julius Caesar and daughter of L. Cornelius Cinna,* 58. 2.

cornū, ūs, N., *horn,* 56. 19.

corōna, ae, F., *garland, wreath,* 70. 26.

corpus, oris, N., *thing formed ; body, form,* 6. 9 ; 9. 1, 3, etc. ; *dead body, corpse,* 45. 16.

corrigō, 3, rēxī, rēctus [regō], *make straight; set right, amend, make up for,* 40. 12 ; 61. 8 ; 63. 2.

corripiō, 3, uī, reptus [rapiō], *seize, snatch up, grasp,* 21. 7 ; 22. 6 ; 25. 13, etc.

corrumpō, 3, rūpī, ruptus, *destroy; bribe, buy over, corrupt,* 71. 18.

corruŏ, 3, uī, —, *fall together ;
fall, sink down,* 53. 4.

✔ corvus, ī, M., *raven,* 54. 5, 7.

cōs, cōtis, F., *flint-stone, whet-
stone,* 43. 5.

cottīdiē, adv. [quot, diēs], *daily,
every day,* 50. 12.

Crassus, ī, M., *Marcus Crassus,*
a contemporary of Caesar,
60. 6.

crātēra, ae, F., *mixing-bowl ;
wine* or *punch-bowl, bowl,* 22.
24 ; 23. 2, 4.

crēbrŏ, adv. [crēber, *frequent*],
*repeatedly, frequently, often,
many times,* 55. 14.

crēdŏ, 3, didī, ditus, *put faith in ;
believe, suppose, hold true,* 26.
18 ; 28. 2 ; 36. 15, etc.

cremŏ, 1, *burn, consume with
fire,* 74. 25.

✔ creŏ, 1, *bring forth ; cause to be,
choose, make, select,* 15. 19 ; 37.
2 ; 38. 5, etc.

Creŏn, ontis, M., *king of Corinth,*
15. 21.

crēscŏ, 3, ēvī, ētus, *come into
being ; be enlarged, increase,
grow,* 40. 22 ; 69. 18 ; 72. 2.

✔ crīmen, inis, N., *judgment ; crime,
fault, offence,* 67. 27.

✔ crīnis, is, M., *hair, locks, tresses,*
36. 2 ; 39. 18.

Critiās, ae (ī), M., *one of the
Thirty Tyrants at Athens,*
73. 26.

✔ cruciātus, ūs, M. [cruciō, *put to
the rack*], *torture, torment,* 16.
12.

crūdēlis, e, adj. [crūdus, *bloody*],
*cruel, fierce, pitiless, barbarous,
painful,* 27. 13 ; superl., 6. 7.

crūdēlitās, ātis, F. [crūdēlis],
cruelty, harshness, severity,
68. 15.

cruentus, a, um, adj., *spotted with
blood ; stained, marked,* 56. 7.

crux, crucis, F., *gallows, cross,*
59. 10.

culex, icis, M., *gnat, midge,* 56. 19.

culpa, ae, F., *fault, error, blame,* ✔
neglect, 70. 18 ; 71. 17.

culpŏ, 1 [culpa], *blame, censure,
reproach.*

culter, trī, M., *that which cuts ;* ✔
knife, razor, 46. 23.

cultus, ūs, M., *care ; way of life,
personal life,* 75. 14.

cum, prep. w. abl., *with, together
with, attended by,* 4. 17 ; 5.
1, 5, etc.

cum, conj., *when, while, after,
since, although,* 2. 9, 10, 13,
etc. ; cum prīmum, *as soon as,*
53. 12 ; 54. 7 ; cum . . . tum,
not only . . . but also, 72. 2.

cūnae, ārum, F., *cradle,* 56. 2, 5, ✔
7, etc.

cunctor, 1, *delay, linger, hesitate.* ✔
Cf. moror.

cupiditās, ātis, F. [cupidus], ✔
*longing; desire, ambition, eager-
ness,* 2. 3 ; 14. 14 ; 27. 4.

cupīdŏ, inis, F., *desire, wish,
longing,* 18. 12.

cupidus, a, um, adj., *longing,* ✔
desirous, eager, anxious, 26. 3 ;
56. 13.

cupiŏ, 3, īvī, ītus, *long for; desire,
wish,* 58. 15 ; 73. 20.

cūr, interrog. adv. [cuī reī], *why?*
10. 11 ; 35. 2 ; 48. 16.

Curēs, ium, F., *ancient capital of
the Sabines,* 36. 24.

cūria, ae, F., *court, ward, curia*,
36. 11 ; *senate-house*, 45. 11, 14 ;
60. 14.

Cūriātius, ī, M., one of the
Curiatii, 38. 11.

cūrō, 1 [cūra, *care*], *care for, take
care.*

currō, 3, cucurrī, cursus, *move
quickly ; run, rush, hasten*,
15. 2.

currus, ūs, M., *a running ; chariot,
car*, 16. 18, 20.

cursus, ūs, M., *running*, 39. 11 ;
course (of a ship), 4. 24; 6. 1 ;
18. 15, etc.; *passage, movement,
course*, 13. 10; 37. 17 ; 63.
3.

curūlis, e, adj., w. sella, *curule
chair, official seat*, 37. 3.

custōdiō, 4 [custōs], *watch ; protect, watch over, guard, preserve*,
11. 15; 37. 15 ; 56. 2.

custōs, ōdis, M. and F., *guard ;* ✓
*watchman, watcher, guardian,
guard*, 56. 4, 8 ; 68. 17, etc.

Cyclōps, ōpis, M. [Grk., *round
eye*], one of the fabulous giants
on the coast of Italy, 20. 11.

Cȳmē, ēs, F., a city of Aetolia,
71. 14.

Cȳrus, ī, M., brother of the Persian king Artaxerxes, 73. 22.

Cyzicus, ī, F., a city in Mysia,
4. 20.

D

Dācī, ōrum, M., *Dacians*, a warlike tribe in modern upper
Hungary, 63. 16.

damnō, 1 [damnum], *adjudge
guilty ; sentence, doom, condemn*, 68. 18 ; 71. 5.

damnum, ī, N., *damage, hurt,
harm, injury*, 25. 16.

Dārēius, ī, M., king of Persia,
69. 16.

dē, prep. w. abl., *about, concern-
ing, for*, 2. 14; 12. 3 ; 20. 12,
etc. ; *over*, 42. 22.

dea, ae, F., *goddess ; nymph*, 37.
24, 27.

dēbeō, 2, uī, itus [for dehibeō
(habeō)], *withhold, owe ;* w.
infin., *ought, must, should*, 45.
1 ; 55. 4 ; pass. *be due*, 54. 17.

dēbitus, a, um, adj. [p. of dēbeō],
*owed ; due, appropriate, be-
coming*, 25. 10 ; 30. 22.

dēcēdō, 3, cessī, cessus, *go away;
withdraw, depart, go away*,
45. 15.

Decelēa, ae, F., a town in northern
Attica, 69. 2.

decem, num. adj., indecl., *ten*, 3.
24 ; 17. 1 ; 18. 11, etc.

dēcernō, 3, crēvī, crētus, *decide,
determine*, 34. 13 ; 68. 6 ; *vote,
decree*, 63. 28 ; 64. 23 ; 71. 10.

decimus, a, um, adj. [decem],
tenth, 18. 17 ; sextus et decimus, *sixteenth*, 58. 2.

dēcipiō, 3, cēpī, ceptus [capiō], ✓
*take off one's guard ; deceive,
entrap, ensnare, catch*, 69. 14.

dēclārō, 1, *disclose ; set forth,
make manifest, prove, show*.
49. 8.

decōrus, a, um, adj. [decor, *come-
liness*], *becoming ; beautiful,
handsome, adorned*, 48. 13.

dēcrētus. See dēcernō.

√ dēcurrō, 3, cucurrī or currī, cursus, *run* or *hasten down, rush to the shore,* 5. 6.

decus, oris, N., *grace ; splendor, ornament, adornment,* 44. 19.

√ dēcutiō, 3, cussī, cussus [quatiō], *shake off ; strike off,* 46. 8.

dēdō, 3, didī, ditus, *give from ; give up, resign, surrender, yield,* 22. 13; 31. 10; 41. 17, etc.

dēdūcō, 3, dūxī, ductus, *take* or *carry down, bring,* 27. 16; *conduct, escort, accompany,* 39. 15; *launch,* 4. 16 ; 11. 6; 12. 21, etc.

dēfatīgātiō, ōnis, F. [dēfatīgō], *a wearying ; weariness, fatigue, exhaustion.*

dēfatīgō, 1, *weary out ; exhaust, tire,* 51. 5 ; 53. 20.

dēfendō, 3, ndī, ēnsus, *ward off ; protect, defend,* 19. 11 ; 33. 19; 55. 4, etc.

dēferō, ferre, tulī, lātus, *bring away ; drive off, carry, force,* 18. 17 ; *refer, bring before,* 60. 9.

dēficiō, 3, fēcī, fectus [faciō], *make from ;* intr., *be wanting, fail, run out,* 5. 15 ; 27. 10.

dēfōrmitās, ātis, F. [dēfōrmis, *misshapen*], *blemish, deformity,* 64. 21 ; *ugliness, hideousness,* 48. 6.

dēfūnctus, a, um, adj. ~~(p. of dēfungor, have done with),~~ *dead,* 61. 10.

dēiciō, 3, iēcī, iectus [iaciō], *throw down ; bring down, let fall,* 43. 19 ; *throw down, push down,* 45. 12 ; 55. 8; 67. 8 ; *cast, drive, force,* 5. 2.

dein, adv. = deinde, 64. 15; 68. 17 ; 69. 2.

deinceps, adv. *one after another, in turn,* 38. 2.

deinde, adv., *from here ; then, afterwards, next,* 24. 16; 33. 15, 16, etc. ; *from that time on, thereafter,* 40. 25 ; *hereafter,* 34. 19. Cf. tum.

dēlābor, 3, lapsus, *glide down ; fall, descend,* 16. 26; 37. 10 ; 54. 12.

dēleō, 2, ēvī, ētus, *erase ; destroy, overthrow,* 41. 24 ; *bring to an end, finish,* 73. 4.

dēlīberābundus, a, um, adj. [dēlīberō, *ponder*], *pondering, reflecting, in a "brown study,"* 46. 6.

dēlīrō, 1, —, — [dēlīrus, *silly*], *be crazy, dote, rave,* 47. 8.

dēlīctum, ī, N., *failing ; fault, offence, crime,* 72. 22. Cf. culpa, 70. 18.

dēligō, 3, lēgī, lēctus [legō], *choose from ; pick out, select, choose,* 4. 14 ; 22. 18; 24. 14, etc.

dēlinquō, 3, līquī, lictus, *fail ; do wrong, transgress, sin,* 57. 5.

Delphī, ōrum, M., a Phocian city, famous for its oracle, 2. 17.

dēmigrō, 1, *go off, depart, emigrate,* 68. 23.

dēmittō, 3, mīsī, mīssus, *send down, let fall, hurl,* 37. 5 ; *lose,* 22. 1; pf. p. dēmīssus, *downcast, dejected, low,* 13. 20.

dēmōnstrō, 1, *point out ; show, indicate, tell, prove,* 2. 19 ; 3. 7, 14, etc.

dēnegō, 1, *reject, refuse, deny,* 58. 13.

dēns, dentis, M., *tooth*, 8. 15; 9. 18, 20, etc.

dēnuō, adv. [dē novō], *once more, a second time, again*, 47. 10. Cf. iterum.

dēpellō, 3, pulī, pulsus, *drive out, drive from*, 72. 16; *remove, banish, satisfy, appease*, 21. 13; 30. 5; *turn aside, divert*, 21. 1.

dēplōrō, 1, *weep bitterly, bewail, lament*, 53. 7.

dēpōnō, 3, posuī, positus, *put down* or *away, lay aside*, 53. 20; *give up*, 13. 5; 21. 11; *appease*, 21. 13.

dēportō, 1, *carry off, bring home*, 68. 13.

dēprecor, 1, *avert by prayer; pray, intercede, plead*, 58. 12.

dēprehendō, 3, dī, ēnsus, *take away; surprise, come upon, discover*, 46. 17; 55. 1.

dēpulsō, 1, —, —, freq., *thrust away; keep off, repel*, 55. 4.

dērīdeō, 2, rīsī, rīsus, *laugh at; scoff at, mock*, 47. 5.

dēripiō, 3, uī, reptus [rapiō], *tear from* or *away, snatch*, 11. 17, 21.

dēscendō, 3, dī, ēnsus [scandō, *climb*], *climb down; come down, go down*, 31. 20; 45. 2; 49. 1, etc.; *descend, alight*, 37. 5.

dēscīscō, 3, īvī, ītus, *withdraw, desert, be unfaithful*, 69. 11.

dēscrībō, 3, psī, ptus, *write off; portion off, allot, assign, divide*, 37. 17.

dēserō, 3, uī, rtus, *unbind; leave, forsake, desert*, 10. 26; 38. 23; 56. 12.

dēsīderium, ī, N., [dēsīderō] *longing, wish, desire*, 31. 18.

dēsīderō, 1, *greatly desire, long for.* Cf. cupiō, 58. 15.

dēsiliō, 4, iluī, ultus [saliō,], *leap down, jump overboard*, 29. 7.

dēsipiō, 3, —, — [sapiō], *be void of understanding, be silly, act foolishly*, 47. 4.

dēsistō, 3, stitī, stitus, *stay from; leave off, cease, stop, give up*, 13. 17; 21. 23; 31. 27.

dēspērō, 1, *be hopeless; have no hope, despair of, give up*, 12. 3; 21. 25; 22. 16; 51. 9.

dēspondeō, 2, dī, ōnsus, *promise to give; promise in marriage, betroth*, 39. 16; w. animōs, *be despondent.*

dēstinō, 1, *make fast; fix upon, design, resolve*, 63. 10.

dēstituō, 3, uī, ūtus [statuō], *set down; forsake, abandon, desert, disappoint*, 69. 23.

dēsum, esse, fuī, *be from; be wanting, fail*, 34. 22.

dēsuper, adv., *from above, from overhead*, 7. 4.

dētegō, 3, ēxī, ēctus, *uncover, expose, bare*, 65. 3.

dēterior, ius, gen. iōris [dē], *lower; worse, poorer, harder*, 53. 14.

dēterreō, 2, uī, itus, *frighten off; discourage, prevent, deter*, 29. 19; 42. 24.

dētineō, 2, uī, tentus [teneō], *hold off; detain, keep a prisoner*, 61. 15.

dētractor, ōris, M., *disparager.*

dētrahō, 3, āxī, actus, *draw off; take* or *throw off, remove*, 53. 6; 61. 5.

deūrō, 3, ūssī, ūstus, *burn up, destroy*, 47. 6.

deus, ī, M., *god, deity,* 7. 24, 26;
8. 8, etc.

✓ dēvinciō, 4, nxī, nctus, *bind fast;
lay under obligation, attach to
oneself,* 67. 17.

dēvincō, 3, vīcī, vīctus, *conquer
completely, overcome, subdue,*
62. 26.

dēvorō, 1, *swallow eagerly; gulp
down, devour, consume,* 21. 8;
22. 7; 23. 8, etc.

✓ dēvōtiō, ōnis, F. [dēvoveō], *curs-
ing, outlawry,* 68. 21; 71. 7.

dēvoveō, 2, vōvī, vōtus, *vow away;
curse, execrate,* 68. 20; 71. 7.

✓ dextera or dextra, ae, F. [dexter,
right, sc. manus], *right hand,*
61. 5.

diadēma, atis, N., *royal head-
dress, crown,* 63. 25.

Diāna, ae, F. [for Dīvāna], *shining one; goddess Diana,* 44. 20.

dīcō, 3, dīxī, dictus, *say,* 14. 23;
declare, tell, assert, 8. 11;
18. 6, etc.; *call, name,* 45.
18; *name, appoint,* 2. 24; 3.
20; *plead,* 68. 10; dīcendī,
speaking, oratory, 58. 19; *pronounce (judgment),* 63. 6.

dictātor, ōris, M. [dictō, *dictate*],
dictator, a Roman magistrate
with unlimited power, chosen
in great emergencies, 63. 20.

dictum, ī, N. [dīcō], *something
said; command, order, words,*
44. 13.

✓ diēs, iēī, M., *light; day,* 2. 9, 23,
24, etc., in diēs, *day by day,*
63. 10.

difficilis, e, adj. [facilis], *not easy;
hard, difficult, perilous,* 3. 16;
8. 10.

difficultās, ātis, F. [difficilis],
difficulty, trouble, 9. 12; 11. 13.

diffīdō, 3, fīsus sum, *distrust;
despair, have no hope,* 74. 15.

digitus, ī, M., *finger,* 55. 2.

dīgnitās, ātis, F. [dīgnus], *worthi-
ness; rank, authority, distinction, honor,* 42. 18; 44. 1; 61.
14; *magnificence, splendor,*
75. 8.

dīgredior, 3, gressus, *go apart;
go away, depart,* 47. 15.

dīlaniō, 1, *tear to pieces, strip off,* ✓
55. 21.

dīligentia, ae, F. [dīligēns, *industrious*], *attentiveness; care, in-
dustry, diligence, application,* 4.
1; 9. 16, 19, etc.

dīligō, 3, lēxī, lēctus [legō], *single
out; esteem, love,* 71. 21.

dīlūoēscō, 3, lūxī, —, inch. [dīlū- ✓
ceō, *shine forth*], *grow light,
dawn,* 5. 7.

dīmicātiō, ōnis, F. [dīmicō], *fighting, struggle, fight,* 46. 11.

dīmicō, 1, *contend, fight,* 35. 25;
38. 12; 44. 5, etc.

dīmittō, 3, mīsī, mīssus, *send
different ways; send out, despatch,* 2. 23; 3. 18; 59. 2;
let go, drop, 55. 2; *renounce,
divorce, neglect,* 73. 3.

dīrigō, 3, ēxī, ēctus [regō], *lay
straight; direct, aim, steer,
drive,* 62. 9.

dīruō, 3, uī, utus, *tear apart;
overthrow, demolish, destroy,*
40. 20.

dīrus, a, um, adj, *ill-omened;
fearful, dreadful, violent,* 6. 6;
16. 5, 12.

discēdō, 3, cessī, cessus, *go apart;*

depart, go away, leave, 31. 12; 51. 5; 61. 16, etc. ; ē vītā, *die*, 14. 10; *separate, open*, 7. 21.

discordia, ae, F. [discors, *inharmonious*], *disunion, dissension, discord*, 52. 21.

discordō, 1, —, — [discors, *inharmonious*], *be at variance, quarrel*, 52. 16.

discrīmen, inis, N., *that which decides ; peril, risk, danger,* 10. 25 ; 12. 23 ; 22. 3, etc.

discurrō, 3, rī and cucurrī, cursus, *run different ways, run hither and thither, run about*, 35. 9.

disertus, a, um, adj. [p. of disserō, *examine*], *tested ; skilful, clever, fluent*, 66. 8.

dīsiciō, 3, iēcī, iectus [iaciō], *throw about ; scatter, disperse*, 18. 16.

dīspergō, 3, sī, sus [spargō], *scatter, disperse.*

displiceō, 2, uī, itus · [placeō], *displease, be unsatisfactory*, 60. 7.

disputō, 1, *weigh apart ; argue, discuss, have a dispute*, 59. 13.

dissēnsiō, ōnis, F. [dissentiō, *differ*], *difference ; disagreement, quarrel.*

dissidium, ī, N., *sitting apart ; dissension, dispute, quarrel*, 50. 3.

dissimilis, e, adj. [similis], *not like ; unlike, different*, 38. 6.

dissimilitūdō, inis, F. [dissimilis], *unlikeness, difference*, 66. 16.

dissimulō, 1, *represent as unlike; conceal, keep secret, hide, repress*, 35. 4.

dissolūtus, a, um, adj. [p. of dissolvō, *loosen*], *loosened ; careless, free, dissolute*, 66. 14.

distrahō, 3, āxī, actus, *drag apart ; draw away, separate, divide*, 39. 1 ; *drag, pull asunder, tear apart*, 40. 19.

distribuō, 3, uī, ūtus, *assign apart ; assign, divide, distribute*, 36. 11 ; 44. 17 ; 52. 19.

dītissimus, a, um, adj., superl. of dīs, dītis, *wealthy, rich*, 66. 20.

diū, adv., *by day ; a long time, long*, 5. 24 ; 8. 6 ; 14. 6, etc.; diūtius, 31. 16 ; 62. 4 ; 69. 13; diūtissimē, 72. 8.

diūturnus, a, um, adj. [diū], *long, of long duration, lasting, lingering*, 41. 1 ; 53. 13 ; 71. 9.

dīvellō, 3, vellī, volsus or vulsus, *tear apart*, 21. 8.

dīversus, a, um, adj. [p. of dīvertō, *turn different ways*], *opposite, different, contrary*, 23. 15 ; 40. 19 ; 66. 16.

dīves, itis, adj., *wealthy, rich*, 66. 10.

dīvidō, 3, vīsī, vīsus, *divide, separate*, 27. 17 ; 54. 16; *divide (among), distribute*, 60. 8.

dīvīnitus, adv. [dīvīnus], *from heaven ; by divine influence, miraculously*, 36. 1.

dīvīnus, a, um, adj. [dīvus, *god*], *of a god, divine*, 47. 2.

dīvitiae, ārum, F. [dīves], *riches, treasures, wealth*, 50. 16.

dō, dare, dedī, datus, *hand over ; give over, give, commit, consign*, 9. 2, 14 ; 10. 8, etc.; *give up, resign*, 21. 13; *bestow*, 6. 22 ;

34. 12 ; 45. 6; *grant, allow,* 35.
15 ; *offer,* 30. 6; *pay,* 50. 9 ;
propose, 15. 8 ; w. negōtium,
charge, assign, entrust, 3. 12,
22 ; 74. 12 ; w. sē, *rush, plunge,*
29. 7 ; w. vēnum, *sell,* 47. 2.

doceō, 2, uī, ctus, *cause to know ;*
instruct, teach, show, tell, 3. 19 ;
7. 15 ; 19. 9, etc.

doleō, 2, uī, itūrus, *feel pain ; be*
grieved, lament, feel sorry,
59. 24.

dolor, ōris, M., *pain,* 16. 11 ; 23.
16, 24 ; *grief, sorrow,* 2. 12, 13 ;
5. 9, etc.; *chagrin, anger,* 12. 20.

✓ dolōsē, adv. [dolōsus, *crafty*],
craftily, cunningly, deceitfully,
35. 18.

dolus, ī, M., *device ; fraud,*
trickery, cunning, 10. 18 ; 14.
14 ; 18. 6, etc.

domicilium, ī, N., *habitation ;*
home, dwelling-place, 42. 17.

✓ domina, ae, F. [dominus], *mis-*
tress, 28. 13 ; 48. 11 ; 53. 15.

dominātiō, ōnis, F. [dominor,
rule], *rule, dominion, power,*
control, 59. 16.

✓ dominus, ī, M., *master ; ruler,*
lord, master, 36. 20.

domō, 1, uī, itus, *tame ; subdue,*
vanquish, overcome, 42. 21 ;
45. 21.

domus, ūs, F., *something built ;*
house, home, 13. 20 ; 18. 2 ; 28.
26, etc.; domī, *at home,* 40. 28 ;
64. 3 ; 71. 11.

dōnō, 1 [dōnum], *give as a*
present ; bestow, give, confer,
w. abl. and acc., 43. 8 ; 70. 26.

dōnum, ī, N., *thing given ; gift,*
present, 16. 8 ; 26. 8.

dormiō, 4, *sleep, slumber,* 10. 3 ;
11. 21 ; 16. 24, etc.

dorsum, ī, N., *back ; slope, ridge,*
63. 16.

dracō, ōnis, M., *serpent, dragon,* ✓
8. 15 ; 9. 18 ; 11. 14, etc.

dubitō, 1 [dubium], *go to and*
fro ; doubt, question, 6. 19 ; 10.
18 ; 12. 3, etc.

dubius, a, um, adj., *moving two*
ways ; doubtful, uncertain, 14.
8 ; 22. 3 ; 24. 1 ; procul dubiō,
without doubt, 47. 8.

ducentī, ae, a, num. adj., *two hun-* ✓
dred, 70. 4.

dūcō, 3, dūxī, ductus, *lead ; lead,*
induce, 69. 10 ; *draw (by lot),*
27. 22 ; *extend, protract,* 72. 8 ;
extend, construct, make, 44. 16 ;
take (as wife), 58. 3 ; w. in
mātrimōnium, *wed, marry,* 16.
1 ; 18. 10 ; *think,* 71. 16.

dulcēdō, inis, F. [dulcis], *sweet-*
ness ; charm, 28. 7.

• dulcis, e, adj., *sweet ; agreeable,*
pleasant, delightful, 19. 1 ; 49.
3 ; superl. dulcissimus, 28. 6.

dum, conj., *while, whilst, until,*
3. 2 ; 9. 18 ; 10. 2, etc.; *as*
long as (w. subj.), 14. 9, 26.

duo, ae, o, num. adj., *two,* 2. 1 ;
7. 10 ; 8. 10, etc.

duodecim, num. adj., indecl.,
twelve, 19. 22 ; 34. 14 ; 37. 13,
etc.

duplicō, 1 [duplex, *double*],
double ; enlarge, increase, 40.
22 ; 42. 23.

dūritia, ae, F. [dūrus], *hardness ;*
hardship, rigorous life, fru-
gality, 75. 14.

dūrō, 1 [dūrus], *last, endure.*

dux, ducis, M., *one who leads ;*
leader, commander, general, **12.**
5, 12 ; 38. 8, etc.

Dyrrachium, ī, N., a town on the
coast of Illyricum, now Epi-
damnus, **62. 2.**

E

Ē, prep. w. abl. See **ex.**

✓ **ēbrius,** a, um, adj., *full ; drunk,*
intoxicated, **19. 8.**

ecquid, interrog. adv., *whether, if*
at all, **47.** 6 ; **64.** 6, 7.

ēdīcō, 3, xī, dictus, *speak forth ;*
proclaim, decree, announce,
make known, **4.** 7 ; **9.** 8.

ēdō, 3, didī, ditus, *give out ; give*
out, breathe forth, **8.** 13; *utter,*
21. 10 ; *bring forth, give birth*
to, bear, **33.** 5 ; *perform, perpe-*
trate, **62.** 5; *bring about, pro-*
duce, hold, **60.** 1.

ᵛ **ēdūcō, 1,** *bring up, rear, educate,*
33. 14; **34.** 11 ; **43.** 23, etc.

ēdūcō, 3, xī, ductus, *lead out,*
lead forth.

efferō, ferre, extulī, ēlātus, *bear*
out ; raise, lift, **43.** 18 ; *extol,*
75. 2 ; *puff up, elate, make*
proud, **40.** 25 ; **71.** 22.

effervēscō, 3, ferbuī, — , *boil up,*
boil over, **14.** 26.

efficiō, 3, fēcī, fectus [faciō],
make out ; bring about, effect,
accomplish, **23.** 19 ; **30.** 13 ;
51. 20, etc.

efflō, 1, *blow out ; breathe out,* **53.** 4.

effugiō, 3, fūgī, — , *flee away ;*
escape from, escape, avoid, **74.**
22.

effundō, 3, fūdī, fūsus, *pour forth;*
pour out, empty, **60.** 12 ; **63.** 16;
waste, spend, squander, **60.** 2 ;
rise (above), overflow, **33.** 8.

Egeria, ae, F., a nymph, **37.** 24.

ego, meī, personal pron., *I,* **14.**
7, 8, 9, etc.

ēgredior, 3, gressus [gradior], *go*
out, depart, **62.** 6; *disembark,*
land, **4.** 20 ; **5.** 4, 16, etc.

ēgregiē, adv. [ēgregius], *excel-*
lently, splendidly, very well,
11. 14.

ēgregius, a, um, adj. [grex], *out* ✓
of the flock ; excellent, noble,
glorious, **40.** 2 ; *surpassing,* **54.**
19; *unusual, remarkable,* **60.**
28.

ēiciō, 3, iēcī, iectus [iaciō], *cast*
out ; banish, drive away, exile,
68. 26.

ēlābor, 3, lapsus, *slip away, get*
off, escape, **58.** 7.   Cf. **effugiō.**

ēlātus, p. of **effero,** **71.** 22.

ēliciō, 3, uī, — , *draw out ; call*
down, evoke, bring down, **37.** 4.

ēligō, 3, lēgī, lēctus [legō], *pluck*
out ; pick out ; choose, select,
36. 8 ; **46.** 3.

Ēlis, idis, F., a state in the western part of the Peloponnesus,
68. 17.

ēloquēns, entis, adj. [p. of ēlo-
quor], *eloquent.*

ēmineō, 2, uī, — , *stand out, pro-* ᵛ
ject, show oneself, **50.** 8.

ēminus, adv. [ex, manus], *out of*
reach ; from a distance, **74.**
22.

ēmittō, 3, mīsī, mīssus, *send*

from; cast, hurl, 41. 18 ; *let go, send out,* 7. 18 ; 24. 20.

√ emō, 3, ēmī, ēmptus, *buy, purchase,* 47. 7, 11.

enim, conj. [nam], usually after the first word in its clause, *for, in fact, you see,* 3. 6, 12, 24, etc.

eō, īre, īvī or iī, itūrus, *go, set out, pass, walk, march,* 28. 1 ; 35. 13 ; 39. 15; *go, perish, die,* 39. 23.

eō, adv. [is], *to this; to that place, thither,* 6. 21 ; 10. 24 ; 11. 8, etc.

Ephesius, a, um, adj., *of Ephesus,* in Ionia, *of the Ephesians,* 44. 20.

Ēpīrus, ī, F., a province in the north of Greece, 62. 1.

eques, itis, M. [equus], *horseman, knight,* 36. 10; 42. 23.

equitō, 1 [eques], *ride, practice horsemanship,* 65. 1.

equus, ī, M., *swift thing; horse, steed,* 46. 16; 52. 7, 9, etc.

ērēctus, a, um, adj. [p. of ērigō], *upright, erect,* 16. 25.

ergā, prep. w. acc., *towards, in relation to,* 68. 15.

ergō, adv., *exactly ; then, thereupon,* 43. 6; *accordingly, therefore,* 46. 19; 71. 5 ; 74. 5.

Ēridanus, ī, M., Greek name for the Po River, 13. 18.

ērigō, 3, ērēxī, ērēctus [regō], *raise up ; lift, set up, erect.*

ēripiō, 3, uī, reptus [rapiō], *snatch from,* 74. 18 ; *snatch, rescue, save,* 2. 7 ; 7. 25.

errō, 1, *wander ; wander, go back and forth,* 23. 18; *be in error, mistake, be wrong,* 5. 7.

ērudiō, 4 [rudis, *rough*], *educate, instruct, teach, polish,* 66. 19.

ērumpō, 3, rūpī, ruptus, *cause to break forth ; burst forth, rush out,* 61. 12.

Esquilīnus, ī, M., *Esquiline hill,* largest of the seven hills of Rome, 44. 15.

et, conj., *and,* 2. 8, 12, 16, etc. ; *too, also,* 2. 25 ; 35. 19 ; et . . . et, *both . . . and,* 35. 17 ; 66. 7.

etiam, *and also ; even, besides,* √ *too,* 6. 5 ; 21. 2 ; 35. 2, etc. ; nōn modo . . . sed etiam, *not only . . . but also,* 2. 5 ; 11. 14 ; 12. 19.

Etrūria, ae, F., a province of Italy, 42. 8.

etsī, conj., *and if ; though, al-* √ *though,* 2. 10 ; 3. 15; 8. 15, etc.

Eumolpidae, ārum, M., descendants of Eumolpus, son of Neptune ; Athenian priests who had charge of the Elusinian mysteries, 68. 19.

Eurīpidēs, is, M., a famous Greek poet [B.C. 480–406], 59. 17.

Eurylochus, ī, M., one of Ulysses' men, 27. 17.

ēvādō, 3, sī, sus, *go out ; come forth, get away, escape,* 7. 20 ; 8. 24 ; 10. 22, etc. Cf. effugiō, 74. 22.

ēvānēscō, 3, nuī, —, inch., *vanish* √ or *fade away, disappear,* 29. 26.

ēveniō, 4, vēnī, ventus, *come out; happen, take place, occur, succeed, result, end,* 7. 27 ; 10. 4 ; 12. 13, etc.; sorte ēvēnit, *the lot fell to,* etc., 27. 20.

ēventus, ūs, M., *a coming out ;*

issue, consequence, result, end, 43. 24.

ēvertō, 3, tī, sus, *turn from; overturn,* 56. 5, 7 ; *overthrow, destroy, ruin, abolish,* 64. 28.

ēvītō, 1, *shun, avoid,* 68. 16.

ēvocō, 1, *call out; call forth, summon,* 45. 14.

ēvolō, 1, *fly out ; fly off* or *away,* 48. 6.

ex or (only before consonants) ē, prep. w. abl., *out of ; from, away from, out from, from among, of,* 2. 7, 8, 25, etc. ; ex ōrdine, *in succession,* 24. 20 ; *according to,* 71. 14.

exanimō, 1 [exanimus, *lifeless*], *put out of breath ; tire, weaken, exhaust,* 10. 1 ; 20. 18.

exārdēscō, 3, ārsī, ārsus, inch., *blaze out; be inflamed, be provoked, rage,* 12. 20; 27. 4.

excēdō, 3, cessī, cessus, *go out, depart ; ē vītā, die, perish,* 16. 13. Cf. discēdō, 14. 10.

excellentior, ius, adj., compar. of excellēns, entis [p. of excellō], *eminent ; surpassing, superior, extraordinary,* 66. 4.

excellō, 3, —, celsus, *be eminent; be superior, surpass, excel,* 48. 13.

excelsus, a, um, adj. .[p. of excellō], *elevated ; high, lofty, noble,* 42. 15; 64. 20. Cf. altus, 42. 15.

excipiō, 3, cēpī, ceptus [capiō], *take out; receive, welcome,* 4. 21 ; 11. 2; 12. 12, etc.

excitō, 1, freq. [exciō, *call out*], *wake, rouse,* 10. 4 ; 22. 5 ; 23. 17, etc.

exclāmō, 1, *call* or *cry out, shout, exclaim,* 20. 24 ; 25. 9; 61. 26.

exclūdō, 3, sī, sus [claudō], *shut out ; cut off, prevent, hinder,* 26. 1 ; 32. 1.

excōgitō, 1, *think out, contrive, devise,* 18. 6.

exemplum, ī, N., *specimen ; example, pattern, model,* 49. 19 ; *copy,* 68. 21.

exeō, īre, iī, itus, *go out ; go away, depart,* 22. 12 ; 24. 8, 10, etc.; *come out, issue,* 28. 8 ; 73. 2.

exerceō, 2, uī, itus [arceō], *drive; practice, carry into effect,* 63. 8.

exercitus, ūs, M., *trained body ; army, force, band,* 35. 15; 36. 1, 12, etc.

exhauriō, 4, hausī, stus, *draw out ; empty, drink up,* 30. 8 ; *use up, exhaust,* 72. 9.

exhibeō, 2, uī, itus [habeō], *hold forth ; produce, show, give.*

exīstimō, 1 [aestimō, *value*], *think, judge, consider,* 21. 17 ; 32. 2; 55. 19, etc.

exitium, ī, N., *a going out ; destruction, 'ruin, overthrow,* 46. 24 ; 58. 16.

exorior, 4, ortus, *come forth ; arise, begin, break out,* 38. 8 ; 52. 9.

exōrō, 1, *pray out ; move, prevail upon, persuade, induce,* 55. 7.

expediō, 4 [pēs], *extricate ; procure, get,* 59. 1.

expellō, 3, pulī, pulsus, *drive out; thrust out, banish, expel,* 2. 4 ; 15. 19, 20, etc.

experīmentum, ī, N. [experior], *trial ; proof, test,* 43. 2.

experior, 4, pertus, *try, prove, test, make a test,* 46. 16; 66. 2.

expetō, 3, īvī, ītus, *seek out; demand, ask,* 55. 11.

expiō, 1, *atone by sacred means; make amends for, atone for, expiate,* 40. 5.

explicō, 1, āvī and uī, ātus and itus, *unfold; display, spread out,* 48. 5.

explōrō, 1, *cause to flow forth; examine, investigate, spy out,* 19. 22; 21. 17.

expōnō, 3, posuī, positus, *set forth; leave to die, expose, set forth, explain, tell,* 44. 28; 46. 22; *in lītore, in terram, set ashore, land,* 18. 19; 19. 6; 59. 4.

exposcō, 3, poposcī, —, *ask from; demand, claim,* 41. 17.

expositiō, ōnis, F. [expōnō], *a setting forth; being exposed, exposing, exposure,* 34. 6.

exprimō, 3, pressī, pressus [premō], *press out, squeeze out, extract,* 8. 25.

expūgnō 1, *fight out; take by assault, take, capture,* 45. 23; 70. 7 ; *overcome,* 58. 14.

expulī. See **expellō.**

exsequor, 3, secūtus, *follow after ; carry out, enforce.*

exsiliō, 4, uī, — [saliō, *leap*], *spring out ; leap forth, dart out,* 15. 1.

exsilium, ī, N. [exsul], *banishment, exile,* 18. 11 ; 46. 26.

exsistō, 3, stitī, —, *step out; come forth, become, be,* 36. 21 ; *happen, be,* 67. 14.

exspectātiō, ōnis, F. [exspectō], *awaiting ; eagerness, longing, desire,* 70. 13. Cf. cupiditās, 2. 3.

exspectō, 1, *look out for, watch, wait to see,* 37. 10; 40. 14; *wait, wait for, await,* 5. 14 ; 11. 19, 24, etc.

exspīrō, 1, *breathe out; breathe one's last, expire,* 38. 21.

exstinctus, a, um, adj. [p. of exstinguō], *dead,* 52. 1 ; 56. 6.

exstinguō, 3, nxī, nctus, *put out; deprive of life,* 56. 3 ; pass., *die,* 38. 1.

exsultō, 1, āvī, —, freq. [exsiliō], *spring vigorously ; exult, rejoice,* 39. 12.

extemplō, adv. [tempus], *immediately, forthwith, at once,* 26. 23. ✓

extrā, prep. w. acc. [ex], *on the outside ; outside of, without, beyond,* 35. 13.

extrahō, 3, āxī, actus, *draw or pull out, remove,* 51. 19, 23.

extrēmus, a, um, adj. [exter, *on the outside*], superl., *outmost, the end of,* 23. 13.

extulī. See **efferō.**

exūrō, 3, ussī, ūstus, *burn up, destroy,* 47. 9.

F

✓ **faber,** brī, M., *workman ; artisan, carpenter, smith,* 20. 15 ; 37. 12.

fabricō, 1 [fabrica, *workshop*], *work ; construct, forge, make,* 37. 13 ; 60. 25.

fābula, ae, F., *speaking; story, tale,* 2. 14; 42. 10; *fable,* 48. 8; **49.** 8, 18, etc.

facētus, a, um, adj., *fine, polite, witty, humorous, jocose.*

facile, adv. [facilis], *with ease; easily, readily, without effort,* **51.** 20; **73.** 21; superl. facillimē, **73.** 7.

facilis, e, adj., *easy to do, easy,* **72.** 15.

✓ **facinus,** oris, N., *deed; act, deed, action,* 39. 25; **56.** 11; **62.** 5; *evil deed, crime,* 42. 1; **43.** 12.

faciō, 3, fēcī, factus, *make, cause to be,* 3. 2; **7.** 5, 8, etc.; *do,* 5. 21; **7.** 15, 24, etc.; *make, build,* 4. 5; **34.** 21; **42.** 5; *form,* **69.** 2; **73.** 9; *perform,* **2.** 22; **18.** 21; **67.** 23; *appoint,* 37. 18; *cause, give,* **36.** 15; certiōrem, *inform,* **6.** 4; **30.** 20; 31. 3, etc.; verba, *speak,* **71.** 1.

factum, ī, N. [faciō], *thing done; deed, act, action,* **46.** 9. Cf. facinus, **39.** 25.

✓ **facultās,** ātis, F. [facilis], *capability; chance, opportunity,* **23.** 11.

fallō, 3, fefellī, falsus, *trip; cheat, deceive, fail, disappoint,* **13.** 12; **72.** 27.

falsō, adv. [falsus], *untruly; falsely, erroneously,* **73.** 8.

falsus, a, um, adj. [p. of fallō], *deceived; feigned, pretended, false,* **2.** 13.

fāma, ae, F., *that which people say; report, rumor, tradition,* **20.** 12; **33.** 10; **44.** 21; *fame,* · *renown,* **72.** 2.

famēs, is, F., *that which devours; hunger, starvation, want,* 21. 12; **30.** 5; fame morior, *starve to death,* **6.** 14.

familia, ae, F. [famulus, *slave*], *slaves of a household; so household, family, race,* **58.** 1.

familiāris, e, adj. [familia], *of a household; as noun,* M., *friend, companion,* **74.** 17.

familiāritās, ātis, F. [familiāris], *familiar intercourse, intimacy, intimate acquaintance,* **42.** 18.

famula, ae, F. [famulus, *slave*], *serving woman, maidservant, slave,* **43.** 22; **53.** 16.

fānum, ī, N. [for], *thing spoken; shrine, sanctuary, temple,* **44.** 20, 22, 27.

fās (only nom. and acc. sing.), N., ✓ *divine law; right, justice.*

fascis, is, M., *bundle, parcel,* **52.** 17, 18; **53.** 20; pl., *fasces, rods-and-axe,* symbol of power over life and death, **60.** 12.

fāstus, a, um, adj. [fās], *according to divine law;* diēs, *day on which the praetor's court was open, secular day,* 37. 18; **63.** 2.

fātālis, e, adj. [fātum, *fate*], *of fate; dangerous, deadly,* **64.** 4.

fatīgō, 1 [agō], *weary, tire, fatigue,* **53.** 13.

faucēs, ium, F., *throat,* **51.** 18, 23; ✓ **61.** 4; *jaws,* 11. 19.

Faustulus, ī, M., the herdsman of Amulius, **33.** 13.

fautor, ōris, M., *favorer, promoter, patron,* **69.** 23.

fefellit. See fallō.

fēlēs, is, F., *cat,* **51.** 10, 14. ✓

fēlīciter, adv. [fēlīx], *abundantly;* ✓

happily, fortunately, favorably,
7. 27 ; 12. 13 ; 24. 19.

fēlīx, īcis, adj., *fruitful; happy,
fortunate.*

fēmina, ae, F., *she who bears ;
woman, female,* 16. 9 ; 35. 2 ;
43. 22.

✓ **fera,** ae, F. [ferus], *wild animal,
beast,* 50. 2, 3.

ferē, adv., *closely ; almost, nearly,*
26. 10; 60. 23.

ferō, ferre, tulī, lātus, *bear, carry,
take, render,* 6. 19 ; 10. 19; 12.
5, etc.; *bear, drive,* 73. 18; *endure,* 40. 3 ; 61. 14; 74. 7 ; *propose, pass, make,* 37. 22 ; 60. 8 ;
say, tell, 42. 24 ; 43. 23; 44.
21, etc.; aegrē or indīgnē, *take
ill, be displeased at,* 8. 19 ;
14. 13 ; 15. 18, etc.

ferōx, ōcis, adj., *fierce, savage,
bold, warlike,* 39. 10, 19; 41.
3, etc.; comp. ferōcior, 38. 6 ;
superl. ferōcissimus, 43. 12.

ferrum, ī, N., *iron ; sword, blade,*
38. 12 ; 39. 10 ; 74. 13.

ferus, a, um, adj., *wild, savage,
untamed,* 36. 25; *hard-hearted,
cruel,* 71. 2.

fessus, a, um, adj., *wearied,
fatigued, worn out, weak, ex-
hausted,* 18. 1 ; 39. 11 ; 46.
8.

fētiālis, e, adj., *speaking; fetial,
diplomatic,* 41. 19, 20.

fictus, a, um, adj. [p. of fingō],
made ; feigned, false, pretended,
46. 2.

fidēlis, e, adj. [fidēs], *of trust ;
faithful, trusty,* 56. 2, 4.

Fīdēnātēs, ium, M., the people of
Fidenae, in Latium, 40. 12.

fidēs, gen. fidē (rare), *trust ; be-* ✓
lief, credence, credit, trust, 36.
15 ; 41. 16 ; 65. 1 ; *pledge,
word of honor,* 37. 28.

fidūcia, ae, F. [fidus, *faithful*],
*trusting; confidence, reliance,
trust,* 40. 25.

fierī. See fiō.

figūra, ae, F., *form, figure, appearance,* 20. 8.

fīlia, ae, F., *daughter,* 8. 18; 9.
14 ; 12. 18, etc.

fīliolus, ī, M., dim. [fīlius], *little
son,* 56. 1, 8.

fīlius, ī, M., *son,* 2. 5; 6. 7 ; 13.
6, etc.

fingō, 3, finxī, fīctus, *touch ;* ✓
make up, invent, pretend, 2. 14 ;
55. 16; 66. 21.

fīniō, 4 [fīnis], *limit ; end, decide,*
38. 9; 40. 11.

fīnis, is, M., *separating thing,
boundary,* 61. 21 ; *borders,* so
pl., *country, land,* 6. 17 ; 8. 2 ;
41. 15, etc.

fīnitimus, a, um, adj. [fīnis],
*bordering upon ; neighboring,
near by,* 8. 24; as noun, M. pl.,
neighboring tribes, neighbors,
35. 5.

fīō, fierī, factus sum, *be made,* 69.
24 ; *be done,* 3. 14; 14. 23; 22.
20, etc.; *become,* 14. 18, 20;
result, happen, 67. 18 ; 71. 16;
obviam, *meet, fall in with,* 18.
23 ; 49. 12.

firmitās, ātis, F. [firmus],
strength, vigor, endurance,
75. 11.

firmus, a, um, adj., *firm, strong,
powerful,* 52. 20.

flagrāns, antis, adj. [p. of flagrō,

flame], *blazing ; burning, glowing,* 23. 14.

✓ **flāmen,** inis, M., *one who lights a sacrificial fire ; special priest, flamen,* 37. 2.

flamma, ae, F., *blazing ; flame, fire,* 8. 13; 43. 24; 74. 16, etc.

fleō, 2, ēvī, ētus, *flow ; weep, lament, shed tears,* 39. 18; 71. 4.

flōreō, 2, uī, — [flōs, *flower*], *bloom ; flourish, prosper, be distinguished.*

fluctus, ūs, M., *flowing ; tide, wave, billow,* 62. 12.

flūmen, inis, N., *that which flows; stream, river,* 3. 3; 8. 1; 13. 18, etc.

foculus, ī, M. [focus, *fireplace*], *sacrificial hearth ; fire pan, brazier,* 47. 5.

foedus, eris, N., *a trusting; compact, treaty, league,* 36. 5; 38. 12, 14, etc.

᷑ **fōns,** fontis, M., *spring, fountain,* 5. 18, 19; 18. 22, etc.

forās, adv., *to the doors ; out through the doors, out of doors, out,* 28. 8 ; 43. 19.

fore, foret. See **sum.**

forēnsis, e, adj. [forum], *of the forum ; public, legal,* 67. 17.

foris, is, F., *door ;* pl., *folding doors, double door,* 30. 2.

forīs, adv., *out at the doors ; out of doors, outside, without,* 28. 10. Cf. forās.

fōrma, ae, F., *form, figure, appearance,* 29. 12 ; 36. 18 ; *form, shape,* 37. 13 ; 60. 23 ; *beauty,* 5. 17 ; 54. 7.

formīdō, inis, F., *fearfulness ; fear, dread, terror,* 49. 10.

fōrmōsitās, ātis, F. [fōrmōsus], *beauty,* 48. 6. Cf. fōrma, 5. 17.

fōrmōsus, a, um, adj. [fōrma], *full of beauty ; beautiful, handsome* (superl.), 18. 9 ; 66. 6.

fōrtasse, adv., *perhaps, probably,* ✓ *possibly,* 48. 10.

fōrte, adv. [abl. of fōrs, *chance*], *by a chance ; by chance, as it happened, accidentally,* 22. 23 ; 33. 7 ; 35. 13, etc.

fortiter, adv. [fortis, *brave*], *strongly ; bravely, valiantly, manfully,* 75. 16 ; superl. fortissimē, 35. 25.

fortitūdō, inis, F. [fortis, *brave*], *braveness ; manliness, courage, bravery,* 44. 3.

fōrtūna, ae, F. [fōrs, *chance*], *that which belongs to chance ; fortune, fate, chance,* 21. 25 ; 40. 14 ; 52. 14, etc.; pl., *property, fortune,* 42. 9.

Forum, ī, N., *open space ; public square, Forum,* the open space between the Capitoline and Palatine hills, surrounded by porticoes and shops, 35. 23 ; 45. 13 ; 59. 27, etc.

fossa, ae, F. [fossus, p. of fodiō, *dig*], *thing dug ; ditch, trench,* 44. 16.

foveō, 2, fōvī,ꞌ fōtus, *warm, keep warm,*. 52. 2 ; *assist, support, favor.*

fragor, ōris, M., *a breaking ; crash, crashing, noise, din,* 36. 14.

frangō, 3, frēgī, frāctus, *break in pieces, break,* 52. 18, 20 ; 60. 12 ; *shatter, break down, weaken,* 41. 2.

frāter, tris, M., *brother*, 2. 1, 4; 10. 22, etc.

fraudō, 1 [fraus], *cheat, defraud, rob*, 43. 11.

✓ fraus, audis, F., *cheating; deceit, trickery, crime*, 2. 16 ; 24. 23 ; 45. 8, etc.

frēnō, 1 [frēnum], *furnish with a bridle; curb, check, restrain*, 25. 22.

frēnum, ī, N., *holding thing; bridle, curb, bit*, pl., *reins*, 45. 16.

frequentius, adv., comp. of frequenter [frequēns, *repeated*], *often ; in greater numbers, by many*, 40. 24.

frīgus, oris, N., *cold, frost*, 52. 1.

frōns, frontis, F., *forehead, brow*, 20. 11.

frūctus, ūs, M., *an enjoying; product, fruit*, 18. 24.

frūmentor, 1 [frūmentum], *get corn; forage*, 27. 8.

frūmentum, ī, N., *corn, grain*, 27. 9.

frūstrā, adv., *in error; without effect, in vain, to no purpose*, 5. 24 ; 12. 2 ; 15. 14, etc.

frūstror, 1 [frūstrā], *deceive, disappoint, trick*, 55. 16.

Fūfetius, ī, M., *Mettius Fufetius*, leader of the Albans, 38. 8.

fuga, ae, F., *a fleeing; flight, running away*, 10. 20, 21 ; 39. 1, etc.

fugiō, 3, fūgī, —, *flee, fly, take flight, run away*, 12. 22 ; 13. 8, 17, etc.

fugō, 1 [fuga], *cause, to flee; put to flight, rout*, 59. 7. ✓

fulgeō, 2, fulsī, —, *flash; gleam, glisten, shine*, 38. 18.

fulmen, inis, N., *flashing thing; lightning, thunderbolt*, 37. 4, 6; 41. 4, etc. ✓

fundō, 3, fūdī, fūsus, *pour; shed, let fall*, 59. 23 ; *scatter, rout, overcome, defeat*, 41. 23 ; 62. 14.

fungor, 3, fūnctus, *busy oneself; perform, discharge*, 60. 21.

furor, ōris, M. [furō, *rage*], *raging; rage, fury, passion*, 16. 13 ; 24. 5.

fūrtō, adv. [abl. of fūrtum], *by stealth, secretly*, 37. 12.

futūrus, a, um [fut. p. of sum], *future, destined, coming*, 64. 1.

G

Gabiī, ōrum, M., an ancient city of Latium, 45. 22.

Gabīnī, ōrum, M., *people of Gabii, Gabines*, 45. 24.

Gadēs, ium, F., a Phoenician colony in Spain, 59. 21.

✓ galea, ae, F., *covering; helmet*, 10. 6.

Gallia, ae, F., the province of *Gaul*, now France, 60. 21.

gallīna, ae, F. [gallus], *hen, fowl*, 50. 12, 14, 15.

gallus, ī, M., *cock*, 53. 12, 14.

gaudeō, 2, gāvīsus sum, *rejoice*, ✓ *be glad, be pleased*, 6. 17.

gaudium, ī, N., *inward joy; joy*,

rejoicing, gladness, delight, 2.
11 ; **12.** 11 ; **18.** 4, etc.

geminātus, a, um, adj. [p. of
geminō, *double*], *doubled ; two-
fold, double,* **39.** 10.

geminus, a, um, adj., *born together ; double, two-faced,* 37.
18 ; as noun, M. pl., *twin sons,
twins,* **33.** 5.

gener, erī, M., *daughter's husband,
son-in-law,* **44.** 8 ; **61.** 11.

genitus. See **gīgnō.**

gēns, gentis, F., *race ; nation,
people, tribe,* **34.** 25 ; **36.** 20.

genus, eris, N., *birth, family,* **66.**
5 ; *kind, manner, method, style,
form,* **6.** 8.

Germānī, ōrum, M., *Germans,*
60. 23.

gerō, 3, gessī, gestus, *bear ; bear,
carry, wield, have,* **28.** 17 ; **29.**
13 ; **38.** 17, etc. ; *wear,* **2.** 21 ;
35. 17 ; *wage, carry on,* **37.** 30 ;
68. 24 ; *do, accomplish,* pass., *be
done, go on, take place,* **11.** 23 ;
12. 14 ; **13.** 15, etc. ; *manage,*
69. 17 ; **71.** 11, 14, etc. ; w. sē,
*conduct oneself, act, behave,
play part (of),* **33.** 11 ; **58.** 22 ;
rem bene gerō, *strike a successful blow,* **8.** 17 ; **21.** 14 ; **23.**
12. etc. ; rēs gestae, *deeds,
achievements,* **74.** 3.

gestō, 1, freq. [gerō], *bear continually ; wear,* **64.** 25.

∨ **gigās,** antis, M., *giant,* **20.** 10, 20;
23. 1.

⅄ **gīgnō,** 3, genuī, genitus, *produce;*
pass., *spring up, arise,* **9.** 22,
25; **10.** 2; genitus, w. ex,
descended from, son of, **43.** 21 ;
58. 1.

gladius, ī, M., *sword,* **7.** 2 ; **10.** 6,
12, etc.

Glaucē, ēs or ae, F., *daughter of
Creon, king of Corinth,* **15.** 23.

glōria, ae, F., *glory, fame, renown,*
4. 8 ; **41.** 5; **45.** 3.

glōriōsior, ius, adj., comp. of
glōriōsus [glōria], *full of glory;
glorious, brilliant, to be proud of,*
71. 28.

Gnaeus. See **Pompēius,** **60.** 6.

gradus, ūs, M., *step, stair,* **45.** 12. ∨

Graecia, ae, F., *Greece,* **4.** 7.

Graecus, a, um, adj., *of Greece,
Greek,* **63.** 13; as noun, M. pl.,
Greeks, **17.** 1.

Grāius, a, um, adj., *of the Greeks;*
as noun, M. pl., *Greeks,* **72.** 1.

graphium, ī, N., *writing-style,*
64. 14.

grassor, 1, intens. [gradior, *step*],
advance, make an attack, **55.**
21.

grātia, ae, F. [grātus, *pleasing*],
*that which gives pleasure ;
favor, esteem,* **69.** 11 ; **73.** 24 ;
gratitude, thanks, **7.** 9, 24 ; **12.**
12, etc.; abl. as prep. w. gen.,
*on account of, for the sake of,
for,* **44.** 6; **59.** 19; **60.** 17.

grātulor, 1 [grātus], *manifest joy;
rejoice, exult,* **39.** 14 ; *rejoice
with, congratulate,* **40.** 18.

gravis, e, adj., *heavy,* **57.** 3 ;
weighty, important, **75.** 1 ;
annoying, **61.** 14; *serious,
painful, dangerous,* **16.** 11 ; **25.**
3 ; **29.** 2, etc.; *heavy, deep,* **28.**
15 ; *severe,* **62.** 3.

graviter, adv. [gravis], *heavily ;
severely, seriously, dangerously,*
23. 23 ; *bitterly,* **48.** 11 ; *deeply,*

violently, 10. 17 ; **12.** 20 ; **16.** 2, etc.

gravŏ, 1 [gravis], *make heavy ; burden, oppress,* **56.** 21 ; *overcome,* **23.** 9.

gressus, ūs, M., *stepping ; step,* **49.** 15.

√ **grex,** gis, M., *flock, herd,* **55.** 15, 18.

grūs, gruis, M. and F., *crane,* **48.** 5, 6 ; **51.** 19.

Grȳnium, ī, N., a town and fort in Phrygia, **73.** 14.

gubernātor, ōris, M. [gubernō], *steersman, helmsman, pilot,* **62.** 9, 11.

gubernō, 1, *steer, pilot,* **26.** 14.

gustō, 1 [gustus, *tasting*], *take a little of, taste,* **18.** 26 ; **23.** 2.

H

habeō, 2, uī, itus, *grasp ; have, possess, own,* 3. 23 ; 5. 15 ; 6. 10, etc. ; *have, carry, wear,* **35.** 20 ; **46.** 23 ; *hold, call,* **36.** 13 ; *regard, consider,* **64.** 18 ; **75.** 19 ; *carry on, hold,* **68.** 3 ; in animō, *intend,* **2.** 5 ; **16.** 2 ; **31.** 11, etc.

habitō, 1, freq. [habeō], *keep possession of ; have as a house, dwell, live, live in, inhabit,* **20.** 1 ; **40.** 24, 25.

haedus, ī, M., *young goat, kid,* **48.** 1.

Harpȳiae, ārum, F., *Harpies,* loathsome birds with maidens' faces, 6. 10.

harūspex, icis, M., *interpreter of the entrails of victims ; soothsayer,* **64.** 3.

√ **hasta,** ae, F., *spear, javelin,* **41.** 17.

haud, adv., *not, not at all,* 4. 18 ; 6. 13 ; **24.** 1, etc.

√ **hauriō,** 4, sī, stus, *draw up ; drain, drink up,* **23.** 3.

Hellēspontus, ī, M., *the Hellespont,* modern strait of Dardanelles, **70.** 6.

herba, ae, F., *springing vegetation ;* √ *herb, plant,* 8. 24 ; **14.** 25 ; **15.** 7, etc.

herbidus, a, um, adj. [herba], *full of grass ; grassy,* **49.** 1.

Herculēs, is, M., son of Jupiter and Alcmena ; god of strength, **4.** 9.

hermae, ārum, F., *hermae,* pillars bearing heads of Hermes, **67.** 7.

hĕsternus, a, um, adj., *of yesterday ;* w. diēs, *yesterday, the day previous,* **22.** 6.

hīc, adv., *here,* **25.** 20 ; **29.** 15.

hīc, haec, hōc, demonst. pron., *this, the latter, he, she,* etc., **2.** 2, 10 ; **3.** 7, etc.

hiems, emis, F., *winter, cold,* **62.** 3.

hinc, adv., *from this place ; from here, hence,* **39.** 22 ; hinc . . . hinc, *on this side . . . on the other,* **36.** 3, 4 ; *hence, so,* **50.** 13.

Hipponīcus, ī, M., father-in-law of Socrates, **66.** 19.

Hispānia, ae, F., the Roman province of *Spain,* **59.** 11.

historicus, a, um, adj., *of history ;*

as noun, M., *writer of history, historian,* **75.** 1.

Homērus, ī, M., *the poet Homer* [about B.C. 900], **17.** 2.

homō, inis, M. and F., *human being; man,* **2.** 24; **3.** 7; **4.** 3, etc.

honōs or **honor,** ōris, M., *that which profits; honor, distinction, office, duty,* **50.** 10; **64.** 24; **71.** 10.

hōra, ae, F., *hour; time, hour,* **4.** 21; **5.** 13; **6.** 24, etc.; in hōrās, *every hour,* **25.** 3.

Horātius, ī, M., one of the Horatii, **38.** 10.

horribilis, e, adj. [horreō, *shudder*], *to be shuddered at; terrible, fearful, dreadful,* **6.** 9; **8.** 13; **20.** 8, etc.

horror, ōris, M., *shaking; fear, dread, terror,* **38.** 19.

hortor, 1, *urge, bid,* **11.** 3; **19.** 15; **22.** 1, etc.

hortus, ī, M., *garden,* **46.** 6.

hospes, itis, M., *entertainer; host,* **35.** 27; *guest, stranger,* **25.** 9; *guest-friend,* **74.** 18.

hospitium, ī, N. [hospes], *that*

pertaining to a guest; entertainment, welcome, hospitality, **4.** 21; **18.** 23; **25.** 23, etc.

(hospitus), a, (um), adj., only F. sing., *hospitable; strange, foreign,* **46.** 28.

Hostīlius, ī, M. See **Tullus,** **38.** 5.

Hostīlius, ī, M., a famous Roman who fell in the war with the Sabines, **35.** 24.

hostis, is, M. and F., *enemy, foe,* **13.** 17; **35.** 27; **39.** 1, etc.

hūc, adv., *to this place, hither,* **48.** 17; **58.** 20.

hūmānitās, ātis, F. [hūmānus], ✔ *human nature; kindness, politeness, refinement, elegance,* **73.** 13.

hūmānus, a, um, adj. [homō], *of man; human, man's,* **20.** 8; **29.** 16; **30.** 18, etc.

humī, adv. [loc. of humus], *on the ground,* **21.** 13.

hydrus, ī, M., *water-serpent, snake,* **55.** 12.

Hylās, ae, M., one of the Argonauts, **5.** 17.

I

iaceō, 2, uī, —, *lie,* **16.** 26; **49.** 4; **56.** 2; *lie dead, be prostrate,* **39.** 13.

iaciō, 3, iēcī, iactus, *throw; cast, throw, let fall, let go,* **18.** 18; **61.** 25.

iam, adv., *at this moment; at once, straightway,* **35.** 26; *now, already,* **5.** 7, 15; **14.** 7, etc.; *soon, at length, at last,* **5.** 11;

22. 5; *already, even,* **12.** 17; **22.** 2; **44.** 20, etc.

iamdūdum, adv. [iam, diū, dum], ✔ *now a long time; for a long time, long,* **26.** 15.

Iāniculum, ī, N., *of Janus;* one of the hills of Rome, *Mt. Janiculum,* **38.** 2.

iānua, ae, F., *door, gate, entrance,* ✔ **28.** 7; **67.** 9.

Iānus, ī, M., *Janus*, an old Italian god, 37. 18.

Iāsōn, onis, M., *Jason*, son of Aeson, 2. 5.

ibi, adv., *in that place, there*, 3. 11 ; 4. 21 ; 5. 13, etc.

ibīdem, adv., [ibi + dem] *in the same place, on the spot*, 47. 9.

(īcō), 3, īcī, ictus, *strike, smite*, 41. 4 ; w. foedus, *make a treaty, enter into a compact*, 36. 5 ; 38. 12, 14, etc.

īdem, eadem, idem, pron., *that or the very person* or *thing ; same, that same, and he*, etc., 4. 24 ; 12. 25 ; 13. 22, etc.

√ ideō, adv., *for that reason, on that account, therefore*, 64. 23 ; 73. 20.

idōneus, a, um, adj. *fit, suitable, proper*, 4. 16 ; 5. 10 ; 11. 6, etc.

Īdūs, uum, F., *Ides, middle of the month* (the 13th day, but the 15th in March, May, July, October), 63. 28.

iēiūnus, a, um, adj., *fasting ; hungry*, 56. 14.

igitur, conj., *therefore, thereupon, accordingly, consequently*, 2. 8, 17; 3. 4, etc. Cf. ideō, 64. 23.

īgnārus, a, um, adj. [gnārus, *knowing*], *not knowing, ignorant of*, 28. 19.

īgnāvē, adv. [īgnāvus, *sluggish*], *slothfully, without spirit.*

īgnis, is, M., *fire*, 14. 25 ; 16. 7 ; 20. 15, etc.

īgnōrō, 1, *not know ; be unacquainted, be ignorant*, 19. 21 ; 68. 1.

īgnōscō, 3, nōvī, nōtus, *pardon, forgive, overlook*, 62. 28.

īgnōtus, a, um, adj., *unknown, strange, unfamiliar*, 19. 20 ; 60. 26.

Īlias, ados, F., *the Iliad*, a Greek epic poem, 17. 3.

īlicō, adv. [for inlocō], *in that very place, suddenly, on the spot*, 56. 21 ; 64. 10. √

ille, a, ud, īus, dem. pron., *that yonder, that, the former, he*, 2. 12, 17 ; 3. 9, etc.

illīc, adv. [ille], *in that place, there*, 59. 14; 61. 6.

imāgō, inis, F., *imitation ; empty form, semblance, likeness*, 34. 21 ; *statue*, 59. 23. √

imbēcillus, a, um, adj., *weak, feeble*, 52. 21 ; 54. 21.

imbellis, e, adj. [bellum], *unwarlike, cowardly*, 35. 27.

imber, bris, M., *rain, heavy rain, storm*, 65. 3.

imbuō, 3, uī, ūtus, *cause to drink in ; fill, infect, imbue*, 37. 28.

imitor, 1, freq., *imitate, copy after*, 75. 17.

immānis, e, adj., *monstrous, enormous, huge*, 56. 3.

immānitās, ātis, F. [immānis], *savageness, cruelty, barbarism*, 25. 10.

immātūrus, a, um, adj., *not ripe; unseasonable, untimely*, 39. 22 ; 42. 7.

immēnsus, a, um, adj., *immeasurable, vast, very great, excessive*, 47. 4 ; 63. 12.

immeritus, a, um, adj., *undeserving ; undeserved, unmerited*, 50. 10.

immittō, 3, mīsī, mīssus, *send in ; let in, admit, drive in*, 30. 25.

immoderātus, a, um, adj., *boundless ; unrestrained, excessive,* 68. 14.

immodestia, ae, F. [immodestus, *unrestrained*], *insubordination, lawlessness,* 72. 26.

immolō, 1, *sprinkle with sacrificial meal ; offer up, sacrifice,* 44. 27 ; 45. 2.

immortālis, e, adj., *undying, immortal,* 47. 18 ; 64. 1.

impār, paris, adj., *not equal ; not a match for ; unable to cope with,* 39. 1.

impatiēns, entis, adj., *that cannot bear ; intolerant, not bearing, impatient,* 62. 6.

impediō, 4, *entangle the feet ; hinder, retard, delay,* 13. 10.

impellō, 3, pulī, pulsus, *strike against, move, impel, induce, lead,* 16. 14 ; 24. 6.

impendeō, 2, —, —, *hang over ; threaten, be near* or *at hand,* 68. 16.

imperātor, ōris, M. [imperō], *he who commands ; commander, leader, chief,* 66. 7.

imperātum, ī, N. [p. of imperō], *that which is ordered ; command, order,* 18. 21.

imperfectus, a, um, adj., *unfinished, not ended,* 61. 16.

imperītus, a, um, adj., *inexperienced ; unskilled,* 50. 20.

imperium, ī, N. [imperō] *empire,* 63. 10 ; *command, authority, power, sway,* 34. 13, 20 ; 37. 7, etc.

imperō, 1 [parō], *command, order, bid,* 9. 23 ; 28. 25 ; 30. 24 ; *demand, levy, raise,* 60. 27.

impetrō, 1 [patrō, *gain*], *gain one's end ; obtain, procure, get,* 31. 15 ; 58. 11.

impetus, ūs, M., *attack, charge, onset,* 7. 5; 29. 23 ; 30. 14, etc.; *violence, fury,* 39. 5.

impius, a, um, adj., *not reverent ; wicked, foul, unnatural, unpatriotic,* 35. 20.

implicō, 1, āvī or uī, ātus or itus, ✓ *fold in; seize, attack, disable,* 41. 1.

implōrō, 1, *invoke with tears ; beg, entreat, beseech,* 55. 15.

impōnō, 3, posuī, positus, *place* or *put upon,* 9. 12 ; 24. 18 ; 53. 6, etc. ; *place, put,* or *lay in,* 33. 7 ; 57. 1 ; *place on board, man,* 12. 21.

imprīmīs or in prīmīs, adv., *among the first ; chiefly, especially, principally,* 63. 10.

impudentia, ae, F. [impudēns, *shameless*], *shamelessness, impudence.*

in, prep., *in :* w. acc., *into, upon, to, for,* 2. 23; 3. 5, 19, etc.; *according to, after,* 10. 6; 12. 7 ; *toward,* 6. 7 ; 12. 17; in aeternum, *forever,* 19. 2 ; w. abl., *in, on, among,* 2. 1, 5; 3, 2. etc.; *at,* 2. 19; 5. 13; *amid, at a time of,* 39. 20 ; in proximō, *near by, in the vicinity,* 34. 22.

inambulō, 1, —, —, *walk up and down, pass to and fro,* 46. 6.

inānis, e, adj., `empty, deserted, ✓ 73. 3; fruitless, useless, vain, unprofitable,* 51. 5.

incēdō, 3, cessī, cessus, *fall upon; advance, march, move,* 49. 15.

incendium, ī, N., *a burning; fire, flames, conflagration,* 74. 15, 22, 25.

incendō, 3, dī, ēnsus, *set on fire; kindle, light, make* (a fire).

incertus, a, um, adj., *not fixed; not certain, undecided, doubtful,* 53. 16.

incīdō, 3, dī, — [cadō], *fall into,* 24. 4 ; 25. 3 ; *happen to be, be made by chance,* 46. 15.

incīdō, 3, dī, sus [caedō, *cut*], *cut into; cut upon, carve,* 68. 22.

incipiō, 3, cēpī, ceptus [capiō], *take hold, take in hand, begin.*

incitō, 1, *set in rapid motion; spur on, incite, drive,* 45. 9 ; 50. 21.

inclāmō, 1, *call on; shout to, call upon,* 39. 6.

inclūdō, 3, sī, sus [claudō], *shut in; enclose, confine, keep,* 9. 10 ; 26. 6, 16, etc.

✓inclutus, a, um, adj., *celebrated, renowned, famous,* 36. 23 ; 43. 1 ; 44. 20.

incōgnitus, a, um, adj., *not ex-amined ; not known, unknown,* 46. 28.

incola, ae, M., *one who dwells in a place ; inhabitant, citizen,* 5. 2, 7 ; 6. 3, etc.

incolō, 3, uī, —, *be at home, live,* 60. 24 ; *dwell in, inhabit,* w. acc., 20. 6, 14 ; 27. 7.

✓ incolumis, e, adj., *unimpaired ; unharmed, safe, sound,* 7. 20, 24 ; 16. 21, etc.

incrēdibilis, e, adj., *not to be be-lieved ; incredible, extraordi-nary,* 7. 14 ; 52. 10 ; 65'. 4.

increpō, 1, uī, itus, *crash, re-sound,* 38. 18; *upbraid, rebuke, chide, reprove,* 34. 18 ; 39. 21.

incrēscō, 3, ēvī, —, *grow upon ; increase, grow, rise,* 42. 3.

incursiō, ōnis, F., *running into ; hostile inroad, invasion,* 41. 9 ; 50. 2.

inde, adv., *from there, thence,* 62. 1 ; 68. 17 ; 75. 8 ; *after that, then, thereupon,* 42. 13 ; 46. 18, etc.

index, icis, M. and F., *one who points out ; sign, mark,* 37. 19.

indicium, ī, N., *notice ; evidence, sign, proof, indication,* 64. 1. ✓

indicō, 1 [index], *point out ; de-clare, inform, disclose, make known, reveal,* 33. 20.

indīcō, 3, xī, dictus, *declare pub-licly, announce, proclaim, de-clare,* 35. 5; 40. 26 ; 41. 11, etc.

indīgnātiō, ōnis, F. [indīgnor, *deem unworthy*], *displeasure, anger,* 27. 4.

indīgnē, adv. [indīgnus, *un-worthy*], *unworthily ; w.* ferō, *take ill, be angry,* 45. 23.

indolēs, is, F., *inborn quality ; nature, character, disposition,* 34. 3 ; 49. 8. ✓

induō, 3, uī, ūtus, *put on,* 16. 6, 10, 11 ; *clothe, dress, wrap,* 50. 6.

industria, ae, F. [industrius, *active*], *activity ; diligence, ac-tivity, zeal,* 42. 18.

ineō, īre, īvī and iī, itus, *go into ; enter upon, form, devise,* 3. 8 ; 8. 23; *begin,* 61. 3; *acquire, obtain,* 73. 24.

✓ inermis, e, adj. [arma], *unarmed,
defenceless*, 50. 18.

īnfāmia, ae, F. [īnfāmis, *of ill
repute*], *ill fame, bad repute,
disgrace, reproach*, 67. 23.

īnfāmō, 1 [īnfāmis, *of ill repute*],
*bring into ill repute; dishonor,
brand*, 75. 1.

＼ ́ īnfandus, a, um, adj., *not to be
spoken; unheard of, unnatural,
shocking, awful*, 13. 5.

īnfāns, fantis, adj., *that cannot
speak;* as noun, M. and F.,
little child, infant, babe, 33. 10.

īnfectus, a, um, adj. [factus],
*not done; unaccomplished, un-
done*, 19. 13.

īnfēlīx, īcis, adj., *not fruitful;
unlucky, unfortunate, ill-fated*,
16. 26.

īnferō, ferre, tulī, lātus, *bear in;
bring upon*, w. acc. and dat.,
14. 15; 23. 25; 62. 16, etc.;
w. sē, *betake oneself, repair,
go into*, 37. 27; *present* or *expose oneself, advance*, 36. 3.

īnfestō, 1, —, — [īnfestus],
*threaten; molest, trouble, in-
fest*, 33. 24.

īnfestus, a, um, adj. [p. of
īnfendō], *striking; hostile,
threatening*, 38. 16; 54. 22.

īnficiō, 3, fēcī, fectus [faciō],
make or *put in; dip, plunge*,
11. 18; *soak, imbue*, 16. 5.

īnfīrmus, a, um, adj., *not strong;
weak, feeble.*

īnflātus, a, um, adj. [p. of īnflō,
blow into], *swelled up; inflated,
filled with air*, 65. 6; *elated,
puffed up, made proud*, 54.
10.

īnflīgō, 3, īxī, īctus, *dash upon;
give to, inflict upon*, 52. 4.

īnfrā, adv. [for īnferā, sc. parte],
*on the under side; below, be-
neath*, 64. 13.

(īnfrendō), 3, —, —, *strike
upon;* only pres. part., *gnash,
grind together*, 51. 21.

īnfundō, 3, fūdī, fūsus, *pour in,
throw in*, 14. 25.

ingemō, 3, uī, —, *groan, mourn,
lament, sigh*, 59. 23.

ingenium, ī, N., *that which is* ✓
*born in; nature, temperament,
disposition*, 45. 7; 75. 11; *talent, cleverness, ability*, 71. 20.
Cf. indolēs.

ingēns, entis, adj., *not of its kind*, ✓
*unnatural; huge, mighty, ter-
rible*, 7. 11; 9. 10; 10. 5, etc.

ingenuus, a, um, adj., *born in,
native; free-born, of free
parents*, 43. 8.

ingredior, 3, gressus [gradior],
go into, enter, 42. 16; 56. 16.

inhaereō, 2, sī, sus, *cling upon;
stick fast, become wedged in*, 51.
18.

inhibeō, 2, uī, itus [habeō], *hold
in; restrain, hold back, draw
in*, 45. 16.

inhiō, 1, *stand open, gape; be
eager for, long for, desire*,
50. 16.

iniciō, 3, iēcī, iectus [iaciō],
*throw in; cast upon, inspire,
occasion, cause*, 67. 13; *throw
over, put on, apply*, 39. 27; w.
manus and dat., *lay hands on,
seize*, 23. 18.

inimīcus, a, um, adj. [amīcus],
*not friendly; hostile, un-

friendly, 5. 3 ; superl., 58. 4 ; as noun, M., *enemy, foe*, 12. 17 ; 54. 21 ; 64. 26, etc.

initium, ī, N., *a going into; beginning; abl.* as adv., *in the beginning, at first*, 69. 19.

iniūria, ae, F. [iniūrius, *unlawful*], *injustice ; wrong, outrage, injury*, 16. 3 ; 21. 2 ; *hurt, harm*, 61. 19.

inlacrimō, 1 [lacrima], *weep upon ; sorrow for, bewail, lament*, 71. 2.

innītor, 3, nīxus, *lean upon ; support oneself on*, 65. 6.

inopia, ae, F. [inops, *without resources*], *want ; want, need, poverty*, 53. 21.

inquam, defect. verb, *say*, 23. 11 ; 24. 1 ; 29. 15, etc.

inrīdeō, 2, rīsī, rīsus, *laugh at ; mock, ridicule, make fun of*, 34. 17.

inrītō, 1, *incite, stimulate, instigate, stir up*, 51. 2.

inruō, 3, ruī, —, *rush in, press in, enter eagerly*, 31. 1 ; *rush upon, attack*, 55. 17 ; 64. 18.

īnsānia, ae, F. [īnsānus], *unsoundness of mind, insanity, madness*, 24. 4.

īnsānus, a, um, adj., *of unsound mind, insane, mad*.

īnsciēns, entis, adj., *not knowing, unaware ;* patre, *without his father's knowledge*, 10. 22.

īnsequor, 3, secūtus, *follow upon ; follow, come after*, 40. 26 ; *pursue, start in pursuit*, 12. 22.

īnserō, 3, sēvī, situs, *plant in ; implant, plant, sow*, 9. 21.

īnserviō, 4, —, ītus, *be serviceable ; devote oneself*, 75. 9, 12.

īnsideō, 2, sēdī, — [sedeō], *sit upon, occupy*, 42. 12.

īnsidiae, ārum, F., *a lying in ambush ; plot, scheme, trick*, 28. 10 ; 43. 11 ; 62. 16, etc.; *treachery*, 18. 1. ✓

īnsidior, 1 [īnsidiae], *lie in ambush ; lie in wait for, waylay*, 33. 18 ; 54. 14.

īnsīgne, is, N. [īnsīgnis], *mark, sign*, 43. 9 ; 63. 25.

īnsīgnis, e, adj., *distinguished by a mark ; famous, noted, eminent, prominent, conspicuous*, 35. 24 ; 37. 2 ; 44. 3 ; N. as noun, *remarkable deed, exploit*, 60. 28.

īnsolentius, adv., comp. of īnsolenter [īnsolēns, *excessive*], *immoderately ; rather insolently, haughtily*, 63. 20.

īnstituō, 3, uī, ūtus [statuō], *put in place ; institute, establish, organize*, 36. 26 ; 63. 8 ; *determine on, decide, resolve*, 29. 19 ; 69. 12.

īnstitūtum, ī, N. [p. of īnstituō], *thing established ; institution, law, custom*, 37. 23.

īnstō, 1, stitī, statūrus, *stand upon ; approach, press upon, be at hand*, 67. 28.

īnstruō, 3, ūxī, ūctus, *build in ;* ✓ *build up, fit out*, 63. 9 ; *prepare, furnish, provide, equip*, 7. 4 ; 16. 19 ; 28. 12, etc. ; *teach, inform, instruct*, 49. 19.

īnsula, ae, F., *island, isle*, 4. 19 ; 5. 1 ; 18. 8, etc.

īnsum, inesse, īnfuī, *be in or upon ; be contained in, be in*, 58. 17.

īnsuper, adv., *above; over and above, in addition, besides*, 53. 5.

intāctus, a, um, adj., *not touched; untouched, uninjured, unharmed*, 39. 10.

integer, gra, grum, adj., *untouched; unhurt, unwounded, sound*, 38. 24.

intellegō, 3, ēxī, ēctus, *come to know; perceive, find out, learn, know*, 2. 7, 13; 3. 6, etc.

intemperāns, antis, adj., *without self-control, unrestrained, extravagant*, 66. 14.

intentus, a, um, adj. [p. of intendō], *held upon; attentive, intent, with attention fixed*, 43. 18.

inter, prep. w. acc., *in the midst of, between*, 34. 11; 36. 16; 38. 7, etc.; *in, among, in the number* or *society of*, 2. 25; 12. 7; 18. 4, etc.; inter sē, *together, with one another*, 10. 12; 24. 14; 27. 19, etc.

intercalārius, a, um, adj. [intercalāris, *to be inserted*], *for insertion, intercalary*, 63. 4.

intercalō, 1, *proclaim an insertion in the calendar, insert*, 63. 5.

intercipiō, 3, cēpī, ceptus, *seize in passing; take away, snatch, usurp*, 42. 20.

interdum, adv., *sometimes, occasionally, now and then*, 52. 16.

intereā, adv., *among these; in the meantime, meanwhile*, 3. 20; 4. 6; 23. 20, *etc.*

interfector, ōris, M. [interficiō], *one who kills; slayer, murderer*, 62. 15.

interficiō, 3, fēcī, fectus [faciō], *make between; put out of the way, destroy, kill, slay*, 2. 5; 9. 25; 10. 14, etc.

intericiō, 3, iēcī, iectus [iaciō], *throw between;* pass., *interpose, pass, go by, elapse*, 46. 20.

interim, adv., *between this; meanwhile, in the meantime*, 40. 22; 44. 12; 59. 1.

interimō, 3, ēmī, ēmptus [emō], *take from the midst; destroy, kill, slay*, 34. 8; 46. 10; 50. 20, etc.

interior, ius, adj., comp. [inter], *inner, interior*, 20. 18, 23; 27. 23.

interitus, ūs, M., *a going between; overthrow, fate, death*, 35. 25.

intermittō, 3, mīsī, mīssus, *let go in the midst; leave off, suspend, interrupt*, 4. 2; 13. 15; pass., *elapse, intervene*, 8. 1; 27. 6; 30. 1.

internūntius, ī, M., *go-between; mediator, messenger*, 69. 20.

interrogō, 1, *ask, inquire, question*, 43. 2; 47. 7.

intersum, esse, fuī, *be between, intervene*, 13. 3.

intervāllum, ī, N., *space between palisades; space between, distance apart, interval*, 7. 13; 39. 2.

intimus, a, um, adj., superl., *inmost; intimate, close, near*, 69. 16.

intrā, prep. w. acc. [in], *in the inner part; within, inside*, 42. 6; 62. 18.

intrō, 1, *go into, enter*, 7. 1; 20. 4; 28. 11, etc.

introeō, īre, īvī and iī, —, *go in, enter,* 71. 28.

introitus, ūs, M., *a going in ; entrance,* 20. 1 ; 21. 19 ; 23. 21, etc.

intueor, 2, itus, *look upon, gaze at, behold,* 15. 3 ; *consider, regard,* 68. 1.

intumēscō, 3, muī, —, *swell up ; rise, become angry, rage,* 62. 8.

intus, adv., *within, inside,* 50. 14.

inūtilis, e, adj., *useless, unserviceable,* 31. 22.

invehō, 3, vēxī, vēctus, *carry in ;* pass., *ride into, be borne into, enter,* 59. 6.

inveniō, 4, vēnī, ventus, *come on; come upon, find, discover,* 20. 5 ; 24. 7 ; 28. 12 ; 46. 19, etc.

inventor, ōris, M., *contriver, discoverer.*

invicem, adv., *by turns, in turn, one after another,* 43. 17.

invidia, ae, F. [invidus, *envious*], *envy ; grudging, jealousy, meanness,* 49. 6, 8 ; 68. 3 ; *disrepute, disfavor,* 71. 15.

invidiōsus, a, um, adj. [invidia], *full of envy ; an object of hatred, hated, odious,* 40. 10.

invīsus, a, um, adj. [p. of invideō, *hate*], *hated, hateful, detested.*

invītō, 1 [for invocitō], *keep calling upon ; invite, urge to enter,* 28. 9.

invītus, a, um, adj., *against the will ; unwilling, with reluctance,* 19. 16 ; 29. 4.

invocō, 1, *call upon, invoke,* 53. 21.

involnerātus, a, um, adj., *unwounded.*

iocus, ī, M. (pl. also ioca, N.), *jest, joke,* 59. 9, 13 ; 60. 17, etc.

Iōnia, ae, F., the middle part of the western coast of Asia Minor, 69. 4.

ipse, a, um, intens. dem. pron., *that* or *this very; self, himself, herself, very, very same,* etc., 5. 5 ; 8. 21 ; 11. 10, etc.

īra, ae, F., *anger, wrath,* 8. 6 ; 10. 17 ; 11. 3, etc.

īrātus, a, um [p. of īrāscor, 3, īrātus, *be angry*], *angered, enraged, furious,* 34. 18 ; 43. 1 ; 63. 22.

is, ea, id, dem. pron., *that, this, he, she,* etc., 2. 9, 13, 21, etc. ; in eō ut, *on the point of,* 21. 15 ; 29. 11.

iste, a, ud, dem. pron., referring to that which is at hand or to the person addressed, *that, that of yours,* 4. 19 ; 9. 3 ; 10. 2, etc.

ita, adv., *in this manner ; in this wise, so, thus,* 4. 18 ; 6. 13 ; 7. 27, etc.; nōn ita multō post, *not very long afterward,* 36. 6.

Ītalia, ae, F., *Italy,* 61. 19.

itaque, conj., *and so, and thus, accordingly,* 15. 13 ; 34. 1.

item, adv., *likewise, also, as well,* 63. 9.

iter, itineris, N., *a going ; way, march, journey, voyage,* 3. 2, 13, 17, etc.; aliquantum itineris, *a little way,* 28. 4 ; 29. 8.

iterum, adv., *again, a second time, once more,* 23. 4 ; 24. 6 ; 28. 3, etc.

Ithaca, ae, F., an island in the Ionian Sea, 18. 8.

Iuba, ae, M., king of Numidia, 62. 25.

iubeō, 2, iŭssī, iŭssus, *order, give orders, command, bid*, 3. 21; 12. 21; 13. 15, etc.

iūdex, icis, M. and F. [iūs], *judge, juror*, 39. 26.

iūdicium, ī, N. [iūdex], *judgment, trial, decision.*

iūdicō, 1[iūdex], *be a judge; judge, decide, declare*, 46. 20.

iugulum, ī, N., dim. [iugum], *collar bone; throat, neck*, 64. 13.

iugum, ī, N., *joining thing; yoke*, 9. 12; of spears, 40. 7.

Iūlia, ae, F., Caesar's daughter and wife of Pompey, 61. 11.

Iūlius, ī, M. See Caesar, Proculus.

iungō, 3, iūnxī, iūnctus, *fasten; join, unite, bind*, 45. 7; *form*, 54. 15; 60. 6; *yoke*, 8. 12, 14; 16. 19.

Iūnō, ōnis, F., daughter of Saturn, and sister and wife of Jupiter, 48. 11, 13.

Iuppiter, Iovis, M., *heaven; Jupiter*, king of the gods, 6. 8; 7. 11; 35. 29, etc.

iūrō, 1 [iūs], *swear, make oath.*

iūs, iūris, N., *that which binds* ✓ (morally); *right, privilege*, 25. 9; 64. 25; *justice, right*, 40. 5; 59. 19; 63. 5; *law*, 41. 19; 63. 11; *law court, trial*, 39. 26; abl. as adv., *with justice, justly, rightly*, 39. 29; 42. 20; 56. 15.

iūs iūrandum (iūsiūrandum), iūris iūrandī, N., *oath to be sworn; oath*, 16. 2; 30. 24; 36. 17, etc.

(iūssus, ūs), M., only abl. sing., *order, command*, 28. 12; 40. 16, 19, etc.

iūstitia, ae, F. [iūstus], *justness; uprightness, justice*, 36. 23.

iūstus, a, um, adj. [iūs], *according to right; just, right, proper*, 25. 10.

iuvenca, ae, F. [iuvencus, *bullock*], *young cow, heifer*, 54. 15.

iuvenis, e, adj., *young*, 14. 18, 20; ✓ as noun, M., *young man, youth, warrior*, 5. 20; 35. 9; 38. 16, etc.

iuventūs, ūtis, F. [iuvenis], *youth.*

iūxtā, adv., *near to, hard by, close* ✓ *to*, 72. 24.

K

Kalendae, ārum, F., *Calends*, the first day of the month, 37. 15.

Cf. the Nones, the fifth, and the Ides, the thirteenth.

L

labor, ōris, M., *work, labor, task, effort, exertion*, 4. 2; 8. 10, 20, etc.

labōriōsē, adv. [labōriōsus], *with fatigue; with an effort, with painstaking*, 63. 5.

labōriōsus, a, um, adj. [labor], *full of labor; industrious, tireless*, 66. 10.

labōrō, 1 [labor], *labor; suffer, be afflicted*, 58. 8.

lāc, lactis, N., *milk*, 20. 5.

Lacedaemōn, onis, F., *Sparta*, 68. 22.

Lacedaemoniī, ōrum, M., *Spartans, Lacedaemonians*, 69. 1.

Lacō, ōnis, M., *a Laconian, Spartan*, 74. 4.

lacrima, ae, F., *tear*, 10. 25; 22. 13; 28. 2, etc.

lacrimō, 1 [lacrima], *shed tears, weep*, 70. 26.

lacus, ūs, M., *opening; lake, pond*, 55. 7.

laetitia, ae, F. [laetus], *gladness; joy, exultation, rejoicing*, 25. 1; 31. 9; 71. 9.

laetus, a, um, adj., *feeling joy; glad, delighted, pleased, with joy*, 37. 8; *pleasant, grateful, rich, abundant*, 49. 1.

✓ **laeva**, ae, F. [laevus, *on the left*], *left hand* (sc. manus), 35. 20.

Lamachus, ī, M., an Athenian general, 67. 6.

lambō, 3, bī, —, *lick, lap*, 33. 11.

lāmenta, ōrum, N., *wailing, weeping, lamentation*, 22. 13.

lāna, ae, F., *wool, spinning*, 46. 19.

laniō, 1 [lanius, *butcher*], *tear in pieces, rend, mangle*, 50. 3.

lapideus, a, um, adj. [lapis, *stone*], *of stone, stone*, 42. 23; 68. 22.

laqueus, ī, M., *loop; noose, rope*, 39. 27.

lassitūdō, inis, F. [lassus, *faint*], *faintness; weariness, fatigue*, 10. 1; 26. 14.

latebra, ae, F., *hiding-place, covert, retreat*, 58. 8.

✓ **lateō**, 2, uī, —, *lurk; be hidden* or *concealed, be out of sight, escape notice*, 24. 15.

Lārentia, ae, F. See **Acca**.

Latīnus, a, um, adj., *of Latium; Latin*, 63. 13; M. pl. as noun, *Latins*, 41. 8.

lātrō, 1, *bark, yelp*, 49. 4.

latrō, ōnis, M., *hired soldier;* ✓ *robber, brigand, bandit*, 20. 25; 33. 17, 18, etc.

lātūrus. See **ferō**.

lātus, a, um, adj., *broad, wide;* comp. lātior, 4. 4.

laudō, 1 [laus], *praise, honor, extol*, 46. 16; 54. 8; 75. 5.

laurea, ae, F. [laureus], *laurel tree; laurel wreath*, 64. 25.

laureus, a, um, adj. [laurus, *laurel-tree*], *of laurel, of bay leaves, laurel*, 70. 26.

laus, laudis, F., *praise, flattery,* ✓ 54. 10; 75. 2; *title to praise, merit*, 75. 16.

lēgātiō, ōnis, F. [lēgō], *office of embassador; embassy, legation*, 35. 2.

lēgātus, ī, M. [p. of lēgō], *one sent on a commission; embassador, envoy*, 34. 25; 41. 11, 13, etc.

legiō, ōnis, F., *legion*, a body of soldiers containing ten cohorts of foot-soldiers and 300 cavalry, in all between 4200 and 6000 men, 61. 3.

legō, 3, lēgī, lēctus, *bring together; choose, select, appoint*, 37. 14.

lēnis, e, adj., *smooth; gentle,* ✓ *light, soft*, 7. 16.

leō, ōnis, M., *lion*, 49. 9; 50. 6, 7, etc.

lētālis, e, adj. [lētum, *death*], ✓ *deadly; fatal, mortal*, 44. 11; 52. 4.

levitās, ātis, F. [levis, *light*], *lightness, quickness, nimbleness,* 48. 7.

levō, 1 [levis, *light*], *lift up; lighten, relieve, ease,* 53. 2.

lēx, lēgis, F., *that which is fixed; rule, law,* 37. 22, 29; **60.** 8, etc.; *terms, condition, stipulation,* 38. 12.

liber, brī, M., *inner bark of a tree; book, roll,* 47. 1, 6, 9, etc.

libenter, adv. [libēns, *willing*], *willingly; gladly, with pleasure,* 3. 16; **6.** 24; 7. 25, etc.; comp. libentius, 64. 25; superl. libentissimē, 28. 13.

līberālis, e, adj. [līber, *free*], *of freedom; generous, liberal, courteous, gracious,* 66. 11.

līberālitās, ātis, F. [līberālis], *frankness; generosity, liberality,* 67. 17.

līberē, adv. [līber, *free*], *freely, without hindrance,* 55. 20.

līberī, ōrum, M. [līber, *free*], *children of free parents; children,* 35. 7; 40. 3.

līberō, 1 [līber, *free*], *make free, set free, deliver, liberate,* 34. 8; 53. 22; 73. 18.

lībertās, ātis, F. [līber, *free*], *free, dom, liberty,* 67. 14.

lībertus, ī, M. [līber, *free*], *one set free; freedman,* 58. 9.

libīdinōsus, a, um, adj. [libīdō, *pleasure*], *full of desire; licentious, sensual, fond of pleasure,* 66. 14.

Libya, ae, F., 18. 18.

licentia, ae, F. [licēns, p. of licet], *freedom; lawlessness, license, lack of restraint,* 68. 15.

licet, 2, uit, itum est, impers., *it is lawful; it is permitted* or *allowed, one may,* 14. 9; 21. 2; 29. 5, etc.

lictor, ōris, M., *lictor,* an officer attending upon a magistrate, 39. 27.

lignum, ī, N., *that which is gathered; wood, woodwork, piece of wood,* 22. 17; 23. 14; 53. 18. etc.

ligō, 1, *tie; bind, fasten,* 26. 9.

ligō, ōnis, M., *mattock, hoe,* 56. 9.

līmen, inis, N., *crosspiece; threshold,* 29. 11.

līneāmentum, ī, N. [līnea, *line*], *line, feature, lineament,* 34. 5.

lingua, ae, F., *tongue,* 33. 10; *language,* 66. 20.

lītus, oris, N., *that covered by the* √ *sea; shore, beach,* 5. 5, 26; 16. 24, etc.

locuplētō, 1 [locuplēs, *rich in lands*], *make rich, enrich,* 70. 10; 72. 1.

locus, ī, M., *place, spot, region,* 3. 17; 9. 9, 17, etc.; *place, room, chance,* 59. 14; *position, place,* 48. 4; 64. 18; 71. 24; *condition, situation,* 6. 15; 13. 4; 21. 24, etc.

locūtus. See loquor.

longē, adv. [longus], *a long way off; widely, greatly, by far, far,* 19. 7; 35. 28; 72. 6; comp. longius, *farther, rather far, to some distance,* 5. 25; 13. 2, 11, etc.

longitūdō, inis, F. [longus], *length,* 51. 19.

longus, a, um, adj., *long, extended,* 18. 1; *tedious,* 32. 5; nāvis, *ship*

of war, **12.** 21 ; superl. longissi-
mus, **65.** 3.

loquor, 3, cūtus, *speak, talk, say,*
14. 7, 16; **15.** 4, etc.

lōtus, ī, F., *lotus,* **18.** 25.

lūcidē, adv. [lūcidus, *full of
light*], *clearly, distinctly,* **28.**
23.

Lucius, ī, M. See **Tarquinius,**
42. 8.

Lucrētia, ae, F., wife of Tarquinius Collatinus, **46.** 18.

lucrum, ī, N., *gain; riches,
wealth,* **26.** 19.

✓ **lūctor, 1,** *wrestle; strive, struggle,
contend,* **25.** 21.

lūctus, ūs, M., *sorrow, mourning,
grief.*

lūcus, ī, M., *shining place; sacred
grove, grove,* **34.** 22 ; **37.** 25.

lūdibrium, ī, N. [lūdus], *thing
causing mockery; taunt, jest,
scoff, ridicule,* **35.** 2.

(lūdicer), cra, crum, adj. [lūdus],
*belonging to play; done in
sport, sportive,* **33.** 15.

✓ **lūdō, 3,** sī, sus, *play; deceive,
trick,* **55.** 19.

lūdus, ī, M., *play;* pl., *public
games, sports, spectacle, shows,*
35. 4 ; **59.** 28.

✓ **lugeō, 2,** lūxī, lūctus, *mourn,*

lament, bewail, grieve for, **39.**
23.

lūmen, inis, N., *that which shines;
rays, light,* **12.** 6, 10.

lūna, ae, F. *shining one ; moon,*
37. 17.

lupa, ae, F. [lupus], *she-wolf,*
33. 9, 12.

lupus, ī, M., *wolf,* **48.** 1, 2, 16, etc. ✓

luscinia, ae, F., *nightingale,* ✓
48. 12.

lūstrō, 1 [lūstrum, *sacrifice for
purification*], *review, examine,*
36. 12.

lūsus, ūs, M. [lūdō], *playing; for
sport, in fun,* **55.** 14.

lūx, lūcis, F., *that which shines ;
light, daylight,* **9.** 11 ; lūce
ortā, *at sunrise, at daybreak,* **9.**
9; **11.** 5; **22.** 5.

lūxuriōsē, adv. [lūxuriōsus],
luxuriously, voluptuously, **75.**
16.

lūxuriōsus, a, um, adj. [lūxuria,
extravagance], *extravagant,
luxurious,* **66.** 14.

lūxus, ūs, M., *excess ; luxury, en-* ✓
joyment, pleasure, **46.** 17.

Lycus, ī, M., father of Thrasy-
bulus, **69.** 24.

Lysander, drī, M., a Spartan general, **72.** 6.

M

M., abbreviation for **Mārcus.**

magicus, a, um, adj., *of magic,
magical,* **14.** 26 ; **15.** 7 ; **28.** 16.

magis, adv., comp., *more, rather,*
24. 12 ; **34.** 21 ; **40.** 4, etc.

magister, trī, M., *master ; teacher,
exponent,* **58.** 19.

magistrātus, ūs, M. [magister],
office of master ; office, **71.** 24 ;
*body of magistrates, administra-
tion,* **68.** 9.

māgnificē, adv. [māgnificus],
*nobly ; grandly, richly, sumptu-
ously, splendidly,* **30.** 4.

māgnificentia, ae, F. [māgnifi-
cus], *loftiness ; splendor, gran-
deur, elegance*, 28. 5.

māgnificus, a, um, adj. [māgnus],
*made great ; splendid, fine,
sumptuous, grand*, 28. 12 ; 29.
8.

māgnitūdō, inis, F. [māgnus],
greatness ; size, proportions, 7.
11 ; 9. 4 ; 10. 5, etc.

māgnopere or māgnō opere, adv.,
*very much, greatly, exceed-
ingly, heartily.*

māgnus, a, um, adj., *increased ;
great, large, mighty*, 2. 11, 22,
24, etc.; *loud, heavy*, 20. 24 ;
25. 8 ; 29. 6, etc.

māior, ius, adj., comp. of māgnus ; *greater*, 33. 2 ; 37. 23 ;
50. 16, etc.

male, adv. [malus], *badly,
wickedly*, 51. 2 ; *scarcely, with
difficulty*, 39. 12 ; *unsuccess-
fully*, 69. 17.

maledīcentissimus, a, um, adj.,
superl. of maledicus [male-
dīcō], *abusive, slanderous*,
75. 4.

maledīcō, 3, xī, dictus, *speak ill
of ; abuse, revile, rail at*, 48.
1, 3.

maleficus, a, um, adj. [male],
evil-doing ; wicked, vicious,
51. 1.

malitiōsē, adv. [malitiōsus, *full
of wickedness*], *wickedly, kna-
vishly*, 71. 17.

mālō, mālle, māluī, — [magis,
volō], *wish rather ; choose,
prefer*, 29. 5 ; 59. 15 ; 74. 9.

malus, a, um, adj., *bad, evil ;* as
noun, N., *evil*, 16. 8 ; 53. 21, 22,

etc.; as noun, M. pl., *the bad*,
52. 5.

mālus, ī, M., *upright pole ; mast*,
26. 9.

Māmurius, ī, M., Numa's smith,
37. 12.

māne, adv. [māne, *morning*], *in* ✓
*the morning, early in the morn-
ing*, 9. 4.

maneō, 2, mānsī, mānsus, *stay ;
abide, stay, remain*, 5. 21 ; 10.
20 ; 12. 17, etc.; *last, endure,
continue*, 40. 9 ; 74. 3.

manifestus, a, um, adj. [manus],
*struck with the hand ; evident,
plain, apparent*, 40. 5.

manūs, ūs, F., *measuring thing ;
hand*, 7. 18 ; 19. 10, 16, etc. ;
band, force, 71. 27 ; w. cōnserō,
engage hand to hand, 38. 20.

Mārcius, ī, M. See Ancus, 41. 6.

Mārcus, ī, M. See Bibulus, 60.
1 ; Brūtus, 64. 18 ; Crassus,
60. 6.

mare, is, N., *sea*, 4. 4 ; 7. 13,
etc.; mare superum, *Adriatic
Sea*, 63. 15.

Marius, ī, M., *Caius Marius* [B.C.
157–86], leader of the popular
party at Rome, 58. 17.

Mārs, Mārtis, M., god of war,
37. 14.

Mārtius, a, um, *of Mars ;* hence
of the month of March, 37. 15.

massa, ae, F., *kneaded dough ;*
hence *mass, lump*, 50. 14.

māter, tris, F., *she that bears ;
mother*, 33. 11, 21.

mātrimōnium, ī, N. [māter],
marriage, wedlock, 15. 24 ; 18.
10 ; 45. 6, etc.

mātūrō, 1 [mātūrus, *ripe*], *make*

ripen; *make haste, hurry, hasten,* 12. 4 ; 18. 2; 32. 1.

māximē, adv. [māximus], *in the highest degree; especially, particularly, principally,* 15. 11 ; 21. 4; **24.** 22, etc.

māximus, a, um, adj., superl. of māgnus ; *greatest, very great,* 17. 2 ; **27.** 3; **42.** 22, etc.

Mēdēa, ae, F., daughter of Aeetes, king of Colchis, 8. 18.

medicāmentum, ī, N. [medicō, *drug*], *drug, potion,* **28.** 14.

medicīna, ae, F. [medicus], *healing art; medicine,* 8. 22 ; 11. 15 ; **14.** 21, etc.

✓ **meditor,** 1, *reflect; plan, devise,* 63. 19.

medius, a, um, adj., *in the middle, in the midst of,* 7. 13, 19; 10. 9, etc.; media nox, *midnight,* 8. 23 ; 10. 21 ; as noun, N., *space between, middle,* 38. 14.

mehercule, interj. [Herculēs], *by Hercules; indeed, assuredly,* 55. 3.

membrum, ī, N., *small part; limb, member,* 13. 9, 11, 14, etc.

memorābilis, e, adj. [memorō], *that may be told; worthy of remembrance, remarkable, notable,* 59. 25.

memoria, ae, F. [memor, *mindful*], *remembrance, memory,* 46. 27; 66. 3; 68. 21 ; w. teneō, *remember, bear in mind,* 11. 1 ; 27. 12.

memorō, 1 [memor, *mindful*], *bring to remembrance; recount, relate, tell,* 41. 4.

✓ **mendāx,** ācis, adj., *given to lying, untruthful, lying,* (p. 55).

mēns, mentis, F., *thinking; mind,* ✓ 43. 3 ; *attention, notice,* 35. 8.

mēnsis, is, M., *month,* 37. 17 ; ✓ 63. 4.

mentiō, ōnis, F., *calling to mind; mention, allusion,* 29. 11 ; 46. 15; 69. 21.

mercātor, ōris, M. [mercor], *trader, merchant,* 20. 25, 26.

mercēs, ēdis, F., *price; fee, reward, offer of a reward,* 51. 18, 20; *return, reward,* 51. 22 ; 52. 5.

mercor, 1 [merx], *trade; buy, purchase,* 47. 13.

Mercurius, ī, M. [merx, *goods*], god of trades, *Mercury,* 29. 18.

mereor, 2, itus, *deserve, be entitled to,* 54. 18.

mergō, 3, sī, sus, *dip; sink, disable,* 59. 8. ✓

merīdiānus, a, um, adj. [merī- ✓ diēs], *of midday, of noon,* **26.** 10.

merīdiēs, acc. em, M. [for medidiēs, medius], *midday, noon,* 9. 16; *south,* 18. 17.

meritō, adv. [abl. of meritum, ✓ *desert*], *according to desert; deservedly, justly,* 48. 14.

meritus, a, um, adj. [p. of mereor], *deserving; due, fit, proper, right,* 7. 8.

merx, cis, F., *goods, wares, commodities,* 63. 7.

Mettius, ī, M., *M. Fufetius,* leader of the Albans, 40. 9.

metus, ūs, M., *fear, dread,* 37. 29.

meus, a, um, adj., *of me ; my, mine,* 14. 10; 34. 19; 41. 16, etc.

micāns, antis, adj. [p. of micō,

move quickly to and fro], *twinkling; glittering, flashing, gleaming,* 38. 19.

mīles, itis, M., *one of many; soldier, man,* 12. 21 ; 44. 5 ; 60. 28, etc.

Mīlētus, ī, F., a noted port of Ionia, 59. 5.

mīliēns, adv. [mīlle], *a thousand times,* 60. 3.

mīlitāris, e, adj. [mīles], *of a soldier ; of war, military, martial,* 9. 6 ; 36. 20.

mīlitia, ae, F. [mīles], *military service;* mīlitiae, *in the field, at war,* 40. 28.

mīlle, pl. mīlia, num. adj., *one thousand,* 4. 23 ; 5. 12 ; 11. 11, etc.

minimē, adv., superl. of parum, *least of all, very little, by no means,* 34. 3.

minimus, a, um, adj., superl., *least, smallest ;* minimum āfuit quīn, *came very near,* 13. 1 ; 25. 15.

minitor, 1, freq.[minor], *threaten, menace,* 30. 15.

minor, 1 [minae], *project; threaten, menace,* 59. 9.

minor, us, adj. comp. of parvus, *less, smaller,* 47. 14 ; 50. 16.

minuō, 3, uī, ūtus, *make small; lessen, diminish, reduce, weaken,* 74. 8.

minus, adv. comp. of parvum, *less,* 37. 29, 30 ; 66. 11, etc. ; neque minus multās, *and as many,* 70. 8.

mīrābilis, e, adj. [mīror], *to be wondered at ; wonderful, singular, strange,* 43. 24. Cf. mīrus.

mīrāculum, ī, N. [mīror], *marvellous thing; marvel, wonder,* 15. 3.

mīror, 1 [mīrus], *wonder, marvel, be astonished* or *amazed,* 9. 13; 12. 8 ; 20. 6, etc.

mīrus, a, um, adj., *wonderful, marvellous, extraordinary,* 9. 21 ; 10. 6 ; 12. 7, etc. Cf. mīrābilis.

misceō, 2, uī, mīxtus, *mix, mingle, prepare,* 28. 14.

miser, era, erum, adj., *wretched ; unfortunate, miserable, poor,* 53. 7.

misericordia, ae, F. [misericors, *tender-hearted*], *pity, compassion, kindness,* 52. 2.

Mithridātēs, is, M., king of Pontus, 62. 17.

mītigō, 1 [mītis], *make soft; soften, subdue, refine,* 36. 26.

mītis, e, adj., *soft ; gentle, kind, mild,* 45. 4, 6, 7.

mittō, 3, mīsī, mīssus, *cause to go ; hurl, throw,* 74. 22 ; *send, send off, despatch,* 2. 17 ; 6. 8, 20, etc.

modo, adv. [abl. of modus], *by a measure ; only, merely, simply,* 73. 21 ; nōn modo . . . sed etiam, *not only . . . but also,* 2. 4 ; 11. 13 ; 12. 18 ; as conj., *if only, provided that,* 55. 4.

modus, ī, M., *measure ; limit, bounds,* 63. 11 ; *way, manner, method,* 3. 4 ; 9. 21 ; 10. 6, etc.

moenia, ium, N., *defensive walls ; ramparts, city walls,* 34. 19 ; 35. 13 ; 42. 3.

mōlēs, is, F., *shapeless mass; weight, mass,* 56. 20.

molestia, ae, F. [molestus], *trouble; annoyance, vexation, distress,* 6. 11.

molestus, a, um, adj. [mōlēs, *mass*], *troublesome, irksome,* 52. 8.

mōlior, 4 [mōlēs], *make exertion; labor at, struggle to accomplish, be busy about,* 73. 25; *undertake, attempt,* 61. 22. Cf. cōnor, 5. 20.

Molō, ōnis, M., *Apollonius Molo,* a famous rhetorician in the time of Caesar, 58. 19.

√ **mōmentum,** ī, N., *movement; weight, importance, influence,* 72. 20; *moment, instant,* 62. 21.

moneō, 2, uī, itus, *make to think; remind, advise, warn,* 2. 20; 48. 8; 63. 22.

monitus, ūs, M. [moneō], *reminding; advice, counsel,* 37. 25.

mōns, montis, M., *projecting; mountain, mount,* 8. 24; 20. 14; 38. 2, etc.

mōnstrō, 1 [mōnstrum], *point out; show, display, point to,* 14. 2; 28. 26.

mōnstrum, ī, N., *that which warns; monster, pest, fiend,* 6. 8; 20. 7, 17, etc.

'mora, ae, F., *delay; hesitation, stopping, delay,* 12. 14; 19. 5; 22. 7, etc.

morbus, ī, M., *sickness, disease,* 41. 1; 58. 8; morbō extinguī, *die a natural death,* 38. 1.

morior, 3, mortuus, *die, expire,* 2. 10; 8. 21; 38. 5, etc.; fame, *starve to death,* 6. 14.

√ **moror,** 1 [mora], *wait; delay, retard, hinder,* 31. 15; 65. 5.

mors, rtis, F., *end, death,* 2. 12, √ 14; 14. 14, etc.

morsus, ūs, M. [mordeō, *bite*], *biting, bite,* 55. 2.

mortālis, e, adj. [mors], *subject to death; mortal, human, of men,* 29. 25.

mortiferus, a, um, adj. [mors], *death-bearing; fatal, deadly.*

mortuus, a, um, adj. [p. of morior], *dead,* 2. 10; 15. 15; 74. 7, etc.

mōs, mōris, M., *will; custom,* √ *practice, habit,* 41. 12; 45. 8; 60. 17, etc.; *way, manner,* 16. 9; 62. 20.

moveō, 2, mōvī, mōtus, *move,* 50. 7; *stir, inspire,* 4. 8; 31. 18; 52. 2; *rouse to anger, arouse, provoke,* 39. 19; *remove, expel, degrade,* 63. 7.

mox, adv., *soon, at length, pres-* √ *ently, afterwards,* 5. 6; 7. 16; 10. 12, etc.

mulier, eris, F., *she who grinds; woman,* 10. 25; 36. 2; 47. 3, etc.

muliebris, e, adj. [mulier], *of a woman, woman's, feminine,* 74. 24.

mūliō, ōnis, M., *mule-keeper; muleteer, driver,* 45. 16.

multiplex, icis, adj. [mŭltus], *with many folds; repeated, frequent,* 62. 18.

multitūdō, inis, F. [multus], *many together; large number, host, throng, crowd;* 4. 3; 42. 1; 67. 12.

multō, adv. [multus], *by much; much, far, very,* 47. 8; 66. 6; 69. 5; nōn ita multō post, *not very long after,* 36. 6.

multum, adv. [multus], *much ;
great deal, greatly, much, long,*
4. 18; 6. 13.

multus, a, um, adj., *much ;* pl.,
many, a great number, 3. 17 ;
4. 7, 11, etc.

mūniō, 4 [moenia], *wall ; build,*
63. 15 ; *fortify, protect, defend,*
11. 14; 20. 2; 69. 2.

√ mūnus, eris, N., *service ; offering,
present, gift,* 35. 15.

mūrus, ī, M., *enclosing thing ;*

wall, city wall, 42. 22; 44.
16.

mūs, mūris, M. and F., *mouse,*
51. 10, 13; 55. 1.

mūtō, 1, freq. [moveō], *keep moving, change, alter,* 8. 9; 42. 24;
58. 6.

Mȳsia, ae, F., a state of Asia
Minor, 5. 13.

mystērium, ī, N., *secret service ;
sacred rite, divine mystery,* 67.
23.

N

nactus. See nancīscor.

nam, conj., *for, you know,* 34. 4 ;
35. 19 ; 37. 19, etc. Cf. enim,
3. 6.

namque, conj., connecting closely
with what precedes; *for, and in
fact,* 66. 7 ; 73. 14, 18, etc.

nancīscor, 3, nactus or nanctus,
get, obtain, 4. 16 ; 11. 6; 18. 4,
etc.; *encounter, fall in with,
meet,* 35. 12.

nārrō, 1 [gnārus, *known*], *make
known ; tell, relate, recount,* 28.
23; 60. 28.

nāscor, 3, nātus, *be born, be pro-
duced,* 44. 24; 56. 16; 66. 4,
etc. ; p. nātus, *born,* i.e. *old,* 74.
27; *son of* (w. abl.), 46. 13.

natō, 1, freq. [nō, *swim*], *swim
about, float,* 55. 9.

nātūra, ae, F., *birth ; quality, nature, character,* 9. 20; 11. 14;
18. 20, etc.

(nātus, ūs), M., only abl. sing.,
being born ; birth, age, years ;
māior nātū, *elder, older,* 33. 2.

nauta, ae, M. [for nāvita, nāvis],
sailor, seaman, 5. 14.

nauticus, a, um, adj. [nāvis], *of
ships ; ship-, naval, nautical,* 3.
23 ; 72. 25.

nāvālis, e, adj. [nāvīs], *of ships ;
naval, sea-,* 70. 3.

nāvicula, ae, F. [nāvis], *small
vessel ; boat, skiff,* 62. 6.

nāvigātiō, ōnis, F. [nāvigō], *sail-
ing, navigation, voyage,* 26. 1 ;
32. 1.

nāvigium, ī, N. [nāvis], *vessel,
ship, boat,* 62. 9.

nāvigō, 1 [nāvis], *make a ship
go ; sail, navigate,* 4. 16; 26.
7 ; 31. 21.

nāvis, is, F., *ship, vessel,* 3. 21,
23 ; 4. 3, etc.; n. longa, *ship
of war,* 12. 20.

Navius, ī, M. See Attus, 42. 25.

nē, adv. and conj., *not,* 10. 25 ;
11. 3; with quidem, *not even,*
4. 1 ; 21. 10, 21, etc.; *that,* 2.
15 ; *that not,* 7. 12; 8. 16,
etc.

-ne, interrog. part., *whether*, 14.
18; 43. 2.

√ nē, interj., *truly, really*, 56. 15.

√ nec or neque, conj., *and not, but
not*, 6. 19; 7. 6; 10. 18, etc.;
nec . . . nec, *neither . . . nor*,
20. 26; 24. 2; 30. 12, etc.

necessāriō, adv. [necessārius],
unavoidably, inevitably, 72. 16.

necessārius, a, um, adj. [necesse,
unavoidable], *indispensable,
needful, requisite*, 63. 12.

necesse, adj., only nom. and acc.,
*unavoidable, inevitable, neces-
sary*, 13. 16; 23. 16.

necessitās, ātis, F. [necesse],
being inevitable ; need, necessity,
33. 19.

√ necō, 1, *kill, slay, put to death*,
15. 9; 16. 14; 56. 5. Cf. interficiō.

nefāriē, adv. [nefārius, *impious*],
impiously, abominably.

√ nefās, indecl., N., *something contrary to divine law ; crime, sin,
wrong*, 67. 24.

nefāstus, a, um, adj. [nefās],
contrary to divine law ; w. diēs,
day on which public assemblies
must not sit, so *holy day, holi-
day*, 37. 18.

neglegenter, adv. [neglegēns,
heedless], *heedlessly, carelessly,
negligently*, 71. 17.

neglegō, 3, ēxī, ēctus [nec, legō],
*disregard, not heed, slight, pass
by*, 9. 7 ; 47. 13; 55. 20.

negō, 1, *say no ; deny, say . . .
not*, 5. 21 ; 43. 1 ; 64. 26 ; *deny,
refuse*, 8. 7 ; 48. 12 ; 61. 18.

negōtium, ī, N. [nec, ōtium], *absence from ease ; business, em-

ployment, task*, 3. 16; 6. 24;
8. 8, etc.; *trouble, effort*, 10.
14 ; w. dare, *charge, commission*,
etc., 3. 11, 22; 74. 12.

nēmō, —, dat. nēminī [nē homō],
no man ; no one, nobody, 24. 1 ;
27. 14; 29. 4.

nemus, oris, N., *feeding thing ;
wood, forest, grove*, 37. 5.

Neontīchos, ī, N., a fortress in
Thrace, 71. 27.

nepōs, ōtis, M., *child's son ;
grandson*, 34. 4; 41. 7.

nēquāquam, adv., *in no wise, by √
no means*, 49. 11.

neque. See nec.

nervus, ī, M., *sinew, muscle, nerve,
strength*, 9. 1.

nēsciō, 4, īvī, —, *not know, be
unaware*, 9. 14; 10. 11; w.
quis as indef. pron., *I know
not who, some, a certain*, 2. 14 ;
3. 3; w. quō modō, *I know not
how, somehow*, 75. 4.

nex, necis, F., *death, execution*, √
58. 6.

Nīciās, ae, M., an Athenian general, 67. 6.

niger, gra, grum, adj., *black*, 64.
21.

nihil, indecl., N., *not a trifle ;
nothing*, 14. 5; 21. 16; 30.
15, etc. ; w. partit. gen., *no*, 16.
8 ; as adv., *in no respect, not at
all*, 7. 3; 9. 13 ; 13. 18, etc.

nihildum, indecl., N., *nothing as
yet*, 59. 25.

nihilum, ī, N., *not a shred ;
nothing*, 47. 14.

nimis, adv., *beyond measure, too
much ;* w. neg., *not very, not
especially*, 71. 9.

nimius, a, um, adj., *beyond measure; too great, too much*, 47. 3 ; 71. 20.

nisi, conj. [nē, sī], *if not ; unless, except*, 30. 21 ; 41. 3 ; 43. 1, etc.

✓ nitor, ōris, M., *brightness ; lustre, sheen*, 54. 8.

nō, 1, āvī, — , *swim*, 65. 6. Cf. natō, 55. 9.

nōbilis, e, adj., *to be known ; well-born, noble*, 43. 22 ; superl. nōbilissimus, 58. 1 ; *well-known, celebrated, renowned*, 36. 16 ; as noun, M., *noble, man of rank*, 68. 15.

noceō, 2, uī, itūrus, *do harm, injure*, 68. 5.

noctū, adv. [nox], *by night, in the night*, 2. 8 ; 62. 6 ; 74. 13.

nocturnus, a, um, adj. [nox], *of night ; by night, nightly*, 4. 2 ; 37. 24 ; 64. 2.

nōlō, nōlle, nōluī, — [nē, volō], *wish . . . not ; not wish, be unwilling*, 3. 18 ; 53. 8 ; 68. 12, etc.

nōmen, inis, N., *means of knowing ; name*, 3. 8 ; 4. 11, 19, etc.

nōminō, 1 [nōmen], *call by name; call by the name of, term, call*, 36. 9.

nōn, adv. [for old noenum, nē and oenum (ūnum)], *not*, 2. 4 ; 4. 24 ; 5. 3, etc.

nōndum, adv., *not yet*, 9. 23 ; 22. 16 ; 64. 7.

nōnne, interrog. adv., *in direct questions expecting an affirmative answer, not?* 29. 15 ; 59. 24.

nōnnūllus, a, um, adj., *not none ; some, several*, 18. 6, 19; 19. 5, etc.

nōnnumquam, adv., *not never ; sometimes, at times*, 65. 2.

nōscō, 3, nōvī, nōtus, *get knowl-* ✓ *edge of ; come to know, learn*, 52. 17.

noster, tra, trum, adj. [nōs], *our*, 4. 4.

notō, 1 [nota, *mark*], *mark, single out, censure*, 50. 10.

nōtus, a, um, adj. [p. of nōscō], *known ; well-known, familiar*, superl. nōtissimus, 4. 11; 17. 3.

novācula, ae, F. [novō, *make new*], ✓ *sharp knife, razor*, 43. 5.

novem, num. adj., *nine*, 26. 12 ; 47. 1, 6, etc.

novitās, ātis, F. [novus], *newness ; novelty, strangeness*, 4. 8 ; 7. 6 ; 28. 11.

novus, a, um, adj., *new, young*, 16. 9; 34. 12, 16, etc. ; *renewed, new, fresh*, 55. 10.

nox, noctis, F., *night*, 5. 2, 13; 8. 23, etc.

nūbō, 3, psī, ptus, *veil oneself ;* ✓ *marry, wed*, 61. 11.

nūdus, a, um, adj., *ashamed ; bare, naked*, 3. 5 ; *barren*, 48. 17.

nūllus, a, um, adj. [ūllus], *not any ; none, no*, 2. 19 ; 3. 4 ; 10. 14, etc. ; as abl. of nēmō, 29. 7.

num, adv., interrog. partic., *whether* (expecting negative answer), 14. 19; 29. 17 ; 43. 5, etc.

Numa, ae, M., *Numa Pompilius*,

the second king of Rome, 36. 23.

numerō, 1 [numerus], *count; count out, pay over, pay*, 59. 4.

numerus, ī, M., *distributing thing; number*, 2. 24 ; 4. 9, 13, etc.

Numidia, ae, F., a country of northern Africa (in modern Algiers), 62. 25.

Numitor, ōris, M., son of Procas and grandfather of Romulus, 33. 1.

numquam, adv. [nē, umquam], *not ever; at no time, never*, 19. 11 ; 23. 2; 28. 3, etc.

nunc, adv. [num], *now, at the present time*, 14. 22 ; 18. 10 ; 35. 23, etc.

nūntiō, 1 [nūntius], *announce, declare, report, make known*, 37. 8.

nūntius, ī, M., *bringer of news; messenger, herald*, 2. 22 ; 3. 18 ; 4. 6, etc.; *news, tidings*, 65. 4.

nūper, adv., *newly ; recently, not long before, just*, 5. 1 ; 27. 13.

nurus, ūs, F., *daughter-in-law, young matron*, 46. 17.

nusquam, adv. [nē, usquam], *not anywhere; nowhere, in no place*, 35. 1 ; 47. 16.

nūtō, 1, freq [nuō, *nod*], *nod ; waver, falter*, 61. 1.

nympha, ae, F., *bride, nymph*, 5. 19.

O

Ō, interj. of address, *O! Oh!* 52. 12.

ob, prep. w. acc., *towards, on account of, because of, for*, 2. 18 ; 5. 15 ; 8. 5, etc.

obeō, īre, īvī, (iī) itus, *go to meet ; w. diem suprēmum, die, perish*, 74. 27 ; 42. 7.

obiūrgō, 1, *chide, blame, rebuke, reprove*, 27. 4.

oblātus. See **offerō**.

oblinō, 3, lēvī, litus, *daub upon ; smear over, anoint*, 9. 4.

oblīquus, a, um, adj., *sidelong, slanting, sidewise*, 49. 14.

oblītus, a, um, adj. [p. of oblīvīscor], *having forgotten ; forgetful, unmindful, regardless*, 18. 26 ; 39. 22, 23.

obnoxius, a, um, adj., *liable ; exposed, subject*, 64. 22.

obruō, 3, uī, utus, *rush against ; overwhelm, cover over, crush, hide, bury*, 35. 19 ; 62. 12.

obscūrus, a, um, adj., *covered over ; dark, black*, 5. 3.

obsecrō, 1 [sacrō, *consecrate*], *beseech ; implore, entreat, pray, beg*, 10. 25; 29. 1 ; 30. 16, etc. Cf. obtestor, 31. 14.

obsequor, 3, cūtus, *follow, comply, gratify, obey*, w. dat., 49. 16.

obses, idis, M. and F., *hostage, pledge*, 60. 27.

obsideō, 2, sēdī, sessus [sedeō], *sit before ; besiege, beset, lay siege to*, 17. 1 ; 46. 12.

obsidiō, ōnis, F., *siege, blockade*, 69. 3.

obsistō, 3, stitī, stitus, *stand in the way ; oppose, resist, withstand*, 60. 10.

✔ **obstrepŏ, 3, uī, —,** *make a noise against; clamor at, shout against, outbawl,* 43. 16.

obstruŏ, 3, strūxī, strūctus, *build against; block up, bar, barricade,* 20. 21 ; 21. 19 ; 24. 7.

obsum, esse, fuī, —, *be against; injure, harm,* 67. 22.

obtestor, 1, *call as a witness; entreat, implore, beseech,* 31. 14. Cf. obsecrō, 10. 25.

obtineŏ, 2, uī, tentus [teneō], *hold against; hold, occupy, maintain, obtain,* 2. 3 ; 3. 9 ; 6. 4, etc.

obtrectātor, ōris, M. [obtrectō, *detract from*] ; *slanderer, disparager, traducer,* 64. 22.

obtulī. See **offerŏ.**

ʟ **obviam, adv.,** *in the way ; before, in face of,* 29. 12 ; w. fīō, *fall in with, meet,* 18. 23 ; 49. 12 ; w. eō, etc., *go to meet,* 28. 1 ; 70. 12.

obvius, a, um, adj. [via], *in the way, meeting,* w. dat. ; w. esse, *meet,* 39. 16.

obvolvŏ, 3, vī, volūtus, *wrap round, muffle, cover,* 62. 7 ; 64. 17.

occāsiŏ, ōnis, F., *opportunity, chance, favorable moment,* 8. 16 ; 16. 20 ; 21. 14, etc.

occāsus, ūs, M., *a falling ; going down, setting,* 4. 22 ; 12. 2 ; 28. 20.

occīdŏ, 3, cīdī, cīsus [caedō], *cut down ; put to death, kill,* 5. 6, 8 ; 10. 13, etc.

occulŏ, 3, uī, ltus, *cover, hide, conceal,* 73. 8.

occumbŏ, 3, cubuī, cubitus, *fall in death ; die, perish,* 27. 13. Cf. morior, 2. 10.

occupŏ, 1, *take into possession; obtain possession, seize, acquire, occupy,* 2. 16 ; 21. 10 ; 27. 24, etc.; *engage, busy, employ,* 72. 7.

occurrŏ, 3, rī, rsus, *run against; meet, come upon,* 12. 10 ; 49. 10. Cf. obviam fierī, 49. 12.

oculus, ī, M., *sharp thing ; eye,* 20. 7, 10, 22, etc.

odium, ī, N., *hatred, aversion, enmity,* 31. 13.

offendŏ, 3, dī, fēnsus, *strike against ; displease, vex, offend,* 63. 26.

offerŏ, ferre, obtulī, oblātus, *bring before ; present, offer,* 21. 25 ; 49. 2 ; 64. 1.

officīna, ae, F. [for opificīna, from opifex, *workman*], *workshop, laboratory,* 20. 16.

officium, ī, N. [for opificium, opus], *service, office ; courtesy, attention, honor,* 64. 9.

ŏlim, adv., *at that time ; once upon a time, once, formerly,* 2. 1 ; 3. 11 ; 6. 7, etc.

Olympia, ae, F., a town in Elis where national games were held, 70. 25.

omittŏ, 3, mīsī, mīssus, *let go ; pass by, disregard, neglect,* 10. 8 ; 15. 9 ; 16. 19, etc.

omnīnŏ, adv. [omnis], *altogether,* ✔ *wholly, entirely,* 15. 12 ; 18. 25 ; 21. 6, etc.

omnis, e, adj., *all, the whole,* 2. 23 ; 3. 19 ; 4. 7, etc. ; *as noun,* M. pl., *all, everybody,* 4. 17 ; 9. 15, 25 ; N. pl., *everything,* 3. 20.

√ **onus,** eris, N., *load, burden,* 53. 2,
8, 20, etc.

onustus, a, um, adj.[onus], *loaded,
laden, freighted,* 53. 1 ; 70. 10.

opera, ae, F. [opus], *aid, help,
assistance,* 67. 17 ; 69. 4 ; *exertion, effort,* 70. 16 ; 71. 3 ; w.
dare and dat., *give attention,
bestow care, busy* or *exert oneself* (about), 41. 3; 58. 20.

opīniō, ōnis, F. [opīnor, *suppose*],
supposition ; idea, belief, expectation, 13. 12 ; *reputation, renown, name,* 6. 18; 71. 20.

√ **oportet,** 2, uit, —, impers., *it is necessary, is proper, ought,* 48. 15.

oppidum, ī, N., *town,* 6. 2; 36. 24;
41. 24, etc.

oppositus, a, um, adj. [p. of oppōnō], *placed against ; opposed,
opposing, stationed against,* 62. 2.

oppressus. See **opprimō.**

opprimō, 3, pressī, pressus, *press
against ; weigh down, overcome, overpower,* 11. 20; 23.
10; 26. 17, etc.; *crush to death,*
16. 26 ; *ruin, destroy,* 67. 14 ;
72. 27.

(ops), opis, F., no nom. or dat.
sing., *aid, help, assistance,* 39.
6 ; 55. 15 ; *power, might, influence, wealth,* 61. 13 ; 69. 18 ;
71. 22, etc.

optimās, ātis, adj. [optimus], *of
the best ;* as noun, M., *adherent
of the nobility, aristocrat, patrician,* 58. 15 ; 69. 22.

optimus, a, um, adj., superl. of
bonus; *best, excellent,* 63. 12.

optiō, ōnis, F. [optō, *choose*],
choosing; choice, liberty to choose
(w. gen.), 35. 15.

opus, eris, N., *work, labor, task,*
4. 1 ; 9. 17, 23, etc.; *work,
book,* 17. 3 ; *want, need,* 60. 3;
māgnō opere (māgnopere),
greatly, exceedingly, heartily,
6. 17; 9. 13; 12. 7.

ōra, ae, F., *extremity ; shore,* √
coast, 70. 7.

ōrāculum, ī, N. [ōrō], *divine announcement ; response, oracle,*
2. 17, 19 ; 3. 7, etc.

ōrātiō, ōnis, F. [ōrō], *speaking ;
speech, words, appeal,* 14. 11 ;
style, speech, 66. 9.

orbis, is, M., *ring ;* terrārum,
earth, world, universe, 59. 26.

orbus, a, um, adj., *deprived, bereft, robbed,* 40. 3. √

ōrdinō, 1 [ōrdō], *order ; arrange,
adjust, regulate,* 36. 11 ; 63. 1 ;
ordain, first make, 44. 17.

ōrdior, 4, ōrsus, *begin a web ;*
hence, *begin, commence,* 43. 17. ι·

ōrdō, inis, M., *row ; rank,* 63. 7 ;
ex ōrdine, *in succession, one
after another,* 24. 20.

orior, 4, ortus, *stir oneself ;
rise, arise, begin,* 34. 11 ; 36.
16 ; 50. 3; *spring forth, rise,*
10. 7, 12 ; sōle ortō, ortā lūce,
at sunrise, 9. 9; 11. 5; 22. 5, etc.

ōrnāmentum, ī, N. [ōrnō], *equipment ; decoration, adornment,
ornament.*

ōrnātissimus, a, um, adj., superl.
of ōrnātus, *fitted out ; distinguished, excellent, eminent,* 58.
13.

Ornī, ōrum, M., *a fortress in*
Thrace, 71. 26.

ōrnō, 1, *fit out ; adorn, decorate,* √
beautify, 59. 28 ; 63. 9.

√ ōrō, 1 [ōs], *use the mouth, speak ;
beg, implore, entreat, plead,* 16.
16 ; 21. 2 ; 31. 14, etc. Cf.
obtestor, 31. 14.

Orpheus, ī, M., son of Onagrus
and Calliope, 4. 10.

√ ōs, ōris, N., *mouth, lips,* 8. 13 ;
33. 11 ; 59. 17 ; of a river, 42.
5 ; *face, countenance, features,*
34. 5 ; 47. 11 ; 64. 20 ; *lips,*
hence *speech, elocution,* 66. 9.

os, ossis, N., *bone,* 51. 18.

ostendō, 3, dī, tus, *stretch before ;
show, indicate, make known,
tell,* 8. 12 ; 14. 5 ; 22. 20, etc.

\ ostentō, 1, freq. [ostendō], *pre-*

sent to view ; point to, hold up,
40. 1.

Ōstia, ae, F., a city founded by
Ancus Marcius at the mouth
of the Tiber, 42. 5.

ōstium, ī, N. [ōs], *door, entrance,* √
28. 5, 19 ; 30. 2.

ōtium, ī, N., *leisure, vacant time,* √
freedom from care ; w. per, *at
one's ease,* 58. 18.

ovāns, antis, adj. [p. of ovō, *re-* √
joice], *rejoicing, exulting, tri-
umphant,* 39. 14.

ovis, is, F., *sheep,* 22. 12 ; 24. 9,
10, etc.

ōvum, ī, N., *egg,* 50. 13.

P

pābulum, ī, N., *food ; fodder, pas-
turage,* 49. 1, 4.

\ pācō, 1 [pāx], *make peaceful ;
subdue, bring to peace,* 37. 20.

Pactyē, ēs, F., a fortress in
Thrace, on the Propontis, 71.
26.

! paene, adv., *nearly, almost,* 9. 4 ;
13. 4 ; 18. 25, etc.

paenitentia, ae, F. [paeniteō],
repentance, 56. 11.

paeniteō, 2, uī, —, *make sorry ;*
impers., *it repents, grieves,* 54.
2 ; 55. 13.

palea, ae, F., *chaff,* 52. 8.

palūdāmentum, ī, N., (*military*)
cloak, mantle, 39. 17.

pālus, ī, M., *stake, bar, post,* 22.
18 ; 23. 13.

palūs, ūdis, F., *swamp, marsh,*
63. 15 ; Caprae, *Goat's-marsh,*
36. 13.

pandō, 3, dī, passus, *spread out ;*

passus as adj., *outspread ; flying, streaming, dishevelled,* 36.
2.

papāver, eris, M., *poppy ;* capita,
poppy-heads, 46. 7.

pār, paris, adj., *equal, matched,*
39. 9 ; 61. 14 ; 67. 20, etc. ; *like,
similar,* 45. 5.

parātus, a, um, adj. [p. of parō],
prepared ; ready, fitted, 8. 11 ;
superl., 4. 13.

parcissimus, a, um, adj., superl.
of parcus, *frugal, sparing, mod-
erate,* 64. 26.

pāreō, 2, uī, —, *appear ; yield to,*
68. 27 ; *carry out orders, obey,*
68. 12.

pariō, 3, peperī, partus, *bring
forth ; produce,* (ōvum) *lay,* 50.
13 ; *gain, obtain, acquire,* 72. 3.
Cf. cōnsequor, 42. 19.

pariter, adv. [pār], *equally,* 58. √
22 ; *in like manner, just,* 55. 19.

parō, 1, *make* or *get ready, prepare,* 10. 21; 12. 6; 18. 3, etc.; *make,* 16. 4; 8. 25; *contrive, arrange, provide,* 35. 5; 43. 11.

pars, partis, F., *that which is cut; part, portion, share,* 10. 5; 20. 18, 23, etc.; *part, direction,* 2. 23; 3. 19; 5. 1, etc.; plur., *party,* 58. 16; 62. 25.

parsimōnia, ae, F. [parcō], *frugality, thrift,* 75. 14.

Parthī, ōrum, M., a people of Scythia, 61. 10.

parum, adv., *too little; little enough, little,* 48. 13.

parvulus, a, um, adj., dim. [parvus], *very small;* as noun, M., *little one, babe,* 33. 6, 12; 53. 8, etc.

parvus, a, um, adj., *small, little, slight,* 7. 12; 51. 22.

pāscō, 3, pāvī, pāstus, *cause to eat; feed, drive to pasture, attend,* 55. 14; pass., *feed, graze,* 50. 1; 52. 8; 56. 13.

passus, a, um, adj., see **pandō.**

passus, ūs, M., *step, pace;* mīlle passuum, *mile,* 4. 23; 5. 12; 11. 11, etc.

pāstor, ōris, M., *one that feeds; herdsman, shepherd,* 20. 13; 33. 13, 15, etc.

patefaciō, 3, fēcī, factus [pateō, faciō], *make stand open; throw* or *lay open, open,* 30. 2.

pater, tris, M., *he who feeds; father, sire,* 8. 20; 23; 10. 22, etc.; pl., *fathers, patricians,* 36. 16; 39. 25.

paternus, a, um, adj. [pater], *of a father; father's, ancestral, hereditary,* 43. 10; 45. 10.

patiēns, entis, adj. [p. of patior], *bearing; enduring, patient, tolerant,* 65. 1; 66. 10.

patientia, ae, F. [patiēns], *quality of enduring; patience, endurance,* 75. 13.

patior, 3, passus, *bear; suffer, endure, allow, permit,* 24. 19; 49. 6; 62. 11, etc.

patria, ae, F. [patrius, *father's,* sc. terra], *fatherland; native land, country,* 18. 12, 26; 25. 19, etc.

patrimōnium, ī, N. [pater], *inheritance from a father; estate, inheritance,* 60. 2.

patrō, 1, *bring to pass; carry out, execute, perform,* 43. 12. Cf, perficiō, 8. 10.

paucus, a, um, adj., *few,* 2. 3, 21; 4. 14, etc.; as noun, M. pl., *few, a few,* 38. 9; 40. 11.

paulātim, adv. [paulum], *by little and little; by degrees, gradually,* 46. 1. ✓

paulō, adv. [abl. N. of paulus], *by a little; a little, shortly,* 4. 3; 18. 8; 40. 2, etc.

paululum, adv. [paululus, *very little*], *a little, a very little,* 54. 3.

paulum, adv. [paulus, *little*], *a little, somewhat,* 5. 19; 16. 12; 19. 23, etc.

pauper, eris, adj., *not wealthy; poor, small,* 59. 13.

pāvō, ōnis, M., *peacock,* 48. 5, 11.

pāx, pācis, F., *binding thing; peace, reconciliation, harmony,* 36. 4; 37. 19; 38. 3, etc.

peccō, 1, *miss, mistake, transgress, offend, sin.*

pectus, oris, N., *fastened thing;*
breast, bosom, 21. 15; 57. 3.

pecūnia, ae, F. [pecus], *property;*
money, wealth, pl. *funds,* 27. 5;
42. 17; 58. 10, etc.

pecus, oris, N., *thing fastened up;*
flock, cattle, 20. 20; 22. 8; 24.
8, etc.

✓ pedester, tris, tre, adj. [pēs], *on*
foot; w. cōpiae, *infantry, land*
forces, 72. 14.

pēior, ius, adj., comp. of malus,
worse.

Peliās, ae, M., a mythical king of
Thessaly, 2. 2.

✓ pellis, is, F., *skin, hide,* 50. 6;
53. 6, 9.

pellō, 3, pepulī, pulsus, *drive;*
drive out, banish, 33. 3; 71.
3.

Peloponnēsius, a, um, adj., *of*
the Peloponnesus, Peloponne-
sian, 67. 3.

Pēnelopē, ēs, F., wife of Ulysses,
18. 10.

✓ penitus, adv., *from within; with-*
in, completely, far within, 73.
6; perveniō, *penetrate,* 43. 14.

penna, ae, F., *feather, plume,* 48.
5; 54. 8.

per, prep. w. acc., *through,*
throughout, 11. 11; 15. 2; 16.
11, etc.; *across, over, down*
over, 7. 19; 16. 21; 45. 11;
by, at, 39. 2; 58. 18; *by means*
of, 4. 6; 10. 18; 11. 1, etc.

pēra, ae, F., *bag, wallet,* 57. 1.

peragō, 3, ēgī, āctus, *drive*
through; go through with,
carry out, perform, 40. 6; *go*
over, set forth, relate, 41. 16.
Cf. perficiō, 8. 10.

peragrō, 1 [ager], *wander*
through the fields; wander
through, travel, pass through,
33. 16.

percipiō, 3, cēpī, ceptus [capiō],
take wholly; assume, feel, 2.
11; 5. 9; 23. 3.

percontor, 1 [contus, *pole*],
search with a pole; question,
inquire, ask, 47. 3; 54. 2. Cf.
interrogō.

percutiō, 3, cussī, cussus [qua-
tiō], *strike through; strike,* 62.
21; *slay, kill,* 43. 7. Cf. oc-
cīdō, 5. 6.

perdō, 3, didī, ditus, *make away*
with; lose, throw away, 50. 16.

perdūcō, 3, xī, ductus, *bring* or
lead through, 7. 24; *lead, bring,*
conduct, guide, 33. 23; 35. 16,
18, etc.

peregrīnus, a, um, adj. [peregre
(per, agō), *abroad*], *from*
foreign parts, foreign, 63. 7.

perennis, e, adj. [annus], *through*
the year; never failing, un-
ceasing, ever flowing, 37. 26.

pereō, īre, iī, itūrus, *go through;*
disappear, perish, die, 3. 13;
15. 17; 45. 8, etc. Cf. morior,
2. 10.

perferō, ferre, tulī, lātus, *bear*
through; bear, withstand, en-
dure, 4. 5; 14. 17; 66. 14.

perficiō, 3, fēcī, fectus [faciō],
do thoroughly; perform, exe-
cute, do successfully, 8. 10.

perfidia, ae, F. [perfidus], *faith-*
lessness, treachery, 40. 20.

perfidus, a, um, adj., *promise-*
breaking; faithless, dishonest,
treacherous, 35. 27.

perflō, 1, —, —, *blow through* or *over*, 26. 22.

✓ perfringō, 3, frēgī, frāctus [frangō], *break through ; break in pieces, shatter, completely wreck*, 21. 6.

pergō, 3, rēxī, rēctus [regō], *make quite straight, go, go on, proceed, hasten*, 43. 15 ; 46. 18 ; 49. 15.

Periclēs, is, M., a celebrated Athenian statesman and general, 66. 18.

perīculum (perīclum), ī, N., *means of trying ; risk, peril, danger*, 2. 7, 20 ; 3. 13, etc.

✓ perītus, a, um, adj., *experienced, skilled, expert*, 42. 14; superl., 65. 1.

perlūstrō, 1, *go over ; wander all through, view all over, examine carefully*, 20. 22 ; 29. 9.

permaneō, 2, mānsī, mānsūrus, *remain through ; continue, remain, persist*, 14. 6.

perpetuō, adv. [perpetuus], *constantly, without ceasing, forever*, 37. 1 ; 64. 25.

perpetuus, a, um, adj., *continuous ; permanent*, 69. 3 ; in perpetuum, *for all time, for life*, 63. 20.

persaepe, adv., *very often*, 65. 4.

perscrībō, 3, psī, ptus, *write in full ; write at length, describe fully*, 32. 5.

persequor, 3, cūtus, *follow perseveringly, chase, follow up*, 62. 14 ; 74. 4.

Persēs, ae, M., *Persian*, 75. 15; w. rēx, for rēx Persārum, 69. 1.

✓ perspiciō, 3, spēxī, spectus, *look through ; examine, inspect.*

perstringō, 3, inxī, ictus, *bind through ; seize, affect deeply, move*, 38. 19.

persuādeō, 2, suāsī, suāsus, *thoroughly convince ; induce, prevail upon*, 5. 20 ; 19. 9; 25. 23, etc.

perterreō, 2, —, itus, *frighten thoroughly ; frighten, terrify*, 7. 6 ; 30. 18 ; 49. 10, etc.

pertimēscō, 3, timuī, —, inch., *be frightened, be alarmed, fear greatly*, 69. 10.

pertināciter, adv. [pertināx, *per- ✓ severing*], *obstinately, persistently*, 58. 13.

pertineō, 2, uī, — [teneō], *stretch out ; belong, relate, concern*, 67. 12, 25.

perturbō, 1, *confuse thoroughly ; disturb, discompose*, 28. 22.

pervehō, 3, vēxī, vēctus, *bear through ;* pass., *reach, arrive*, 68. 14.

perveniō, 4, vēnī, ventus, *come through ; reach, come*, 3. 5; 7. 12 ; 13. 18, etc.; w. penitus, *penetrate*, 43. 14.

pēs, pedis, M., *going thing ; foot*, ✓ 3. 5 ; 10. 24 ; 30. 23, etc. ; referō, *retreat*, 10. 2.

pestilentia, ae, F. [pestilēns, *unhealthy*], *plague, pestilence*, 40. 26.

petō, 3, īvī (iī), ītus, *fall upon ; ✓ seek, make for, attack*, 7. 2 ; 50. 3; 64. 16 ; *try to gain, strive for, solicit*, 23. 11 ; 35. 1 ; 61. 17, etc.; *get, obtain, seek*, 10. 21; 35. 13 ; *ask, beg, request*, 12. 44; 55. 6 ; 70. 2; *ask, claim as reward*, 35. 16; 47. 14.

petulantia, ae, F. [petulāns, *for-*

ward], *freakishness, impudence,*
50. 9.

Pharnabazus, ī, M., governor of
northwestern Asia Minor, 73.
12.

Pharnacēs, is, M., king of Pontus, a province south of the
Black Sea, 62. 17.

Pharsālicus, a, um, adj., *of* or *at
Pharsalus,* a town in Thessaly,
where, in B.C. 48, Julius Caesar
defeated Pompeius, 62. 13.

Phāsis, idis, M., a river flowing
into the Black Sea, 8. 1.

Philoclēs, ī, M., an Athenian general, 72. 5.

Phīneus, eī, M., a blind king of
Thrace, 6. 5.

Phrīxus, ī, M., son of Athamas,
3. 10.

Phrygia, ae, F., a country of Asia
Minor, 73. 15.

✓ **pietās, ātis, F.** [pius, *dutiful*],
*dutiful conduct; religiousness,
devotion, piety,* 37. 28; *justice,
right,* 59. 20.

∖ **pīgnus, oris** and **eris, N.,** *pledge,
token, assurance,* 37. 7, 15.

pīla, ae, F., *pillar, column,* 68.
22; 71. 7.

pilleus, ī, M. (pilleum, ī, N.),
skull-cap, cap, 42. 11.

pīnguissimus, a, um, adj., superl.
of pīnguis, e, *fat, heavy,* 24. 13.

Pīraeus, ī, M., the port of Athens,
70. 12.

pīrāta, ae, M., *sea-robber, pirate,*
58. 22; 59. 3, 8.

Pīsander, drī, M., an Athenian
general, 69. 19.

pīstrīnum, ī, N. [pīstor, *miller*],
corn-mill, mill, 50. 8.

placeō, 2, uī or **itus sum, itus,**
please, be pleasing, suit, w. dat.,
impers., *(they) decide, determine,
agree,* 38. 9; 46. 16; 51. 11.

placidē, adv. [placidus, *calm*],
gently, calmly, quietly, 47. 10.

plāga, ae, F., *blow, thrust, wound,* ✓
64. 17.

plausus, ūs, M. [plaudō, *clap the
hands*], *clapping, applause,
cheering,* 4. 17.

plēbs, bis, F., *common people,* ✓
plebeians, people, 36. 17 ; 39. 25;
60. 8.

(plectō), 3, —, —, only pass.,
be punished, suffer, 56. 15.

plēnus, a, um, adj., *full, filled,*
60. 12 ; 64. 20 ; 66. 7.

plērusque, raque, rumque, adj.,
the greater part; pl., *about all,
the greater part,* 75. 1.

plūrimum, adv. [plūrimus], *very
much,* 67. 22 ; 68. 26; w. possum, *have great power* or *influence, be of chief importance,*
46. 3.

plūrimus, a, um, adj., superl. of
multus ; *most, very many,
numerous,* 10. 13; 36. 26; 37.
22, etc.

plūs, ris, adj., comp. of multus ;
fuller ; more, many, 42. 6;
63. 10 ; 66. 21, etc. ; as adv.,
68. 27 ; 72. 14.

pōculum, ī, N., *vessel ; cup, vessel,* ✓
30. 6, 7.

poena, ae, F., *compensation ;
penalty, punishment,* 25. 10;
30. 22 ; 35. 20, etc.

poēta, ae, M., *poet,* 17. 3 ; 59. 17.

pol, interj. [Pollux], *by Pollux !
truly ! indeed !* 54. 8.

polliceor, 2, itus [prō-liceor], *hold forth ; promise, bargain, engage,* 14. 3. Cf. prōmittō, 6. 22.

.Polyphēmus, ī, M., a Cyclops, 5. 25.

Pompēiānus, a, um, adj., *of Pompey, Pompey's,* 61. 14.

Pompēius, ī, M., *Gnaeus Pompey,* a Roman general, Caesar's friend and ally, afterwards his rival, 60. 6.

Pompilius, ī, M. See Numa, 36. 23.

Pomptīnus, a, um, adj. [Pontius, *a Roman name*], *Pomptine* or *Pontine ;* palūs, the large marshy region in Italy, exposed to the inundation of the Amasenus and Ufens, 63. 14.

pōnō, 3, posuī, positus, *put down ; set in position, set up, place, fix,* 7. 11 ; 14. 25 ; 20. 11, etc.; *regard, consider,* 67. 20 ; 75. 13, 19 ; pass., *lie, rest, depend* or *consist in,* 7. 23 ; 24. 13.

pōns, pontis, M., *bridge,* 42. 4 ; 60. 25.

ponticulum, ī, N., dim. [pōns], *little bridge,* 61. 24.

Ponticus, a, um, adj., *relating to the Pontus,* 62. 23.

Pontus, ī, M., the region about the Black Sea (Pontus), 62. 17.

populus, ī, M., *the many ; nation, people, citizens,* 34. 24 ; 35. 1 ; 36. 10, etc.

porcus, ī, M., *tame swine ; hog, pig,* 28. 18 ; 29. 16 ; 30. 21, etc.

porta, ae, F., *thing passed through; passage, exit,* 26. 22 ; *gate, door,* 9. 11 ; 20. 7, 21, etc.

portendō, 3, dī, tus, *stretch forth;*

foretell, predict, destine, 42. 14 ; 44. 1.

porticus, ūs, F. [porta], *covered walk between columns ; colonnade, gallery,* 59. 28.

portō, 1, freq., *bear, carry, take,* 42. 16 ; 53. 5.

portōrium, ī, N., *tax, duty, tariff,* 63. 7.

portus, ūs, M., *harbor, port,* 19. 17 ; 26. 10.

poscō, 3, poposcī, —, *ask urgently ; beg, request, demand, require,* 47. 4 ; 66. 10.

possum, posse, potuī, — [potis, *able*], *be able, have power, can,* 3. 5 ; 4. 24 ; 7. 10, etc.; plūrimum, *have great influence, be of chief importance,* 46. 3.

post, adv., *behind ; afterwards, after, later,* 4. 18 ; 16. 12 ; 36. 7, etc.; prep. w. acc., *after, following,* 2. 3, 15, 21, etc.; *behind,* 19. 16 ; 27. 3.

posteā, adv., *after these ; afterwards, then,* 7. 6 ; 34. 14 ; 46. 12, etc.

(posterus), adj. [post], *coming after ; following, next,* 2. 9 ; 40. 18 ; 46. 22 ; pl., M., *descendants,* 41. 12.

posthāc, adv., *after this ; hereafter, henceforth, in future,* 41. 3.

postquam, conj., *after that ; after* (w. indic.), 3. 20 ; 4. 22 ; 5. 23, etc.

postrēmō, adv. [postrēmus], *at last, finally,* 58. 10 ; 61. 25.

postrēmus, a, um, adj., superl. of posterus ; *last;* w. ad, sc. tempus, *at last, finally,* 46. 3.

✓ **postrīdiē**, adv. [for posterō diē], *on the day after, next day,* 5. 10; 11. 5; 19. 19, etc.

✓ **postulātum**, ī, N. [postulō], *demand, claim, request,* 41. 17 ; 72. 19.

ι **postulō**, 1, *ask, demand, request, desire,* 8. 4 ; 9. 18 ; 14. 2, etc.

✓ **potentātus**, ūs, M. [potēns, *able*], *ability ; power, rule, dominion,* 36. 7.

·ι′ **potentia**, ae, F. [potēns, *able*], *might ; political power, influence, authority, sovereignty,* 69. 22; 73. 12. Cf. imperium, 34. 13.

potentior, ius, adj., comp. of potēns [p. of possum], *able ; mighty, strong,* 67. 16.

potestās, ātis, F. [potis, *able*], *ability ; power, control, rule,* 45. 22; 59. 8; 70. 5 ; *chance, opportunity,* 73. 22.

ι **potior**, 4, *become master of ; get possession of, obtain, acquire,* w. abl., 3. 12 ; 34. 20.

potius, adv., comp. [potis, *able*], *rather, more,* 68. 2.

prae, prep. w. abl., *before, in front of,* 39. 16.

praeacūtus, a, um, adj., *sharp in front ; sharpened at the end, pointed,* 22. 19.

praebeō, 2, uī, itus [habeō], *hold before ; offer, furnish, give, show,* 2. 12 ; 4. 1 ; 6. 7, etc.

praecaveō, 2, cāvī, cautus, *take care* or *heed, be on one's guard, beware,* 21. 5.

praeceptum, ī, N. [p. of praecipiō], *rule, precept, direction, order,* 49. 16.

praecipiō, 3, cēpī, ceptus [capiō], *take beforehand ; advise, admonish, instruct, charge, bid, order,* 9. 2 ; 10. 9; 36. 19.

praecipitō, 1 [praeceps, *headlong*], *throw headlong, hurl down, cast,* 71. 8.

praecipuē, adv.[praecipuus, *taken before others*], *chiefly, principally, more than anything else,* 20. 14; 63. 8.

praeclārissimus, a, um, adj., superl. of praeclārus; *very famous, distinguished, noted,* 4. 10.

praeda, ae, F., *property taken in war ; booty, prey, victim,* 54. 15 ; 56. 14; 70. 10, etc.

praedicātiō, ōnis, F. [praedicō], *public proclamation ; vaunting, boast,* 62. 22.

praedicō, 1, *make known by proclamation ; declare, pronounce, assert,* 52. 7 ; 68. 23 ; 75. 6.

praedīcō, 3, xī, dictus, *say before ; predict, tell beforehand, foretell,* 10. 4 ; 64. 4.

praedō, ōnis, M. [praeda], *one who makes booty; robber, pirate,* 58. 20 ; 59. 7.

praedor, 1 [praeda], *make booty; rob, plunder,* 20. 26; 73. 2. ✓

praefectus, ī, M. [p. of praeficiō], *commander, governor, satrap,* 69. 15.

praeferō, ferre, tulī, lātus, *bear in front ; carry in procession, display,* 62. 24.

praeferōx, ōcis, adj., *very violent ; haughty, insolent,* 62. 18.

praeficiō, 3, fēcī, fectus, *place in front ; place in command, put at the head,* 69. 26. ✓

praefīniō, 4, *determine beforehand ; ordain, prescribe,* 56. 17.

praemātūrus, a, um, adj., *too
early, untimely, premature.*

✓ praemium, ī, N. *taking before ;
favor, reward, recompense,* 6.
22.

praepōnō, 3, posuī, positus, *place
in front ; put before, prefer to,*
w. acc. and dat., 49. 3.

praeripiō, 3, uī, reptus [rapiō],
*snatch before ; seize, carry off,
snatch away,* 42. 7.

✓ praesaepe, is, N. [saepēs, *fence*],
enclosure ; stall, crib, manger,
49. 4.

praesēns, entis, adj. [p. of prae-
sum], *at hand ; present,* 52. 13;
68. 2 ; 70. 16, etc.; *instant,
immediate,* 21. 11 ; in praesentī, *for the present,* 68. 4.

praesentia, ae, F. [praesēns],
presence ; w. in, *at* or *for the
time, at present,* 2. 19; 74. 20.

✓ praesertim, adv., *especially, particularly,* 69. 14.

praeses, idis, M. and F., *protector,
guardian,* 20. 15.

✓ praesidium, ī, N. [praeses], *protection ; guard, watch,* 11. 9;
25. 1 ; *garrison,* 69. 3.

praestāns, antis, adj. [p. of prae-
stō], *standing before* (all others); *distinguished, remarkable,
wonderful, very great,* 69. 9;
superl., 5. 18.

praestantia, ae, F. [praestāns],
*preëminence, superiority, ex-
cellence,* 54. 17.

praestō, 1, itī, itus, *stand before ;
be superior, excel, surpass,* w.
dat., 46. 20.

praesum, esse, fuī, *be before ; be
at the head of, command, have
charge of,* w. dat. 4. 1 ; 27. 18;
35. 14, etc.

praeter, prep. w. acc., *besides, except,* 26. 5; 50. 18; 59. 27,
etc.

praetereā, adv., *besides these ; in* ✓
addition, beyond this, moreover,
37. 7 ; 67. 5; 70. 6.

praetereō, īre, iī, itus, *go beyond,*
56. 18; *go by, pass by,* 24. 18;
48. 1 ; 64. 8.

praetermittō, 3, mīsī, mīssus, *let
go by ; let go, pass by, neglect,
disregard,* 26. 6.

praetexta, ae, F. [praetextus, *bordered*], *bordered toga ; toga with
a purple border* (sign of power),
43. 8.

praetor, ōris, M., *leader ; general,*
69. 19, 24; 72. 5, etc.

praeveniō, 4, vēnī, ventus, *come
before ; arrive before, precede,
anticipate,* 63. 19 ; 65. 5.

prātum, ī, N., *meadow, pasture,* ✓
50. 1.

prehendō, 3, dī, ēnsus, *lay hold
of ; grasp, seize, snatch.*

premō, 3, essī, essus, *press ; check,
curb, restrain,* 25. 22.

pretium, ī, N., *price, value, money,* ✓
47. 3, 7, 11, etc.

(prex, precis), F., *a praying ;
prayer, entreaty,* 16. 18; 29.
19; 31. 13, etc.

prīdem, adv., *long ago, long since,*
61. 13.

prīmō, adv. [prīmus], *in the first ;
at first, first, at the beginning,*
33. 15; 43. 15.

(prīmōris, e), adj. [prīmus], *first ;*

as noun, M. pl., *chiefs, leading men, nobles,* **46**. 10.

prīmum, adv. [prīmus], *first ; in the first place, at first,* **2**. 2 ; **7**. 2 ; **8**. 12, etc.; cum (ubi) prīmum, *as soon as,* **13**. 14 ; **53**. 12 ; **54**. 7 ; quam prīmum, *as soon as possible,* **11**. 4.

prīmus, a, um, adj., superl., *the first, first,* **12**. 15 ; **35**. 24 ; **38**. 18, etc.; *earliest,* **59**. 16 ; *chief, foremost,* **18**. 4 ; **59**. 15 ; **66**. 8 ; *first part of,* **53**. 16.

prīnceps, cipis [prīmus, capiō], *taking first place ; first in the procession, at the head, foremost, chief,* **39**. 15 ; **75**. 19.

prior, ius, adj., comp., *former ; first,* **34**. 14 ; **53**. 7.

Prīscus, ī, M. See Tarquinius, **42**. 21.

√ prīstinus, a, um, adj. [for priustinus], *former, early, previous,* **70**. 28.

prius, adv., comp. [prior], *before ; first,* **8**. 10 ; **45**. 1 ; **49**. 17 ; *formerly, before,* **53**. 15.

priusquam or prius quam, adv., *sooner than, before,* **7**. 19 ; **13**. 17 ; **39**. 7, etc.

prīvātus, a, um, adj. [p. of prīvō], *apart from the state ; as private citizen,* **67**. 16 ; w. rēs, *personal property, private life,* **67**. 12.

prīvīgnus, ī, M., *stepson,* **66**. 18.

prīvō, 1, *rob, deprive, bereave,* w. abl., **33**. 3.

prō, prep. w. abl., *before, in front of,* **63**. 25 ; *instead of,* **60**. 20 ; *in behalf of, for,* **38**. 11 ; *for, the same as, as,* **36**. 22 ; prō certō, *beyond a doubt,* **13**. 10 ; *in return for,* **7**. 8 ; **23**. 7 ; **26**. 8, etc.

Proca, ae, M., a king of Alba, **33**. 1.

prōcēdō, 3, cessī, —, *go before ; advance, move forward, go forth,* **35**. 22 ; **36**. 17 ; **38**. 15, etc.

prōclāmō, 1, *call out ; cry loudly, shout, proclaim,* **39**. 29.

procul, adv., *driven forward ;* √ *far, far off, at a distance, a great way,* **29**. 26 ; **34**. 4 ; **39**. 4 ; procul dubiō, *without doubt,* **47**. 8.

Proculus, ī, M., a Roman knight, **36**. 16.

prōcūrō, 1, *take care of ; avert,* √ *ward off,* **37**. 6.

prōdeō, īre, iī, itus, *go forth ; go out, appear,* **67**. 19.

prōdigium, ī, N., *prophetic sign ;* √ *omen, sign, portent,* **42**. 14 ; **43**. 23.

prōditiō, ōnis, F., *a betraying ; treachery, treason,* **35**. 20.

prōdō, 3, didī, ditus, *put forth ; hand down,* w. memoriae, *report, record,* **46**. 27 ; **66**. 3.

proelium, ī, N., *battle, combat, contest,* **36**. 1 ; **39**. 12 ; **43**. 7, etc.

profectiō, ōnis, F., *a going away ; departure, setting out,* **18**. 2 ; **26**. 10 ; **31**. 26.

prōferō, ferre, tulī, lātus, *bring forth ; bring forward, produce.*

proficīscor, 3, fectus [prōficiō, *advance*], *begin to advance oneself ; set out, take the field, start,* **3**. 18 ; **5**. 1 ; **12**. 6, etc.;

set out, go away, depart, **25.**
6; **67.** 28; *go,* **27.** 23; **59.**
11.

✓ **prōflīgō, 1,** *strike to the ground;
completely crush, overthrow,
overcome,* **62.** 20.

prōgeniēs, acc. em., F., *descent,
descendants, race, family.*

prōgredior, 3, gressus [gradior],
*go forward; advance, proceed,
go on,* **4.** 23; **5.** 12; **11.**
11, etc.

prohibeō, 2, uī, itus [habeō], *hold
before; prevent, keep from,
hinder,* **5.** 4.

prōiciō, 3, iēcī, iectus [iaciō],
*throw forth; throw away, let
go, give up,* **27.** 5; w. sē, *throw
oneself, fall prostrate,* 10. 24;
30. 23.

proinde, adv., *henceforward; accordingly, therefore, then,* **11.**
20; *in like manner, equally,
just, even,* **70.** 14; **71.** 3.

prōmittō, 3, mīsī, mīssus, *let go;
engage, promise, assure,* **6.** 22;
8. 9; **11.** 3, etc. Cf. polliceor, **14.** 3.

✓ **prōmō, 3,** mpsī, mptus [emō],
take out; bring forth, produce,
22. 22.

prope, adv., *nearly, almost, about,*
58. 8, 21; comp. propius,
nearer, **49.** 13; **64.** 10.

properō, 1 [properus, *quick*],
*hasten, hurry, proceed with
haste,* 33. 21; **45.** 13; **59.** 5.
Cf. mātūrō.

propinquus, a, um, adj. [prope],
near; as noun, M., *relative,
kinsman,* **58.** 11.

prōpōnō, 3, posuī, positus, *put*

*forth, propose, offer, suggest,
conceive,* **8.** 20; **10.** 16; **51.** 11.

Propontis, idis, F., *the Propontis,*
or *Sea of Marmora,* **73.** 7.

proprius, a, um, adj., *not common* ✓
*with others; own, special, pri-
vate,* **57.** 2.

propter, prep. w. acc. [prope],
*near; on account of, by reason
of, because of,* 36. 9; 40. 20;
50. 19, etc.

prōra, ae, F., *prow, bow,* **7.** 17.

prōripiō, 3, uī, reptus [rapiō],
seize forth; w. sē, *rush, burst
forth,* 43. 20.

prōsequor, 3, cūtus, *follow on;
follow up, pursue, continue, go
on,* 13. 12; 70. 24.

prōsiliō, 4, uī, — [saliō, *leap*],
leap forward, spring up, **64.** 15.

prōsperē, adv. [prōsperus, *accord-* ✓
ing to hope], *hopefully; favorably, fortunately, prosperously,*
71. 16.

prōstrātus, a, um, adj. [p. of prō-
sternō, *strew before*], *cast down,
throw to the ground,* **21.** 13.

prōsum, desse, fuī, *be for; do* ↳
good, benefit, serve, **7.** 3; **10.**
26; **13.** 19, etc.

prōtendō, 3, —, tus, *stretch forth,
reach out, extend.*

prōtinus, adv., *before oneself; at
once, immediately,* **62.** 8.

prōtulī. See **prōferō.**

prōvehō, 3, vēxī, vectus, *carry
forward;* pass., *advance, proceed, progress,* **7.** 16; **25.** 8.

prōvincia, ae, F., *office, duty,
charge,* **68.** 11; *province, state,*
60. 21, 23; **61.** 21.

prōvocō, 1, *call forth; challenge,*

invite, 23. 1 ; appeal, call upon, 39. 28.

proximē, adv., superl. [proximus], nearest, very near, 59. 5.

proximus, a, um, adj., superl. [prope], nearest, next, 11. 17 ; 61. 23; 64. 4 ; last, previous, 38. 6 ; in proximō, near at hand, near by, 34. 22.

prūdentia, ae, F. [prūdēns, for prōvidēns, foreseeing], sagacity, sense, intelligence, discretion, 18. 5 ; 69. 9.

Ptolemaeus, ī, M., a king of Egypt in the time of Caesar, 62. 15.

pūblicē, adv. [pūblicus], on account of the people, 47. 18 ; at the public expense, 71. 5.

pūblicō, 1 [pūblicus], open to the public, 63. 14 ; take for public use, confiscate, 68. 19.

pūblicus, a, um, adj. [populus], of the people ; public, general, common, 39. 20 ; 67. 12 ; nūntius, state messenger, 41. 15; rēs pūblica, state, republic, 60. 7, 15; 63. 2, etc.; in pūblicō, in a public place, 68. 22 ; in pūblicum, in public, 67. 19.

puella, ae, F., dim. [puer], female child ; girl, maiden, 18. 9 ; 39. 21.

puer, erī, M., male child ; boy, lad, 2. 7, 10, 14, etc.; ā puerō, from boyhood, 3. 1.

puerulus, ī, M., dim. [puer], little boy, 56. 3.

pugiō, ōnis, M., short dagger, dirk, poniard, 64. 16.

pūgna, ae, F., hand to hand fight; battle, combat, 35. 23 ; 50. 21.

pūgnō, 1 [pūgna], fight, do battle, contend, 5. 5; 10. 12 ; 35. 28, etc.

pulcher, chra, chrum, adj., beautiful, fair, handsome, 29. 12.

pulchritūdō, inis, F. [pulcher], beauty, 54. 9.

pulsō, 1, freq. [pellō], keep striking ; knock at, 28. 8 ; 30. 2.

pūniō, 4 [poena, punishment], correct ; punish, chastise, 51. 1 ; 55. 12.

pusillus, a, um, adj., dim. [pūsus, boy], very little, small, insignificant, 55. 3.

putō, 1 [putus, pure], clean ; clear up ; think, consider, believe, 10. 8 ; 15. 9 ; 71. 20.

Q

quā, adv. [abl. F. of quī], on which side ; by which way, where, 26. 22.

quadrāgintā, num. adj., indecl. [quattuor], forty, 38. 4 ; 45. 19; 58. 21, etc.

quadrīgae, ārum, F. [quattuor, for quadriugae], team of four, four horses, 40. 19.

quaerō, 3, sīvī, sītus, seek ; hunt for, search for, 5. 16, 18, 24, etc. ; ask, inquire, 2. 12 ; 6. 3 ; 21. 3, etc.

quaestiō, ōnis, F., a questioning ; investigation, inquiry, examination, 68. 3.

quaestor, ōris, M. [for quaesitor], quæstor, a Roman officer (originally a deputy of the consul to *investigate* and try capital crimes) who had charge of the public money, **59.** 11.

✓ quālis, e, pron., interrog., *how constituted? of what sort, what,* **18.** 20; **52.** 5.

quam, adv. [quī], *in what manner; how,* **27.** 12 ; **52.** 20, 21 ; after comps., *than,* **4.** 4; **24.** 12 ; **34.** 21 ; w. superls., *as* . . . *as possible,* **2.** 17 ; **10.** 22 ; **11.** 4, etc.

quamquam, conj., *though, although, notwithstanding that,* **58.** 7 ; **62.** 7 ; **70.** 22.

quamvīs, conj., *as you will; although, albeit,* **61.** 17.

✓ quantum, adv. [quantus], *as much as; how far, to what extent, how,* **15.** 4 ; **61.** 22.

quantus, a, um, pronom. adj., correl. w. tantus, *of what size; how great,* **6.** 18, 21; **48.** 5, etc.; as noun, N., *how much,* **50.** 5.

quā rē, or quārē, adv., *by which thing; wherefore, therefore, whereby, then,* **39.** 25; **41.** 22 ; **44.** 8, etc.

quartānus, a, um, adj. [quartus], *of the fourth;* as noun, F. (sc. febris, *fever*), an ague occurring every fourth day, *quartan ague,* **58.** 7.

✓ quartus, a, um, adj. [quattuor], *fourth,* **54.** 20 ; **63.** 5.

✓ quasi, adv., *as if, just as if,* **16.** 7 ; **18.** 11 ; **19.** 8, etc.

quattuor, num. adj., indecl., *four,* **45.** 19; **54.** 16; **62.** 19.

-que, conj., enclitic, *and,* **4.** 11 ; **6.** 20 ; **10.** 6, etc.

quī, quae, quod, interrog. adj., *which? what?* **2.** 12 ; **3.** 1, etc.

quī, quae, quod, rel. pron., *who, which, what,* **2.** 1, 17 ; **3.** 5, etc.

quia, conj., *because, since,* **39.** 1 ; ✓ **68.** 4.

quīcumque, quaecumque, quodcumque, rel. pron. [quī], *whoever, whosoever, whichsoever,* **34.** 19 ; **39.** 23 ; **75.** 19.

quīdam, quaedum, quoddam and (as substantive) quiddam, indef. pron., *certain, some,* **2.** 6, 16 ; **3.** 1, etc.

quidem, adv., *certainly, indeed,* ✓ *to be sure, however,* **20.** 8 ; **28.** 1 ; **37.** 30, etc.; nē . . . quidem, enclosing an emphatic word, *not* . . . *even,* **4.** 2 ; **21.** 10, 22, etc.

quiēs, ētis, F., *a lying still; rest, freedom,* **10.** 2 ; **26.** 15 ; **40.** 27.

quiēscō, 3, ēvī, ētus [quiēs], *rest, sleep,* **74.** 14; *be inactive, do nothing, remain quiet,* **68.** 4.

quīn, conj. [quī, nē], *by which not; but that, from,* **6.** 14, 19 ; **10.** 18, etc.

quīndecim, num. adj., indecl., ✓ *fifteen,* **47.** 18.

quīnquāgēnī, ae, a, num. adj. ⎣ [quīnquāgintā], *fifty each; fifty each year,* **73.** 15.

quīnquāgintā, num. adj., indecl., ✓ *fifty,* **4.** 13; **59.** 3.

quīnque, num. adj., indecl., *five,* **63.** 4 ; **70.** 3.

quīnquiēns, adv. [quīnque], *five times,* **62.** 28.

quīntus, a, um, adj. [quīnque], *fifth,* **62.** 18.

Quirīnālis, e, adj., *of or belonging to Quirinus, Quirinal,* **36.** 21.

Quirīnus, ī, M., a name of Romulus, 36. 22.

quis, quae, quid, interrog. pron., *who? which? what?* 2. 18; 3. 14; 5. 15, etc.; as indef. pron. w. sī or nē, *anybody, anything*, 2. 20; 7. 12, 13, etc.; w. nēsciō, *I know not what*, i.e., *some*, 2. 14; 3. 3.

quisnam, quaenam, quidnam, interrog. adj., *who then? what pray?* 46. 4.

quisquam, —, quicquam, indef. pron., as noun, M., *any one whatever, anybody no matter who*, 67. 20; N., *anything whatever*, 30. 13; 50. 18.

quisque, quaeque, quidque, and quodque, *whoever it be; each, every*, 10. 11; 24. 9; 38. 11, etc.

quō, *to the place to which, whither*, 12. 9; 13. 3; 19. 7; 29. 14, etc.; *at which*, 68. 6; as rel. adv. = ut eō, *in order that*, etc., 40. 23.

quod, conj. [quī], *because, since*, 6. 6; 8. 7; 10. 26, etc.

quō modo, adv., *in what manner or way? how?* 14. 22; 51. 10.

quondam, adv., *at some time; at one time, once, formerly*, 37. 3; 46. 28; 56. 19. Cf. ōlim.

quoniam, adv., *since now; since then, since, seeing that*, 72. 23.

quoque, conj., after an emphatic word, *also, too*, 35. 3; 37. 22; 41. 1, etc.

quōrsum, adv. [quō versus], *to what place, whither*, 61. 6.

quotiēns, adv. [quot, *how many*], *how often; as often as, as many times as*, 6. 11.

quotiēnscumque, adv. [quotiēns], *how often soever; as often as*, 67. 18.

R

rāmus, ī, M., *growing thing; branch, bough*, 11. 17.

rāna, ae, F., *frog*, 55. 6, 8.

rapīna, ae, F., *a robbing; robbery, plundering, pillage*, 33. 17.

rapiō, 3, puī, ptus, *seize and carry off by force, drag away, snatch, snatch up*, 5. 4; 35. 9, 11, etc.

ratiō, ōnis, F., *a reckoning; manner, way, plan*, 7. 9; 21. 18.

ratus, a, um, adj. [p. of reor], *reckoned; fixed, settled, sure, certain*, 74. 2.

rebellō, 1, *wage war again; revolt, rebel*, 62. 17.

recēdō, 3, cessī, cessus, *go back;* w. abl., *give up, renounce*, 72. 4.

recidō, 3, cidī, cāsūrus [cadō], *fall back; fall again*, 71. 15; *be handed over, revert*, 36. 8.

recipiō, 3, cēpī, ceptus [capiō], *take again; regain, recover, get back*, 3. 4; 26. 1; 31. 7, etc.; *take in, admit, receive*, 36. 6; 53. 8; w. sē, *betake oneself, withdraw, go*, 12. 19.

recondō, 3, didī, ditus, *put up again; conceal, hide, shelter*, 52. 2.

recreō, 1, *make again; revive,
refresh, restore,* 52. 3.

✓ rēctē, adv. [rēctus], *in a straight
line; well, properly, excellently,*
44. 14.

rēctus, a, um, adj. [p. of regō],
*kept straight; in a straight line,
straight, direct,* 7. 18; 21. 1;
49. 15.

✓ recumbō, 3, cubuī, —, *lie down
again; lie down, sink down,*
23. 9; 26. 15.

recuperō, 1, *take again; regain,
recover, be restored to,* 25. 24.

recūsō, 1 [causa], *make an objec-
tion against; decline, refuse,
reject,* 67. 18.

redāctus. See redigō.

reddō, 3, didī, ditus, *give back;
bring again, return, restore,* 31.
5; *cause to appear, make, render,* 48. 4; 52. 6.

redeō, īre, iī, itus, *go again; go
back, return,* 2. 9; 5. 26; 7.
7, etc.; *turn, turn back,* 39. 5.

✓ redigō, 3, ēgī, āctus [agō], *drive
back; reduce, compel, force,
bring,* 45. 22; 59. 8; 60. 23.

rediissem. See redeō.

redimō, 3, ēmī, ēmptus [emō],
*take back; beg off, release, ran-
som, rescue,* 59. 2.

redintegrō, 1, *make whole again;
renew, begin afresh, take up
again,* 36. 2.

reditus, ūs, M., *a going back; returning, return,* 11. 24; 22.
20; 25. 2, etc.

redūcō, 3, xī, ductus, *lead back;
bring back, restore, return,* 15.
6; 30. 19.

referō, ferre, rettulī, lātus. *bring*

back; bear back, carry, 18. 20;
27. 1; 74. 23; *return, repay,
give;* w. grātiam, *make return,
requite, show gratitude,* 7. 9;
12. 12; 23. 8, etc.; *regain, recover, get again,* 14. 4; 44. 7;
w. pedem, *retrace one's steps, go
back, withdraw, retreat,* 11. 22.

reficiō, 3, fēcī, fectus [faciō], ⌐
*make again; restore, renew, re-
pair, regain, recover,* 15. 1; 31.
23.

refluō, 3, —, —, *flow back; flow
off, overflow.*

refoveō, 2, fōvī, —, *warm again;* ⌐
restore, revive, 62. 26.

refugiō, 3, fūgī, —, *flee back;
turn back, flee for refuge,* 20.
18; 45. 12; 55. 8.

refulgeō, 2, sī, —, *flash back;* ⌐
shine, gleam, glisten, 12. 7.

rēgia, ae, F. [rēgius, *sc.* domus], ⌐
royal abode, palace, 3. 5; 6. 20;
10. 20, etc.

regiō, ōnis, F., *directing; part,
district, region, land,* 4. 7, 20;
6. 4; 16. 16, etc.

rēgius, a, um, adj. [rēx], *of the
king; royal, of the king, king's,*
33. 13; 37. 9; 46. 15, etc.

rēgnō, 1 [rēgnum], *have power;
be king, rule, reign, govern,* 14.
17; 33. 3; 38. 4, etc.

rēgnum, ī, N., *power, government,
kingdom, throne,* 2. 2, 3, 15,
etc.

regō, 3, rēxī, rēctus, *rule, govern,*
34. 13.

regredior, 3, gressus [gradior],
go back; turn back, return, 28.
21; 61. 23; 62. 26. Cf. redeō,
2. 9.

✓ **relābor**, 3, lapsus, *slide back; flow back, recede, fall*, 33. 8.

relaxō, 1, *stretch out; relax.*

religiō, ōnis, F., *that which binds; sense of right, devoutness, piety*, 36. 24; 41. 8; *religious observance*, 36. 25; 67. 25.

✓ **religō**, 1, *bind back; fasten, bind fast*, 40. 19.

relinquō, 3, līquī, līctus, *leave behind, abandon, leave*, 3. 11 ; 11. 9, 24, etc.; *bequeath*, 33. 2.

reliquiae, ārum, F., *what is left; remainder, remnant, rest*, 62. 25.

reliquus, a, um, adj., *left;* as noun, M. pl., *the rest, those remaining*, 10. 14; 18. 8; 19. 5, etc.

remaneō, 2, mānsī, —, *stay behind, remain.*

remedium, ī, N., *that which restores health; cure, antidote, remedy*, 6. 23.

rēmigō, 1, —, — [rēmex, *oarsman*], *ply the oar, row*, 13. 16.

reminīscor, 3, —, *recall to mind, recollect, remember*, 70. 28.

remittō, 3, mīsī, mīssus, *let go back; allow oneself rest, relax*, 66. 13.

removeō, 2, mōvī, mōtus, *move back;* pass., *withdraw, pass, disappear*, 13. 17 ; 25. 13.

Remus, ī, M., twin brother of Romulus, 33. 5.

rēmus, ī, M., *oar*, 7. 23; 11. 7; 12. 23, etc.

renūntiō, 1, *bring back word; report, declare, announce*, 2. 9; 74. 5.

renuō, 3, uī, —, *nod back; shake* ✓ *the head, refuse, reject, decline*, 64. 11.

reor, 2, ratus, *reckon ; think, believe, judge*, 39. 2 ; 61. 20 ; 68. 16.

repellō, 3, reppulī, pulsus, *drive back ; reject, refuse*, 63. 26 ; *drive away, cast down, deprive*, 22. 11.

repente, adv. [repēns, *sudden*], ✓ *suddenly, unexpectedly, on a sudden*, 34. 7.

repentīnus, a, um, adj. [repēns, *sudden*], *sudden, unlooked for, unexpected*, 67. 13.

reperiō, 4, repperī, repertus, *find again; find, discover, devise*, 6. 23; 9. 10 ; 19. 8, etc.

repertor, ōris, M. [reperiō], *dis-* ✓ *coverer, inventor*, 20. 15.

repetō, 3, īvī, ītus, *seek again; demand again*, 45. 10 ; w. rēs, *demand restitution, require satisfaction*, 41. 11, 14, 21.

repetundae, ārum, F. [p. of repetō], sc. pecūniae, *money to be recovered by suit*, hence, *extortion*, 63. 6.

repleō, 2, ēvī, ētus, *fill again ; fill up, fill to the brim*, 23. 1, 4; 30. 6, etc.

repōnō, 3, posuī, positus, *put again ; put away, replace, restore*, 42. 13; *put away, store, keep*, 22. 18.

reportō, 1, *bring* or *carry back*, 19. 17.

repudiō, 1 [repudium, *putting away*], *cast off, separate from, put away*, 15. 24 ; 58. 4; *reject, scorn*, 53. 3.

repūgnō, 1, *fight back; object to, oppose, refuse,* 60. 9 ; 72. 24.

reputō, 1, *count over ; reflect, think over, ponder on, meditate,* 61. 22 ; 68. 14.

requīrō, 3, sīvī, sītus [quaerō], *seek again ; look after, search for,* 54. 3.

rēs, reī, F., *that thought* or *spoken of ; thing, fact, occurrence, event, matter,* 3. 12, 15, 23, etc.; *circumstances, condition, life,* 6. 22 ; 70. 16 ; rēs mīlitāris, *art of war,* 9. 6 ; 36. 19; as adv., rē vērā, *in very truth, in reality, really,* 2. 11 ; 15. 14; 55. 17 ; *undertaking,* 19. 12 ; rēs gesta, *deed, achievement,* 74. 3; rēs pūblica, *republic, state,* 60. 7, 15; 63. 2. See also restituō, gerō.

resacrō, 1, —, —, *reconsecrate, release from a curse,* 71. 6.

resistō, 3, stitī, —, *stand back ; make opposition, resist, oppose,* 19. 10 ; 24. 2 ; 66. 9.

resonō, 1, āvī, —, *sound again ; resound, reëcho.*

respiciō, 3, ēxī, ectus, *look again; look back, look behind,* 39. 4; *look at* or *upon, regard,* 63. 22.

respondeō, 2, dī, spōnsus, *answer, reply, make answer,* 2. 19 ; 14. 6, 11, etc.; *correspond to, be equal to, equal,* 54. 10.

respōnsum, ī, N. [p. of respondeō], *that which is answered ; response, reply,* 21. 7 ; *oracle,* 44. 25.

rēspūblica. See rēs pūblica.

restituō, 3, uī, ūtus [statuō], *set up again ; reëstablish, rein-*

state, *restore, replace, revive,* 22. 12; 34. 9 ; 56. 10, etc.

restō, 1, stitī, —, *stand again ; stand one's ground, stand firm, not yield,* 36. 1.

retineō, 2, uī, tentus [teneō], *hold back; restrain, keep, prevent,* 28. 7.

rettulī. See referō.

reus, a, um, adj. [rēs], *concerned in a thing ; at fault, guilty, to blame,* 72. 23 ; w. faciō, *prosecute, arraign, accuse,* 68. 9.

revērā or rē vērā. See rēs.

revertor, 3, sus, pf. usually revertī, *turn back ; come back, return,* 13. 20 ; 33. 12 ; 71. 25.

rēx, rēgis, M., *ruler, king,* 2. 9 ; 3. 8 ; 4. 20, etc.

Rhea, ae, F., *Rhea Silvia,* mother of Romulus and Remus, 33. 4.

Rhēnus, ī, M., *River Rhine,* 60. 24.

Rhodos, ī, F., an island off the southwest coast of Asia Minor, 58. 18.

rictus, ūs, M., *aperture of the mouth ; mouth, gaping jaws,* 56. 7.

rīdeō, 2, sī, sus, *laugh,* 47. 8.

rigō, 1, *guide ; flow through, water,* 37. 26.

rīpa, ae, F., *bank, shore,* 33. 7.

rīte, adv. [rītus], *according to religious usage ; solemnly, with proper ceremonies, according to their custom,* 37. 16.

rītus, ūs, M., *form of religious observance ; rite,* 41. 19.

rīxa, ae, F., *a tearing apart ; dispute, quarrel, brawl,* 43. 13.

rŏbur, oris, N., *hard wood, oak*, 4. 5; *strength, power*, 54. 18.

rogŏ, 1, *ask, request, beg*, 14. 12; 47. 10; 53. 1, etc. Cf. petŏ, 12. 44.

Rŏma, ae, F., *Rome*, 34. 15.

Rŏmānus, a, um, adj. [Rŏma], *of Rome, Roman*, 35. 9; as noun, M., 35. 11.

Rŏmulus, ī, M. [Rŏma], the founder and first king of Rome, 33. 5.

rŏstrum, ī, N. [rŏdŏ, *gnaw*], *beak, bill*, 54. 11; pl., *Rostra*, the platform for speakers in the Roman Forum, 63. 25.

Rubicŏ, ōnis, M., *Rubicon*, a small stream which formed the bound-ary between Italy and Cisalpine Gaul, 61. 20.

ruīna, ae, F., *a rushing down ; destruction, downfall, ruin ;* pl., *ruins*, 40. 22.

ruŏ, 3, uī, ūtus and uitus, *fall with violence ; rush forth*, 26. 22; 29. 14.

rūpēs, is, F., *breaking thing ; cliff, crag*, 7. 11, 19, 20, etc.

rūrsus, adv. [revorsus=reversus], ✔ *turned back ; back again, once more, again*, 4. 22; 7. 21; 12. 14; 42. 12, etc.

rūsticus, a, um, adj. [rūs, *country*], *of the country*, as noun, M., *countryman, rustic, peasant*, 55. 1, 15; 56. 1.

S

Sabīnī, ōrum, M., *Sabines*, a people of central Italy, 35. 7.

saccus, ī, M., *bag, sack*, 26. 4, 9, 16, etc.

sacer, cra, crum, adj., *dedicated ; sacred ;* as noun, N. pl., *sacred rites*, 36. 26; 37. 6; 41. 3, etc.

sacerdōs, ōtis, M. and F. [sacer], *one given to sacred things ; priest*, 37. 2, 14; 44. 28, etc.; *priestess*, 33. 4.

sacrārium, ī, N. [sacrum], *depository of holy things ; shrine*, 47. 16.

sacrificium, ī, N. [sacrificus, *sacrificial*], *sacrifice, offering*, 2. 22; 40. 6.

sacrificŏ, 1, *make a sacrifice ; offer sacrifice, sacrifice.*

sacrilegium, ī, N. [sacrilegus, *stealing sacred things*], *violation of sacred things, profanation*, 71. 4.

saepe, adv., *often, frequently, oftentimes*, 19. 11; 37. 26; 48. 4, etc.

saepius, adv., comp. of saepe, *more often*, 65. 2; *again and again, repeatedly*, 33. 12.

saevitia, ae, F. [saevus], *cruelty*, ✔ *harshness, severity*, 45. 24.

saevus, a, um, adj., *raging ; fierce, furious, savage*, 62. 8.

sagācitās, ātis, F. [sagāx, *of quick perception*], *keenness ; shrewdness, acuteness*, 69. 13.

Saliī, ōrum, M., Roman priests, dedicated to the service of Mars, 37. 14.

Salmydessus, ī, F., a town of Thrace, 6. 2.

saltō, 1, freq. [saliō, leap], *leap about; dance,* **37**. 16.

(saltus, ūs), M., only acc. and abl., *a leaping; leap, bound,* **34**. 17.

saltus, ūs, M., *forest pastures; woodland pastures, woodland, glade,* **33**. 16.

√ salūbris, e, adj. [salūs], *health-giving; healthy, sound, well,* comp., **40**. 28.

(salum, ī), N., only acc. and abl. sing., *open sea, deep,* **56**. 15.

√ salūs, ūtis, F. [salvus], *soundness; health, welfare, safety,* **7**. 22 ; **10**. 20 ; **12**. 3, etc.

salūtō, 1 [salūs], *wish health; greet, hail, salute,* **45**. 14.

salvus, a, um, adj., *in good health; safe, sound, unharmed.*

Samos, ī, F., an island near Ephesus, **69**. 19.

sarcina, ae, F., *package, bundle, load, pack,* **53**. 1, 5, 9.

satis, adv., *enough, sufficiently, fully,* **5**. 10; **12**. 16; **14**. 17, etc.

satrapēs, is, M., *governor of a Persian province, viceroy, satrap,* **74**. 8.

saxum, ī, N., *large, rough stone; stone, broken rock,* **10**. 8, 11; **20**. 21, etc.

√ scelerātus, a, um, adj. [p. of scelerō, *pollute*], *polluted; accursed, impious, wicked,* **45**. 18.

scelestē, adv. [scelestus, *wicked*], *wickedly, impiously, in an infamous manner,* **45**. 20.

scelus, eris, N., *wicked deed, crime, wickedness,* **15**. 18.

scientia, ae, F. [sciēns, p. of sciō], *knowing; knowledge, experi-*

ence, skill, **3**. 22 ; **8**. 22 ; **11**. 16. etc.

sciō, **4**, *know, understand, perceive,* **6**. 17 ; **7**. 26 ; **8**. 8, etc.

Scīpiō, ōnis, M., a Roman noble, friendly to Pompey, **62**. 24.

scīscitor, 1, freq. [scīscor, inch. of sciō], *inform oneself; seek to know, ask, enquire,* **46**. 4.

scissus, a, um, adj. [p. of scindō], √ *cut; rent, cleft, parted, opened,* **37**. 11.

scītum, ī, N. [p. of scīscō, *decree*], *ordinance, decree, resolution, vote,* **69**. 25.

scrībō, **3**, psī, ptus, *scratch; write,* **17**. 3 ; **60**. 18; **75**. 6 ; *inscribe, carve,* **71**. 8.

scūtum, ī, N., *covering; shield, buckler,* **35**. 19 ; **37**. 11, 13, etc.

sēcēdō, **3**, cessī, cessus, *go by oneself; go apart* or *away, draw off, wander, stray,* **5**. 19 ; **58**. 18.

secō, 1, uī, ctus, *cut; cut in two, cut through, divide,* **43**. 5, 6.

sēcrētus, a, um, adj. [p. of sēcernō, *put asunder*], *mysterious, secret,* **37**. 14.

secundus, a, um, adj. [sequor], *following; second,* **54**. 18 ; **59**. 15 ; *successful, favorable, propitious, fair,* **26**. 12 ; **71**. 22 ; **72**. 21 ; w. rēs, *prosperity,* **70**. 16.

secūris, is, F., *that which cuts;* √ *axe, hatchet,* **43**. 18.

secus, adv., *otherwise;* w. neg., √ *not otherwise;* w. āc, *just the same as, equally with,* **44**. 2.

sed, conj., *but, however,* **2**. 4; **11**. 14; **12**. 19, etc.

sedeō, **2**, sēdī, sessum, *sit; take* √

place, sit, 9. 18 ; 24. 9 ; 28. 20, etc.; *remain seated,* 63. 21.

sēdēs, is, F., *a sitting ; seat, place, spot, dwelling,* 20. 6; 40. 24.

sēditiō, ōnis, F., *a going apart; discord, quarrel, strife, disagreement,* 36. 17, 19; 60. 11.

sēgniter, adv. [sēgnis, *slow*], *slowly ; lazily, without spirit,* 44. 5.

sella, ae, F., *seat ; chair, throne, official seat,* 37. 3 ; 63. 24.

semper, adv., *ever, always, continually,* 19. 1; 49. 14; 59. 17.

senātor, ōris, M., *member of the senate ; councillor, senator,* 36. 9.

senātōrius, a, um, adj. [senātor], *of a senator, senatorial,* 63. 7.

senātus, ūs, M., *council of the elders, senate,* 45. 10; 60. 9; 61. 18, etc.

senectūs, ūtis, F. [senex], *old age, extreme age,* 36. 10.

senēscō, 3, senuī, —, inch. [seneō, *be old*], *grow old; lose strength, grow weak, decline,* 69. 18.

senex, senis, adj., *old ;* 52. 15; as noun, M., *old man, aged man,* 14. 20; 39. 28; 53. 18, etc.

senior, ius, adj., comp. of senex, *old ; elder,* 36. 8.

sēnsus, ūs, M., *a perceiving ; feeling, way of thinking, opinion, view,* 69. 22.

sententia, ae, F., *way of thinking, mind,* 8. 9; *intention, purpose, desire, wish,* 2. 6; 71. 14.

sentiō, 4, sēnsī, sēnsus, *perceive by the senses ; feel,* 16. 12 ; *see, perceive, realize, notice,* 5. 7, 23; 7. 5, etc.

sēparātim, adv. [sēparātus, *separated*], *apart, separately,* 60. 1.

sepeliō, 4, īvī, (iī) pultus, *bury, inter,* 38. 2.

septem, num. adj., indecl., *seven,* 38. 3.

septimus, a, um, adj. [septem], *seventh,* 19. 3 ; 25. 25.

sepultūra, ae, F. [sepeliō], *burial,* 13. 21.

sepultus. See sepeliō.

sequor, 3, cūtus, *come after ; follow, give chase, pursue,* 5. 26; 13. 2 ; 29. 7, etc.

sēriō, adv. [sērius], *in earnest, seriously,* 59. 14.

sērius, a, um, adj. [for sevērius], *grave, earnest, serious,* 47. 11.

sermō, ōnis, M., *continued speech ; conversation, talk, discourse,* 29. 25.

serō, 3, sēvī, satus, *plant, sow,* 8. 15.

sērō, adv. [sērus], *late, too late,* 53. 7 ; 55. 13.

sērus, a, um, adj., *late, too late,* 56. 11.

serva, ae, F. [servus], *female slave ; maidservant, maid.*

servīlis, e, adj. [servus], *of a slave ; slavish, servile,* 34. 3.

serviō, 4 [servus], *be a servant ; serve, be subject to, be enslaved to,* 66. 12 ; 73. 17.

servō, 1, *make safe; watch, guard, keep, preserve, save.*

Servius, ī, M., *Servius Tullius,* the sixth king of Rome, 43. 21.

servus, ī, M. [servus, *serving*], *slavish person ; serving man, servant, slave,* 20. 16 ; 28. 14 ; 59. 1.

sēstertius, a, um, num. adj. [for sēmis-tertius], *two and a half;* as noun, M. [sc. nummus], *sesterce,* a coin worth nearly five cents, **60.** 3.

seu. See sīve.

Seuthēs, is, M., a king of Thrace, **72.** 15.

sevērē, adv. [sevērus, *serious*], *rigidly, austerely, strictly,* superl., **63.** 6.

sex, num. adj., indecl., *six,* **34.** 14; **47.** 6.

sexāgintā, num. adj., indecl., *sixty,* **63.** 3, 27.

sextus, a, um, adj. [sex], *sixth;* sextus et decimus, *sixteenth,* **58.** 2.

Sextus, ī, M., *Sextus Tarquinius,* son of Tarquinius Superbus, **45.** 22.

sī, conj., *if, in case,* **2.** 20; **6.** 23; **7.** 13, etc.; *to see if,* **51.** 4.

Sibyllīnus, a, um, adj. [Sibylla, *prophetess*], *of a Sibyl, Sibylline,* **47.** 17.

sīc, adv., *in this way; so, thus,* **34.** 18; **35.** 20; **39.** 23, etc.

✓ siccō, 1 [siccus], *make dry; dry up, drain,* **63.** 14.

siccus, a, um, adj., *dry;* as noun, N., *dry land, dry place,* **33.** 8.

Sicilia, ae, F., *Sicily,* **20.** 14.

sīcut or sīcutī, *so as; just as, as,* **30.** 13; **71.** 18.

sīgnificō, 1 [sīgnum, faciō], *make signs; indicate, show, mean, signify,* **37.** 21.

sīgnō, 1 [sīgnum], *set a mark upon; mark, seal, affix a seal, sign,* **60.** 17.

sīgnum, ī, N., *mark, sign, signal,* **31.** 1; **35.** 8; **38.** 16; *standard,* **44.** 5, 7.

silēns, entis, adj. [p. of sileō, *be still*], *still; in silence, speechless, quiet,* **37.** 9.

silentium, ī, N. [silēns], *a being still; silence, stillness,* **46.** 9.

silva, ae, F., *forest, wood,* **11.** 10, 11; **12.** 7, etc.

Silvia, ae, F. See Rhea, **33.** 4.

similis, e, adj., *of a corresponding nature; like, resembling,* **41.** 8; superl. simillimus, **34.** 5.

similitūdō, inis, F. [similis], *likeness; similarity, likeness,* **45.** 8.

simul, adv., *at the same time,* **39.** ✓ 21; **41.** 2; **56.** 5, etc.; w. atque or āc, *as soon as,* **6.** 16, 25; **20.** 17, etc.; alone, as if with atque, *as soon as,* **57.** 5; w. cum, *in connection with,* **58.** 16; **69.** 26; **70.** 5; simul ... simul, *at the same time ... and, no sooner ... than,* **56.** 13, 14.

simulō, 1 [similis], *make like; pretend, feign, represent,* **37.** 23; **43.** 13.

sine, prep. w. abl., *without, unattended by,* **7.** 26; **8.** 8; **12.** 14, etc.

singulī, ae, a, adj., *one at a time, separately,* **39.** 2; **50.** 3; **52.** 19; *one on each side,* **39.** 9; per singulās noctīs, *each successive night,* **58.** 8.

sinister, tra, trum, adj., *left, on the left;* as noun, F. (sc. manus), *left hand,* **35.** 17.

sinus, ūs, M., *curve, fold; fold of* ✓ *the toga about the breast, bosom,* **52.** 2.

situs, a um, adj. [p. of sinō, *set*], *placed; situated,* **70.** 7.

√ **sīve** or **seu**, conj., *or if;* sīve . . .
sīve, or seu . . . seu, *whether* . . .
or, **16**. 23 ; **36**. 1 ; **45**. 7, 8, etc.

sōbrius, a, um, adj. [sē, *without,*
ēbrius, *full*], *not drunk, sober,*
64. 28.

socer, erī, M., *father-in-law*, **61.**
11 ; **66**. 19.

societās, ātis, F. [socius], *fellow-
ship ; league, alliance*, **34**. 25 ;
54. 15 ; **60**. 5, etc.

√ **sociō**, 1 [socius], *join together ;
hold in common, share*, **36**. 6.

socius, ī, M., *one who shares;
companion, fellow, associate,
friend*, **4**. 14; **6**. 20; **9**. 9, etc.

Sōcratēs, is, M., a celebrated
Athenian philosopher, **66**. 19.

sōl, sōlis, M., *sun*, **4**. 22 ; **12**. 2 ;
28. 20, etc.

soleō, **2**, solitus sum, *sit down to
a thing ; use, be wont, be accustomed*, **34**. 1 ; **50**. 15, 21, etc.

sōlitūdō, inis, F. [sōlus], *being
alone ; lonely place, desert, wil-
derness*, **33**. 9.

sollicitus, a, um, adj., *thoroughly
moved ; troubled, afflicted, dis-
turbed, restless*, **28**. 21.

solum, ī, N., *lowest part ; ground,
land*, **56**. 16.

sōlum, adv. [sōlus], *alone, only,*
38. 6; **51**. 1; **67**. 21.

sōlus, a, um, adj., *alone, only,*
3. 18; **28**. 21 ; **34**. 20, etc.;
without assistance, **9**. 25.

solvō, **3**, vī, ūtus, *loosen ; unbind,
untie, undo, let down*, **26**. 20 ;
27. 2 ; **39**. 18 ; *leave land, set
sail, weigh anchor, depart*, **4**.
17, 22 ; **5**. 26 ; **7**. 16, etc.; *pay,
give*, **25**. 11.

somnium, ī, N. [somnus], *dream,* √
44. 25.

somnus, ī, M., *sleep, slumber*, **10**.
3 ; **11**. 20 ; **21**. 13, etc.

sonitus, ūs, M., *noise, sound,* **20**.
6 ; **51**. 12 ; **55**. 8 ; *crackling*,
74. 16.

sonōrus, a, um, adj. [sonor, *noise*],
noisy, loud, resounding, **25**. 21.

sopor, ōris, M., *deep sleep, slumber*, **28**. 15.

soror, ōris, F., *sister*, **39**. 16, 20 ;
46. 13.

sorōrius, a, um, adj. [soror], *of
a sister, sister's*, **40**. 8.

sors, rtis, F., *lot, drawing of lot,
decision*, **27**. 22 ; sorte ēvēnit,
the lot fell to, **27**. 20.

sortior, **4** [sors], *cast lots, draw
lots*, **27**. 19.

spargō, **3**, sī, sus, *throw about;* √
strew, scatter, sprinkle, **9**. 20;
10. 1 ; **11**. 20.

spatium, ī, N., *space, interval, distance*, **7**. 13, 19; **39**. 3 ; *of time,*
8. 1 ; **27**. 6; **30**. 1, etc.

speciēs, —, acc. em, abl. ē, *sight ;
appearance, likeness, form,
looks*, **2**. 11 ; **6**. 9 ; **8**. 13, etc.;
pretence, **64**. 9.

spectāculum, ī, N. [spectō],
*means of seeing ; public show,
spectacle, exhibition*, **35**. 5, 7.

spectō, 1, freq., *look at ; behold,
look on, see*, **38**. 19.

speculātor, ōris, M. [speculor,
spy out], *looker-out ; spy, scout,*
73. 1.

spēlunca, ae, F., *cave, cavern, den,*
20. 18, 20 ; **23**. 15, etc.

spernō, **3**, sprēvī, sprētus, *separate ; despise, scorn, reject*, **25**. 10.

spērō, 1 [spēs], *hope, look for, expect,* **3.** 13; 13. 13; 15. 12, etc.

spēs, speī, F., *hope,* **4.** 8; **7.** 22; 13. 4, etc.

spīritus, ūs, M., *a breathing; spirit, spirits, pride, haughtiness,* 41. 2.

splendidus, a, um, adj., *bright; magnificent, showy, fine, handsome,* 66. 11; superl., **75.** 7.

splendor, ōris, M., *brightness; splendor, magnificence, sumptuousness,* **75.** 8.

√ spoliō, 1 [spolium], *strip; strip, despoil, rob, plunder,* 39. 13; 58. 6.

spolium, ī, N., *skin;* pl., *arms stripped from an enemy; booty, spoil,* 39. 15; 40. 1.

spondeō, 2, spopondī, spōnsus, *promise sacredly; give assurance, pledge oneself,* 59. 4; 72. 13.

√ (spōns, spontis), F., *free will;* only abl. sing. (w. suā), *of one's own accord, willingly, voluntarily,* 19. 15.

spōnsus, ī, M. [p. of spondeō], *one promised; betrothed, lover,* 39. 18, 22.

spopondī. See spondeō.

Spūrinna, ae, M., a soothsayer in the time of Caesar, **64.** 3.

stabulum, ī, N., *standing-place, stall, enclosure,* **9.** 10.

statim, adv., *at once, immediately, straightway,* 6. 13; **7.** 6; 8. 3; etc.

statuō, 3, uī, ūtus [status, *standing*], *cause to stand; stop, halt,* 13. 14; *decide, conclude, determine,* 26. 2; 27. 9; 29. 10, etc.

statūra, ae, F., *standing; height, size, stature,* 64. 20.

status, ūs, M., *position; state, condition,* 63. 2.

stercus, ī, M., *dung, filth,* 60. 12. √

sterilis, e, adj., *unfruitful, barren, unproductive,* 48. 17.

stirps, pis, F., *trunk* (of plants); *progeny, family, children,* 40. 2.

stō, 1, stetī, status, *stand; take* √ *position, stand still, stop,* **7.** 17; 16. 25; 29. 12, etc.

stolidus, a, um, adj., *dull, rude,* √ *uncultivated, coarse,* 50. 10; 52. 12; 55. 13.

strēnuus, a, um, adj., *brisk; active, vigorous, able,* 45. 21.

stringō, 3, nxī, ictus, *draw tight; draw, unsheathe,* 10. 12; 29. 22; 30. 14, etc.

studeō, 2, uī, —, *give attention; strive, apply oneself,* 56. 5.

studium, ī, N., *application; desire, eagerness,* 35. 6; pl., *pursuits, study, practice,* 9. 6; 75. 9.

stultitia, ae, F. [stultus], *folly,* \ *simplicity, foolishness,* 55. 11.

stultus, a, um, adj., *foolish, simple, stupid.*

stupēns, entis, adj. [p. of stupeō, *be stunned*], *astounded, amazed, struck with astonishment,* 15. 3.

suādeō, 2, sī, sus, *advise, recommend, induce, persuade,* 44. 1, 22; 51. 16, etc.

suāvitās, ātis, F. [suāvis, *sweet*], *sweetness, pleasantness, agreeableness,* 48. 12.

sub, prep.: w. acc., *under, beneath,* 40. 7; *towards, about,* 10. 3; 22. 21; w. abl., *under,* 16. 23; 46. 23.

subālāris, e, adj. [āla], *under the arm ; carried under the arm,* **74. 17.**

subdūcō, 3, xī, ductus, *draw from beneath ; lead away, lead secretly,* 40. 14 ; *draw up, beach,* 10. 23 ; 16. 24 ; *take away, remove,* **74. 17** ; w. reflex. pron., *withdraw, steal away,* 68. 17.

subeō, īre, iī, itus, *go under ; undergo, submit to, sustain, endure,* 4. 12 ; 8. 11, 19, etc. ; *take on one's shoulders,* 54. 4.

subeundus, p. of subeō.

subiciō, 3, iēcī, iectus [iaciō], *throw under ; place under,* 24. 15.

subigō, 3, ēgī, āctus [agō], *drive under ; put down, overcome, conquer, subdue,* **44. 15**; **59. 26.**

subitō, adv. [subitus], *coming on suddenly ; of a sudden, suddenly,* 4. 23 ; 10. 3 ; **12. 6,** etc.

subitus, a, um, adj., *that comes unexpectedly ; sudden,* 3. 6.

sublātus. See tollō.

sublevō, 1, *lift from beneath ; raise, lift, support,* 7. 4.

sublicius, a, um, adj. [sublica, *pile*], *of piles ;* pōns, *the Pile Bridge* (across the Tiber), 42. 4.

sublīmis, e, adj., *uplifted ; into the air, aloft, on high,* 42. 13.

submergō, 3, sī, sus, *dip under ; sink, overwhelm, submerge,* 25. 15.

subolēs, is, F., *shoot ; offspring, progeny, children,* **33. 3.** Cf. stirps, 40. 2.

subrīdeō, 2, sī, —, *laugh slightly; smile,* **51. 21.**

subsequor, 3, cūtus, *follow up ; follow on, come after,* **62. 3.**

subsidium, I, N., *that sitting aside ; reserve, help,* w. comparō, *make provision, provide,* 4. 15.

subsiliō, 4, uī, —, *leap up,* **51. 3.**

subsistō, 3, stitī, —, *take a stand; remain, stay,* **64. 3.**

substituō, 3, uī, ūtus [statuō], *place under ; put in place of, place instead,* 71. 24.

subsum, esse, —, *be under ; be at hand, be near,* **66. 13.**

subter, prep. w. acc., *underneath,* below, under, **52. 2.**

subveniō, 4, vēnī, ventus, *come up ; come to help, aid, assist, succor,* **55. 18.**

subvolō, 1, —, —, *fly up,* **54. 6.**

succēdō, 3, cessī, cessus, *go below ; follow, succeed,* **36. 23.**

succendō, 3, ndī, cēnsus, *kindle beneath ; set on fire, fire,* **74. 14.**

successus, (ūs), M. [succēdō], *coming up ; success, goodness,* **62. 18.**

sūcus, ī, M., *juice, sap,* **8. 25.**

sufficiō, 3, fēcī, fectus [faciō], *make or put under ; be adequate or enough, suffice,* **34. 16.**

suffīgō, 3, —, fīxus, *fasten beneath, attach ;* crucibus, *crucify,* **59. 10.**

suffrāgor, 1, —, *vote for, support,* favor, **69. 25.**

suī, gen., reflex. pron., *himself, herself, itself,* etc., 2. 18 ; 3. 14 ; 4. 14, etc.

Sulla, ae, M., *L. Cornelius Sulla,* [B.C. 138–78], Roman Dictator **58. 3.**

sum, esse, fuī, futūrus, *be*, **2**. **1**, 12, 13, etc.

summus, a, um, adj., superl. [for supimus, superus], *highest, greatest, supreme, very great* or *high*, 3. 22 ; 6. 11 ; 8. 16, etc.; *excellent*, 66. 5 ; *deepest*, 5. 11 ; summā vī, *with might and main*, 7. 23 ; summīs vīribus, *with all one's strength*, 12. 23; as noun, F. (sc. rēs), *highest place, leadership, supremacy*, 44. 25.

✓ **sūmō**, 3, mpsī, mptus [for subimō], *take up ; undertake, enter upon, begin*, 35. 11 ; *inflict*, 30. 22.

sūmptuārius, a, um, adj. [sūmptus, *expense*], *of expense, sumptuary*, 63. 8.

super, adv., *above*, 33. 7 ; 39. 17 ; w. sum, *be left, remain*, 72. 10.

super, prep. w. acc., *over, above, upon, on*, 38. 20 ; 39. 17 ; 42. 11, etc.

✓ **superbē**, adv. [superbus], *arrogantly, proudly, haughtily*, 41. 21 ; 53. 10.

superbia, ae, F. [superbus], *proudness ; haughtiness, arrogance, insolence*, 53. 7.

superbiō, 4, —, — [superbus], *be haughty ; plume oneself, take pride*, 50. 11.

superbus, a, um, adj., *haughty.*

Superbus. See **Tarquinius.**

superior, ius, adj., comp. of superus, *high ; upper, higher*, 44. 10 ; *superior, stronger*, 61. 15 ; 69. 5 ; *former*, 70. 16.

superō, 1 [super], *be above ; outdo, surpass, be superior to*, 75.

8 ; *get the better of, overwhelm*, 60. 26 ; **74. 15.**

supersum, esse, fuī, *be over ; survive, be left, remain*, 39. 9; 43. 10.

superus, a, um, adj. [super], *upper* ; Mare Superum, *upper sea*, i.e., *the Adriatic*, 63. 15.

superveniō, 4, vēnī, ventus, *come in addition ; come upon the scene, appear, arrive*, 34. 7.

suppeditō, 1, freq. [pēs], *give in* ✓ *abundance, furnish bountifully, supply freely*, 72. 9.

supplicium, ī, N., (supplex, *suppliant*), *a kneeling down ; punishment, penalty*, 6. 6, 8; **24**. 3, etc.

suppōnō, 3, posuī, positus, *put below ; place under, apply*, 14. 25.

suprā, adv. [for superā parte], *on the upper side ; above, before, beyond*, 11. 16 ; 13. 7 ; 22. 14, etc.

suprēmus, a, um, adj., superl. of superus, *high ; highest ; last, latest, supreme*, 14. 8 ; 74. 28.

Susamithrēs, ae, M., a Persian noble, 74. 9.

suscipiō, 3, cēpī, ceptus [capiō], *take under ; take upon oneself, undertake, begin*, 3. 16 ; 6. 24 ; 8. 9, etc.

suspendō, 3, dī, pēnsus, *hang up ; hang, suspend*, 11. 12 ; 57. 3.

suspiciō, 3, spēxī, spectus, *look up ; look at secretly, mistrust, suspect*, 61. 13.

suspicor, 1, *mistrust, suspect*, 16. 8 ; 24. 17 ; 25. 4, etc.

sustentō, 1, freq. [sustineō], *hold up ; support, sustain*, 53. 11.

sustineō, 2, uī, tentus [teneō],

hold under; support, sustain, bear the weight of, 39. 12.
sustulī. See tollō.
suus, a, um, poss. adj. [suī], of him, her, etc., 2. 4, 15; 6. 7, etc.; as noun, M., his men, his friends, 46. 4; 69. 11.

Symplēgadēs, um, F., dashing together; the Symplegades, dangerous rocks on the Euxine Pontus, 7. 9.
Syrācūsānī, ōrum, M., Syracusans, the people of Syracuse in Sicily, 67. 4.

T

tacitus, a, um, adj. [p. of taceō, be silent], without speaking, meditating, silent, 14. 6.
taenia, ae, F., band, ribbon, fillet, 70. 26.
talentum, ī, N., talent (about $1200), 59. 3; 73. 15.
tālis, e, adj., of such a kind, such, 9. 20; 16. 6; 22. 23, etc.
tam, adv., in such a degree; so much, so very, so, 21. 12; 44. 6; 52. 7, etc.
tamen, adv., notwithstanding, nevertheless, however, yet, for all that, 2. 6, 11, 13, etc.
tamquam, adv., as much as; as if, just as if, 50. 7.
Tanaquil, īlis, F., wife of Tarquinius Priscus, 42. 13.
tandem, adv. [tam], at length, at last, finally, 5. 26; 8. 7; 13. 22, etc.
tangō, 3, tetigī, tāctus, touch, strike, 28. 17; 29. 22; 30. 9.
tantō opere, adv., so earnestly, so much, so greatly, 58. 15.
tantum, adv. [tantus], so much, 10. 26; only, merely, 7. 20; 20. 10; 26. 6.
tantus, a, um, adj., of such size; so great, such, 2. 7, 16; 4. 1, 23, etc.

tard:tās, ātis [tardus, slow], slowness, heaviness, 48. 7.
tardō, 1 [tardus, slow], make slow, check, stay, prevent, 64. 15.
Tarpēia, ae, F., a Roman girl who betrayed the citadel to the Sabines, 35. 12.
Tarquiniī, ōrum, M., a town in Etruria, 42. 8.
Tarquinius, ī, M., an early Roman name; Priscus, 42. 8; Superbus, 45. 20; Sextus, 46. 13; Collatinus, 46. 13.
Tatius, ī, M., Titus Tatius, leader of the Sabines against the Romans, 35. 14.
taurus, ī, M., bull, 8. 13; 9. 10, 11, etc.
tēctum, ī, N., covering thing; roof, top, 48. 1, 2.
tegō, 3, tēxī, tēctus, cover; cover over, conceal.
tēlum, ī, N., shaft; dart, spear, javelin, weapon, 13. 3; 36. 3; 43. 19, etc.
temerē, adv., by chance; rashly, thoughtlessly, indiscreetly, 21. 16; 56. 8.
tempestās, ātis, F. [tempus], portion of time; time, period, 42. 25; weather, 4. 16; 5. 10;

11. 6, etc.; *storm, tempest,* **4. 5,** 23 ; **18.** 14, etc.

templum, ī, N., *open place for observation ; temple, shrine,* **59.** 22.

tempus, oris, N., *section ; time, hour, season, moment,* **2.** 15 ; **3.** 9 ; **4.** 2, etc.; *opportunity, chance,* **66.** 12 ; **69.** 12 ; pl., *time, season, date,* **34.** 6 ; *occasion,* **66.** 10.

tendō, 3, tetendī, tentus or tēnsus, *stretch, hold out,* 61. 6 ; *spread, lay,* **62.** 16.

teneō, 2, uī, —, *hold ; keep, hold,* 7. 18 ; **34.** 7 ; **56.** 9, etc.; *keep to, hold, follow,* **4.** 24 ; **6.** 1 ; **18.** 15, etc.; *hold back, restrain,* **28.** 2 ; memoriā, *remember,* **11.** 1 ; **27.** 12.

tenuis, e, adj., *drawn out ; thin, light,* **29.** 26.

tergum, ī, N., *back,* **19.** 16; **24.** 9, 18, etc.; ā tergō, *in the rear,* **40.** 16.

ternī, ae, a, distrib. adj. [ter, *thrice*], *three each ; three on a side,* **38.** 16.

terra, ae, F., *dry thing ; ground, land, country,* **5.** 16; **6.** 3; **8.** 3, etc.

terreō, 2, uī, itus, *alarm, frighten, strike with terror,* 40. 17 ; **64.** 2.

terrestris, e, adj. [terra], *of the earth ; on land, land-,* **70.** 3.

terribilis, e, adj., *frightful, dread, terrible,* **11.** 15 ; **20.** 6 ; **23.** 17, etc.

territō, 1, —, —, freq. [terreō], *put in terror ; frighten, alarm, terrify,* **50.** 6.

terror, ōris, M., *frightening ; terror, alarm,* **20.** 17 ; **21.** 9 ; **42.** 2, etc.

tertiō, adv. [tertius], *for the third time,* **49.** 12.

tertium, adv. [tertius], *for the third time,* **23.** 4.

tertius, a, um, num. adj. [ter, *thrice*], *third,* **31.** 24; **39.** 8 ; **54.** 19, etc.

testātior, ius, adj., comp. of testātus [p. of testor], *manifest, evident, published,* **68.** 21. ✓

testis, is, M. and F., *witness.* ✓

testor, 1 [testis], *cause to testify ; bear witness, attest,* 60. 17.

texō, 3, xuī, xtus, *weave,* **53.** 11.

Thēbae, ārum, F., the greatest city of Boeotia, **68.** 18.

Theopompus, ī, M., a Greek historian of Chios, **75.** 3.

Thērāmenēs, is, M., an Athenian general, **69.** 25.

Thēseus, eī, M., a mythical king of Athens, **4.** 10.

Thessalia, ae, F., a country in the northeastern part of Greece, **2.** 1.

Thrācia, ae, F., a country northeast of Greece, **6.** 1.

Thrāx, ācis, adj., *Thracian,* **72.** 15.

Thrasybūlus, ī, M., a famous Athenian general, **69.** 23.

Thūcÿdidēs, is, M., a celebrated Greek historian [B.C. 472–403], **75.** 2.

Thurii, ōrum, M., a city of Lucania, in Italy, **68.** 13.

Tiberis, is, M., the river Tiber, **33.** 7.

tigillum, ī, N., dim. [tīgnum, *timber*], *small beam, bar*, 40. 7, 8.

Timaeus, ī, M., a Greek historian, 75. 3.

timeō, 2, uī, —, *fear, be afraid, dread*, 11. 3; 49. 11; 62. 10, etc.

timidus, a, um, adj., *prone to fear; fearful, afraid, fainthearted*, 48. 4; 51. 17.

timor, ōris, M., *fearing; fear, dread, alarm*, 3. 6; 12. 11; 27. 24, etc.

tingō, 3, nxī, īnctus, *wet; dye, color, tinge*, 16. 5.

tintinnābulum, ī, N. [tintinnō, *ring*], *means of ringing; bell*, 51. 12, 14.

Tissaphernēs, is, M., a Persian, satrap of Lydia and Caria, 69. 15.

titulus, ī, M., *superscription; inscription, placard, notice*, 62. 24.

Titus, ī, M., see Tatius, 35. 14.

toga, ae, F., *covering; cloak, toga*, 64. 11, 16.

tollō, 3, sustulī, sublātus, *lift, raise*, 35. 29; 53. 18; *carry away, bear aloft*, 42. 11; *set up, raise*, 23. 17, 23; *pick up*, 51. 7; of anchors, *weigh*, 5. 12; 7. 16; 12. 15, etc.; w. animōs, *raise one's spirits, become emboldened*, 41. 9; *take away, make away with, remove*, 12. 11; 54. 18; 63. 4; 74. 1.

tonitrus, ūs, M. [tonō, *thunder*], *thundering, thunder*, 36. 14.

tōtus, a, um, adj., *swollen; entire, the whole, all*, 4. 5; 9. 17, 23, etc.

trabs, trabis, F., *beam, timber*, 55. 7, 9.

tractō, 1, freq. [trahō], *keep drawing, feel of, handle*, 24. 10.

trādō, 3, didī, ditus, *hand over, surrender, deliver*, 8. 5; 7. 9, etc.; *entrust, give over*, 71. 11; *give up, abandon*, 10. 2; *hand down*, 33. 10; 64. 20; *relate, recount, tell*, 4. 9; 33. 10.

trādūcō, 3, xī, ductus, *lead across; take, transfer, remove*, 41. 24.

trahō, 3, āxī, actus, *draw, drag along*, 39. 11; *drag, lead by force*, 9. 11.

trāiciō, 3, iēcī, iectus [iaciō], *throw across; cross, pass over, go over*, 34. 17; 58. 20; 61. 26, etc.; *thrust through, pierce, stab*, 64. 14.

tranquillitās, ātis, F. [tranquillus], *calmness; stillness, calm, quiet*, 5. 11.

trāns, prep. w. acc., *across, beyond, on the other side of*, 60. 24.

trānseō, īre, iī, itus, *go across, cross*, 3. 2; 29. 12; 40. 21; 59. 12, etc.; *go over to, go to*, 46. 6; *pass over, ascend*, 36. 15; *pass through*, 74. 21.

trānsfīgō, 3, xī, xus, *pierce through; transfix, stab to the heart*, 21. 16; 39. 21. Cf. trānsfodiō.

trānsfodiō, 3, fōdī, fossus, *pierce through; stab, run through, transfix*, 23. 14.

trānsiliō, 4, uī, —, *leap across, jump over*, 34. 19.

trānsmittō, 3, mīsī, mīssus, *send across, place* or *erect across*, 40.

6 ; *go across, cross over,* **62.** 3.
Cf. trānseō.

trānsportō, 1, *carry over ; carry,
convey, transport,* **4.** 3.

trecentī, ae, a, num. adj. [trēs,
centum], *three hundred,* **63.** 3.

tredecim, num. adj., indecl. [trēs,
decem], *thirteen,* **43.** 7.

trepidātiō, ōnis, F. [trepidō], *confused hurry ; alarm, agitation,
consternation,* **61.** 8.

trepidō, 1 [trepidus, *restless*],
*hurry with alarm ; be agitated,
tremble, be afraid,* **62.** 9.

trēs, tria, num. adj., *three,* **24.** 13;
25. 2 ; **36.** 10, etc.

tribuō, 3, uī, ūtus [tribus, *third
part, division*], *assign, bestow,
confer, give,* **48.** 9; **67.** 2 ; **70.**
18 ; **71.** 17.

trigeminus, a, um, adj., *born
three at a birth ;* pl. M., *triplet
brothers, triplets,* **38.** 10, 14.

trīgintā, num. adj., indecl., *thirty,*
36. 11 ; **38.** 4; **41.** 5, etc.

trirēmis, e, adj. [ter, *thrice,* rē-
mus], *with three banks of oars,*
70. 4; as noun, F. (sc. nāvis),
trireme, **68.** 12 ; **70.** 14.

trīste, adv. [trīstis], *sadly, seriously, unfortunately.*

trīstia, ae, F. [trīstis, *sad*], *sad-
ness, grief, melancholy, gloom,*
14. 6.

triumphō, 1 [triumphus], *cele-
brate a victory, triumph,* **42.**
22 ; **62.** 28.

triumphus, ī, M., *celebration of a
victory by a public entrance into
Rome ; triumphal procession,
triumph,* **62.** 23.

Trōia, ae, F., *Troy,* **17.** 1.

tu, tuī, pron. of second person,
thou, you, **23.** 7 ; **24.** 1, etc.

tuba, ae, F., *trumpet, war-trumpet,*
50. 19.

tubicen, cinis, M. [tuba, canō],
trumpeter, **50.** 17.

tueor, 2, tūtus, *look at ; maintain
guard, defend, protect,* **63.** 9.

tulī. See ferō.

Tullia, ae, F., daughter of Servius Tullius, **45.** 9.

Tullius, ī, M., see **Servius,** **43.**
21.

Tullus, ī, M., *Tullus Hostilius,*
third king of Rome, **38.** 5.

tum, adv., *then, at that time, in
those days,* **4.** 14; **6.** 5 ; **7.** 17,
etc. ; cum . . . tum, *not only* . . .
but also, **72.** 2.

tumultuor, 1 [tumultus], *make a
disturbance, be noisy,* **43.** 13.

tumultus, ūs, M., *swelling ; up-
roar, confusion, commotion,* **45.**
15.

tunc, adv. [tum], *at that very
time ; at that time, then,* **33.** 7 ;
35. 29 ; **41.** 2, etc.

turba, ae, F., *a crowding ; commotion, disturbance,* **45.** 15.

turbō, inis, M. [turba], *that which
whirls ; whirlwind, hurricane,*
26. 22.

tūtēla, ae, F., *watching ; protection, defence,* **34.** 16.

tūtor, ōris, M., *watcher; guardian,
tutor,* **42.** 19.

tūtus, a, um, adj. [p. of tueor,
watch], *guarded ; safe, secure,*
12. 16; **25.** 5 ; **49.** 3, etc.

tuus, a, um, adj. [tu], *thy, thine,
your,* **25.** 10 ; **29.** 16 ; **48.** 6,
etc.

✓ **tyrannis,** idis, F., *sway of a tyrant ; despotic power, absolute control,* 71. 22.

tyrannus, ī, M., *monarch ; despot, tyrant, one of the " Thirty,"* 73. 26.

U

ūber, eris, N., *udder, breast, teats,* 33. 11.

ubi, adv., *in which place ; where,* 9. 17, 21 ; 10. 23, etc.; *when,* 2. 6; 5. 26; 6. 24, etc.

✓ **ulcīscor,** 3, ultus, *avenge oneself on, take vengeance on, punish,* 16. 3.

Ūlixēs, ī or eī, M., *Ulysses,* 18. 5.

ūllus, a, um, adj. [for ūnulus, ūnus], *any one, any,* 21. 7 ; 46. 11 ; 60. 7.

ūltimus, a, um, adj., superl., *last, latest,* 23. 8 ; 24. 21 ; 64. 5.

✓ **ūltrā,** prep. w. acc., *on the other side ; beyond, past,* 65. 1.

umbra, ae, F., *shade, shadow,* 16. 23.

umerus, ī, M., *upper arm, shoulder,* 39. 17 ; 64. 11.

umquam, adv., *at any time, ever* (usu. w. neg.), 7. 6 ; 14. 20.

ūnā, adv. [ūnus], *in the same place; at the same time, together,* 53. 9.

unde, adv., *from which place ; from which, whence, hence,* 5. 1 ; 13. 23; 25. 14, etc.; *where, to the side on which,* 38. 12.

ūndecim, num. adj., indecl. [ūnus, decem], *eleven,* 37. 12.

undique, adv. [unde], *from all parts,* 2. 25 ; 4. 8; 10. 10, etc.; *all around, everywhere, on all sides,* 64. 16.

unguentum, ī, N. [unguō], *ointment, salve,* 8. 25 ; 9. 2 ; 31. 3.

unguō, 3, unxī, ūnctus, *smear, rub, anoint,* 31. 4.

ūniversus, a, um, adj. [ūnus, versus], *all together, all, everybody,* 31. 9 ; 70. 12.

ūnus, a, um, adj., *one,* 2. 21 ; 15. 22 ; 20. 10, etc.; *alone,* 64. 27; 75. 5.

ūnusquisque or **ūnus quisque,** ✓ ūnīuscūiusque, pron., *every single one, each one,* 56. 17.

urbānus, a, um, adj. [urbs], *of the city, cultivated ; witty, facetious, humorous,* 60. 16.

urbs, urbis, F., *walled town, city,* 2. 8 ; 8. 23 ; 13. 8, etc.

ūrō, 3, ussī, ūstus, *burn, consume,* 16. 7.

usque, adv., *all the way ; even,* ✓ *as far as,* 63. 16.

ūsūrpō, 1 [ūsus], *seize for use ; make use of, adopt, enjoy,* 64. 24.

ūsus, ūs, M., *use, service, value ;* pred. dat. w. sum, *be of use,* 3. 21 ; 31. 23; ūsū veniō, *come to pass, really happen,* 68. 19; 70. 25.

ut (utī), conj. w. subj., *that, in order that, so that,* 2. 20, 22 ; 3. 12, etc.; w. indic. *as, when,* 10. 4 ; 11. 16; 13. 7, etc.

ūter, ūtris, M., *bag of hide, leather* ✓

bag, **65.** 6 ; *leather bottle, skin*
(of wine), **22.** 22.

uter, tra, trum, interrog. pron.,
which of two ? which ? **27.** 19 ;
34. 12.

uterque, utraque, utrumque,
pron., *one and the other ; each,
both,* **43.** 15 ; **64.** 11.

ūtilis, e, adj. [ūtor], *of use ; useful, suitable, beneficial, good,* **37.**
22 ; superl., *most expedient, ad-
visable, wise,* **68.** 15.

ūtilitās, ātis, F. [ūtilis], *use ; advantage, profit, benefit, welfare,*
68. 27.

ūtor, 3, ūsus, *use, employ, make
use of,* **4.** 4 ; **15.** 13 ; **70.** 10.

utrimque, adv. [uterque], *on
both sides, one on each side,* **7.**
21 ; **38.** 15.

ūva, ae, F., *grape, cluster of grapes,*
51. 3.

uxor, ōris, F., *wife,* **15.** 24 ; **18.**
12 ; **34.** 24, etc.

V

vāgītus (ūs), M. [vāgiō, *cry*], *crying, screaming, cries,* **33.** 10.

valdē, adv. [for validē], *strongly ;
very much, exceedingly.*

valeō, 2, uī, itūrus, *be strong,* **14.**
18 ; **54.** 11 ; **66.** 8, etc. ; *have
power, avail, succeed,* **9.** 13 ;
15. 4 ; **29.** 21, etc.

validus, a, um, adj., *strong,
sound, stout,* **56.** 2.

vāllum, ī, N. [vāllus, *palisade*],
*line of palisades ; wall, ram-
part,* **34.** 16.

vānus, a, um, adj., *containing
nothing ; empty, idle, ground-
less,* **62.** 21.

varius, a, um, adj., *of different
colors ; different, diverse, vari-
ous,* **16.** 4.

vās, vāsis, N., pl. vāsa, ōrum,
vessel, dish, utensil, **14.** 24 ; **15.**
1, 7, etc.

vāstus, a, um, adj., *hollow,
empty ; vast, boundless, im-
mense,* **25.** 20 ; **33.** 9.

vēctīgal, ālis, N., *payment to the
state ; revenue, tax, tribute,*
73. 16.

vegetus, a, um, adj., *enlivened ;
bright, animated, spirited, active,* **64.** 21.

vehementer, adv. [vehemēns,
eager], *strongly, vigorously,
roughly,* **25.** 11 ; **31.** 27 ; *eagerly,
earnestly,* **22.** 1.

vehō, 3, vēxī, vēctus, *bear,* **62.**
10 ; pass., *be borne, ride, drive,*
16. 21 ; **45.** 13 ; *sail,* **4.** 19 ;
12. 24 ; **18.** 16, etc.

Vēientēs, ium, M., the people of
Veii, in Etruria, **40.** 12.

vel, conj. [old imper. of volō],
choose ; or ; vel ... vel, *either
... or,* **65.** 5, 6 ; **66.** 4 ; **67.** 1.

vellet. See **volō.**

vellus, eris, N., *wool ; pelt, fleece,*
3. 10, 12 ; **8.** 4, etc.

vēlō, 1 [vēlum *veil*], *veil, cover,*
41. 14.

velut or **velutī,** adv., *in a com-
parison, as if, just as,* **26.** 21 ;
33. 12 ; **37.** 27, etc.

√ **vēnātiŏ**, ōnis, F. [vēnor], *hunting, chase*, **9**. 5 ; **59**. 28.

√ **venēnum**, ī, N., *poison, magic drug*, **11**. 18, 20 ; **16**. 5, etc.

venerātiŏ, ōnis, F. [veneror, *reverence*], *profound respect, reverence*, **59**. 1.

⋎ **venia**, ae, F., *desire ; forgiveness, pardon*, **58**. 11.

veniŏ, 4, vēnī, ventus, *come, arrive*, **2**. 18, 20, 25, etc. See also **ūsus**.

vēnor, 1, *hunt*, **33**. 16 ; **75**. 16.

venter, tris, M., *belly*, **24**. 15.

ventus, ī, M., *wind*, **7**. 16 ; **25**. 21 ; **26**. 5, etc.

vēnum, ī, N., usually acc., *that which is for sale, sale ;* w. dŏ, *sell*, **47**. 2.

verbum, ī, N., *that which is spoken ; word*, **30**. 9, 12 ; **34**. 18, etc.; *saying*, **64**. 27 ; w. faciō, *speak*, **71**. 1.

\ **vērē**, adv. [vērus], *according to truth ; truly, rightly*, **72**. 18.

vereor, 2, itus, *respect ; fear, be afraid*, **2**. 15 ; **19**. 4 ; **24**. 23.

⟋ **vērŏ**, adv. [vērus], *in truth, indeed, however, but*, **22**. 14 ; **27**. 3 ; **34**. 24, etc.

versŏ, 1, freq. [vertŏ], *turn often;* pass., *be engaged, be*, **19**. 4 ; **28**. 24.

'∙ **versus**, ūs, M., *line, row ; line, verse*, **59**. 18.

vertŏ, 3, tī, sus, *turn ; turn back, direct*, **20**. 7.

vērum, adv. [vērus], *truly ; but in truth, but*, **36**. 6.

vērus, a, um, adj., *true ;* rē vērā, *in very truth, in fact, actually*, **2**. 11 ; **15**. 14 ; **55**. 17.

vescor, 3, —, *use as food, feed √ upon, eat, enjoy ;* w. abl., **19**. 2 ; **49**. 6.

vesper, erī or eris, M., *evening √ star ; evening*, **10**. 3 ; **19**. 3 ; **22**. 21.

Vesta, ae, F., *daughter of Saturn and Ops, goddess of flocks and of the household*, **33**. 4.

vester, tra, trum, poss. adj., *your*, **14**. 16 ; **15**. 5 ; **72**. 26, etc.

vestibulum, ī, N., *enclosed space before a house ; entrance court, vestibule*, **43**. 13.

vestīgium, ī, N., *bottom of the foot ; trail, track, step, footprint*, **5**. 25.

vestīmentum, ī, N. [vestis], *clothing, garment*, **74**. 20.

vestis, is, F., *covering* (for the √ body) *; clothing, vesture, robe*, **16**. 4, 6, 7, etc.

vetus, eris, adj., *old, aged.* ⟍

via, ae, F., *way, road, street*, **28**. 25 ; **40**. 6 ; **51**. 6, etc.; *path, line*, **7**. 18 ; **49**. 15 ; *way, distance*, **53**. 19 ; w. capiō, *make way, go*, **11**. 10 ; *journey, voyage, march*, **29**. 7 ; **53**. 19 ; **65**. 3.

vīcīnitās, ātis, F. [vīcīnus], *nearness ; neighborhood, vicinity, region*, **74**. 11.

vīcīnus, a, um, adj. [vīcus], *of the neighborhood ; neighboring, near*, **34**. 25 ; as noun, M., *neighbor*, **55**. 18.

victor, ōris, M., *he who conquers ; victor, conqueror*, **34**. 15 ; **62**. 26 ; **70**. 1, etc.

victōria, ae, F., *conquering ; vic-*

tory, triumph, **38.** 12 ; **39.** 10 ;
44. 7, etc.

✓ **vīctus,** ūs, M., *sustenance, nourishment, food,* **18.** 24 ; *manner of
living, private life,* **66.** 11 ;
75. 14.

vīcus, ī, M., *row of dwellings ;
quarter, district, part of a city,*
45. 17 ; *village, hamlet,* **19.** 6 ;
59. 13.

. **vidēlicet,** adv. [vidēre licet], *one
may see ; to wit, of course,
namely,* **35.** 17.

videō, 2, vīdī, vīsus, *see, perceive,
look at, behold,* **3.** 6 ; **5.** 8, 20,
etc.; pass., *seem, appear,* **34.**
16 ; **39.** 25 ; **63.** 26, etc.

✓ **viduus,** a, um, adj., *bereft, deprived of ;* w. mulier, *widow,*
53. 11.

vigeō, 2, uī, —, *be lively ; be
strong, thrive, flourish, be
honored,* **70.** 2.

vigilia, ae, F. [vigil, *awake*],
a watching ; watch, guard, **12.**
15.

vīgintī, num. adj., indecl., *twenty,*
27. 20 ; **59.** 2 ; **64.** 17.

villa, ae, F., *country house, villa,
farm,* **28.** 4 ; **29.** 8.

vīmen, inis, N., *pliant twig ;
withe, osier,* **24.** 14.

Vīminālis, e, adj. [vīmen], *of
osiers ; Viminal Hill* (in
Rome), **44.** 15.

\ · **vinciō,** 4, nxī, nctus, *tie ; bind,
fetter,* **19.** 16.

vinclum. See **vinculum.**

vincō, 3, vīcī, vīctus, *conquer,
overcome, defeat, vanquish,* **35.**
27 ; **40.** 17 ; **61.** 8, etc. ; *surpass, outdo,* **75.** 15.

vinculum or **vinclum,** ī, N. [vin-
ciō], *binding thing ;* pl., *fetters,
chains,* so *prison,* **25.** 22 ;
33. 6.

vindicō, 1 [vindex, *defender*], ✓
*claim as one's own, demand,
appropriate,* **54.** 19 ; *avenge, requite, punish, overtake,* **35.** 20 ;
61. 19.

vīnum, ī, N., *wine,* **19.** 8 ; **22.** 22,
24, etc.

violentus, a, um, adj. [vīs], *full
of force ; impetuous, violent,
fierce,* **45.** 7.

violō, 1 [vīs], *treat with violence ;
abuse, outrage,* **59.** 19, 20 ; **74.**
8 ; *dishonor, pollute, insult,*
68. 8.

vir, ī, M., *male person ; man,
hero,* **9.** 21, 24 ; **10.** 2, etc.;
husband, **36.** 4 ; **42.** 15 ; **46.**
24.

virga, ae, F., *slender green
branch ; rod, stick,* **52.** 19.

virgō, inis, F., *young girl, virgin,* \ !
maiden, **6.** 9 ; **35.** 9, 10, etc. . .

virgula, ae, F., dim. [virga], *little
twig, small rod,* **52.** 17.

virtūs, ūtis, F. [vir], *manhood ;
strength, valor, courage, bra-
very,* **6.** 18 ; **18.** 5 ; **24.** 13, etc.;
virtue, good quality, **66.** 4.

vīs, (vīs), F., *strength, power,* ✓
powers, might, **9.** 1, 5 ; **15.**
1 ; **16.** 6, etc.; *force, strength,
violence,* **2.** 16 ; **4.** 5 ; **5.** 22,
etc.; *quantity, number, crowd,*
34. 23 ; *attack, outbreak,* **67.**
13 ; w. summā or summīs,
*with might and main, with
all one's might,* **7.** 23 ; **12.**
23.

vis. See **volō.**

√ **vīsō,** 3, sī, sus, freq. [videō], *look at attentively ; see, view, behold,* 70. 13.

vīsus, ūs, M. [videō], *a looking; sight, vision,* 29. 25; 43. 25; 64. 2; *appearance, seeming,* 43. 23.

vīta, ae, F., *life,* 9. 5; 14. 10; 16. 13, etc.; *public life,* 66. 11; 75. 8.

vītis, is, F., *vine, grapevine,* 51. 3.

vitium, ī, N., *fault, failing, defect, vice,* 57. 2; 66. 4.

ˑ **vītō,** 1, *shun, avoid,* 54. 13; *seek to escape, avoid, escape,* 7. 10.

vīvidus, a, um, adj., *full of life, animated.*

vīvō, 3, vīxī, —, *be alive,* 14. 9; *live, dwell, reside,* 3. 1; 74. 24; 75. 16.

vīvus, a, um, adj., *alive, living,* 53. 2; 56. 10; 74. 7, etc.; *of water, running,* 45. 1.

ˈ **vix,** adv., *with effort; hardly, scarcely, barely,* 16. 11; 28. 1, 23, etc.

vōciferō, 1, —, ātus [vōx], *cry out, cry aloud, shout, bawl,* 43. 15.

vocitō, 1, freq. [vocō], *be wont to call, call habitually, name,* 67. 10.

vocō, 1, *speak ; call, name, call by the name of,* 34. 15 ; *call, summon,* 6. 20; 43. 14.

Volcānus, ī, M., *Vulcan, god of fire,* 20. 15.

volgō, adv. [volgus], *among the crowd ; generally, commonly,* 36. 15 ; 70. 26.

volgus, ī, N., *mass, multitude, people, crowd,* 70. 14 ; 72. 11 ; 73. 1.

volitō, 1, freq. [volō], *keep flying ; fly about, flutter,* 42. 12 ; *hasten,* 61. 2.

volnerō, 1 [volnus], *wound, injure, hurt,* 23. 24 ; 24. 1 ; 38. 21, etc.

volnus, eris, N., *wound, injury, hurt,* 10. 14; 39. 11; 43. 19, etc.

volō, velle, voluī, —, *be willing ; will, wish, determine,* 3. 14; 8. 12 ; 10. 11, etc.

volō, 1, āvī, ātūrus, *fly, speed,* 7. 19 ; 36. 3.

volpēcula, ae, F., dim. [volpēs], *little fox,* 54. 6.

volpēs, is, F., *fox,* 49. 9 ; 51. 3 ; 54. 10, etc.

voltur, uris, M., *vulture,* 34. 14.

voltus, ūs, M., *expression of the* √ *face ; features, looks, mien,* 34. 2 ; *countenance, face, eyes,* 63. 22.

volucer, cris, cre, adj., *winged; as noun,* F. (sc. avis), *flying creature, bird,* 6. 10; 7. 2.

voluntās, ātis, F. [volō], *will, wishes.*

voluptās, ātis, F., *satisfaction, en-* √ *joyment, pleasure,* 23. 3.

vōs, pl. of **tu,** *you,* 14. 22 ; 15. 5, 6.

vōtum, ī, N. [p. of voveō], *promise to a god ; wish, prayer,* 54. 2.

voveō, 2, vōvī, vōtus, *vow, pledge, promise,* **35**. 29.

vōx, vōcis, F., *that which calls out; voice, word,* **20**. 24; **21**. 10 ; **25**. 9, etc.

Z

Zephyrus, ī, M., *Zephyr*, a gentle west wind, **26**. 6.

Zētes, ae, M., an Argonaut, son of the North Wind, **7**. 3.

Printed in Great Britain
by Amazon